MySQL Troubleshooting

Sveta Smirnova

Beijing · Cambridge · Farnham · Köln · Sebastopol · Tokyo

MySQL Troubleshooting

by Sveta Smirnova

Published by O'Reilly Media, Inc., 1005 Gravenstein Highway North, Sebastopol, CA 95472.

O'Reilly books may be purchased for educational, business, or sales promotional use. Online editions are also available for most titles (*http://my.safaribooksonline.com*). For more information, contact our corporate/institutional sales department: (800) 998-9938 or *corporate@oreilly.com*.

Editor: Andy Oram	**Indexer:** Angela Howard
Production Editors: Jasmine Perez and Teresa Elsey	**Cover Designer:** Karen Montgomery
Copyeditor: Genevieve d'Entremont	**Interior Designer:** David Futato
Proofreader: Jasmine Perez	**Illustrator:** Robert Romano

February 2012:   First Edition.

Revision History for the First Edition:
   2012-02-03   First release
See *http://oreilly.com/catalog/errata.csp?isbn=9781449312008* for release details.

ISBN: 978-1-449-31200-8

[LSI]

1328211598

Table of Contents

Foreword

Solving a system problem can be one of the most frustrating experiences a systems expert can encounter. Repair of the problem or the execution of the solution is typically the easy part. Diagnosing the cause of the problem is the real challenge.

Experienced administrators have learned—some by doing and others by trial and error—that the best way to solve a problem is to use a standardized process for defining the problem, forming a list of possible causes, and then testing each until the solution is found. This may sound naïve, but it generally works (although it is not sufficient for specialized systems).

MySQL is a specialized, complex, mature, and powerful database system capable of meeting the needs of a vast number of organizations. MySQL is also very easy to install and configure. Indeed, most default installations do not need to be configured or tuned at all. However, MySQL is also a system with many layers of functionality that can sometimes go awry and produce a warning or error.

Sometimes the warning or error is specific enough (or has been seen and documented enough) that a solution can be implemented immediately. Other times, and thankfully infrequently, a problem is encountered that does not have a known solution or is specific to your application, database, or environment. Finding a solution for such a warning, error, or other problem with MySQL can be a daunting task.

When encountering such an issue, database professionals typically search various resources looking for clues or at least documentation that describes a similar problem and solution. Most will find that there are simply too many references to problems that are somewhat similar or that contain suggested solutions that simply don't work or don't apply to your situation.

A fine example of this is searching the Internet using the error message as search criteria. More often than not, you will find all manner of hits, varying from archived email logs to blogs and similar commentary that may or may not refer to the error message. This often leads to a lot of wasted time and frustration. What is needed is a reference guide for how to solve problems with MySQL.

Not only does this book fulfill that need, it also establishes a protocol for solving problems that can be applied to almost any system. The methods presented are well structured, thorough, and repeatable. Combined with real-world examples, the text becomes a watershed work that defines the proper way to diagnose and repair MySQL.

Sveta uses her firsthand experiences and in-depth knowledge of MySQL and diagnostic skills to teach the reader fundamental skills to diagnose and repair almost any problem you may encounter with MySQL—making this book a must have for any MySQL professional.

I consider myself a MySQL expert, and while my skills are backed by much experience, I won't claim to know everything there is to know about MySQL. After reading this book, I can say that I've broadened my skills even further. If a seasoned professional like myself can benefit from reading this book, every MySQL user should read this book. More to the point, it should be considered required reading for all MySQL database administrators, consultants, and database developers.

—Dr. Charles Bell, Oracle Corporation,
Author of *MySQL High Availability* (O'Reilly)
and *Expert MySQL* (Apress)

Preface

I have worked since May 2006 as a principal technical support engineer in the Bugs Verification Group of the MySQL Support Group for MySQL AB, then Sun, and finally Oracle. During my daily job, I often see users who are stuck with a problem and have no idea what to do next. Well-verified methods exist to find the cause of the problem and fix it effectively, but they are hard to cull from the numerous information sources. Hundreds of great books, blog posts, and web pages describe different parts of the MySQL server in detail. But here's where I see the difficulty: this information is organized in such a way as to explain how the MySQL server normally works, leaving out methods that can identify failures and ill-posed behavior.

When combined, these information sources explain each and every aspect of MySQL operation. But if you don't know why your problem is occurring, you'll probably miss the cause among dozens of possibilities suggested by the documentation. Even if you ask an expert what could be causing your problem, she can enumerate many suspects, but you still need to find the right one. Otherwise, any changes you make could just mask the real problem temporarily, or even make it worse.

It is very important to know the source of a problem, even when a change to an SQL statement or configuration option can make it go away. Knowledge of the cause or failure will arm you to overcome it permanently and prevent it from popping up again in the future.

I wrote this book to give you the methods I use constantly to identify what caused an error in an SQL application or a MySQL configuration and how to fix it.

Audience

This book is written for people who have some knowledge about MySQL. I tried to include information useful for both beginners and advanced users. You need to know SQL and have some idea of how the MySQL server works, at least from a user manual or beginner's guide. It's better yet if you have real experience with the server or have already encountered problems that were hard to solve.

I don't want to repeat what is in other information sources; rather, I want to fill those gaps that I explained at the beginning of this Preface. So you'll find guidance in this book for fixing an application, but not the details of application and server behavior. For details, consult the MySQL Reference Manual (*http://dev.mysql.com/doc/refman/5.5/en/index.html*).

How to Solve a Problem

This book is shaped around the goal of pursuing problems and finding causes. I step through what I would do to uncover the problem, without showing dozens of distracting details or fancy methods.

> It is very important to identify what the problem is.
>
> For example, when saying that a MySQL installation is slow, you need to identify where it is slow: is only part of the application affected, or do all queries sent to the MySQL server run slowly? It's also good to know whether the same installation was "slow" in the past and whether this problem is consistent or repeatable only periodically.
>
> Another example is wrong behavior. You need to know what behaved wrongly, what results you have, and what you expected.

I have been very disciplined in presenting troubleshooting methods. Most problems can be solved in different ways, and the best solution depends on the application and the user's needs. If I described how to go off in every direction, this book would be 10 times bigger and you would miss the fix that works for you. My purpose is to put you on the right path from the start so that you can deal quickly with each type of problem. Details about fixing the issue can be found in other information sources, many of which I cite and point you to in the course of our journey.

How This Book Is Organized

This book has seven chapters and an appendix.

Chapter 1, *Basics*, describes basic troubleshooting techniques that you'll use in nearly any situation. This chapter covers only single-threaded problems, i.e., problems that are repeatable with a single connection in isolation. I start with this isolated and somewhat unrealistic setting because you will need these techniques to isolate a problem in a multithreaded application.

Chapter 2, *You Are Not Alone: Concurrency Issues*, describes problems that come up when applications run in multiple threads or interfere with transactions in other applications.

Chapter 3, *Effects of Server Options*, consists of two parts. The first is a guide to debugging and fixing a problem caused by a configuration option. The second is a reference to important options and is meant to be consulted as needed instead of being read straight through. The second part also contains recommendations on how to solve problems caused by particular options and information about how to test whether you have solved the problem. I tried to include techniques not described in other references, and to consolidate in one place all the common problems with configuration options. I also grouped them by the kind of problems, so you can easily search for the cause of your symptom.

Chapter 4, *MySQL's Environment*, is about hardware and other aspects of the environment in which the server runs. This is a huge topic, but most of the necessary information is specific to operating systems and often can be solved only by the system administrator. So I list some points a MySQL database administrator (DBA) must look into. After you read this short chapter, you will know when to blame your environment and how to explain the problem to your system administrator.

Chapter 5, *Troubleshooting Replication*, is about problems that come up specifically in replication scenarios. I actually discuss replication issues throughout this book, but other chapters discuss the relationship between replication and other problems. This chapter is for issues that are specific to replication.

Chapter 6, *Troubleshooting Techniques and Tools*, describes extra techniques and tools that I skipped over or failed to discuss in detail during earlier guidelines to troubleshooting. The purpose of this chapter is to close all the gaps left in earlier chapters. You can use it as a reference if you like. I show principles first, then mention available tools. I can't write about tools I don't work with, so I explain the ones I personally use every day, which consequently leads to a focus on tools written by the MySQL Team and now belonging to Oracle. I do include third-party tools that help me deal with bugs and support tickets every day.

Chapter 7, *Best Practices*, describes good habits and behaviors for safe and effective troubleshooting. It does not describe all the best practices for designing MySQL applications, which are covered in many other sources, but instead concentrates on practices that help with problem hunting—or help prevent problems.

The Appendix, *Information Resources*, contains a list of information sources that I use in my daily job and that can help in troubleshooting situations. Of course, some of them influenced this book, and I refer to them where appropriate.

Some Choices Made in This Book

In the past few years, many forks of MySQL were born. The most important are Percona server and MariaDB. I skipped them completely in this book because I work mostly with MySQL and simply cannot describe servers I don't work with daily. However, because they are forks, you can use most of the methods described here. Only if you are dealing with a particular feature added in the fork will you need information specific to that product.

To conserve space and avoid introducing a whole new domain of knowledge with a lot of its own concerns, I left out MySQL Cluster problems. If you use MySQL Cluster and run into an SQL or application issue, you can troubleshoot it in much the same way as any other storage engine issue. Therefore, this book is applicable to such issues on clusters. But issues that are specific to MySQL Cluster need separate MySQL Cluster knowledge that I don't describe here.

But I do devote a lot of space to MyISAM- and InnoDB-specific problems. This was done because they are by far the most popular storage engines, and their installation base is huge. Both also were and are default storage engines: MyISAM before version 5.5 and InnoDB since version 5.5.

A few words about examples. They were all created either specially for this book or for conferences where I have spoken about troubleshooting. Although some of the examples are based on real support cases and bug reports, all the code is new and cannot be associated with any confidential data. In a few places, I describe customer "tickets." These are not real either. At the same time, the problems described here are real and have been seen many times, just with different code, names, and circumstances.

I tried to keep all examples as simple, understandable, and universal as possible. Therefore, I use the MySQL command-line client in most of the examples. You always have this client in the MySQL installation.

This decision also explains why I don't describe all complications specific to particular kinds of installations; it is just impossible to cover them all in single book. Instead, I tried to give starting points that you can extend.

I have decided to use the C API to illustrate the functions discussed in this book. The choice wasn't easy, because there are a lot of programming APIs for MySQL in various languages. I couldn't possibly cover them all, and didn't want to guess which ones would be popular. I realized that many of them look like the C API (many are even wrappers around the C API), so I decided that would be the best choice. Even if you are using an API with a very different syntax, such as ODBC, this section still can be useful because you will know what to look for.

A few examples use PHP. I did so because I use PHP and therefore could show real examples based on my own code. Real examples are always good to show because they reflect real-life problems that readers are likely to encounter. In addition, the MySQL

API in PHP is based on the C API and uses the very same names, so readers should be able to compare it easily to C functions discussed in this book.[1]

I omitted JDBC and ODBC examples because these APIs are very specific. At the same time, their debugging techniques are very similar, if not always the same. Mostly the syntax is different. I decided that adding details about these two connectors might confuse readers without offering any new information about troubleshooting.[2]

Conventions Used in This Book

The following typographical conventions are used in this book:

Italic
> Indicates new terms, URLs, email addresses, filenames, and file extensions.

`Constant width`
> Used for program listings, as well as within paragraphs to refer to program elements such as variable or function names, databases, data types, environment variables, statements, and keywords.

`Constant width bold`
> Shows commands or other text that should be typed literally by the user.

`Constant width italic`
> Shows text that should be replaced with user-supplied values or by values determined by context.

 This icon signifies a tip, suggestion, or general note.

 This icon indicates a warning or caution.

- This square indicates a lesson we just learned.

---

1. `mysqlnd` uses its own client protocol implementation, but still names functions in the same style as the C API.

2. You can find details specific to Connector/J (JDBC) at *http://dev.mysql.com/doc/refman/5.5/en/connector -j-reference.html* and to Connector/ODBC at *http://dev.mysql.com/doc/refman/5.5/en/connector-odbc -reference.html*.

Using Code Examples

This book is here to help you get your job done. In general, you may use the code in this book in your programs and documentation. You do not need to contact us for permission unless you're reproducing a significant portion of the code. For example, writing a program that uses several chunks of code from this book does not require permission. Selling or distributing a CD-ROM of examples from O'Reilly books does require permission. Answering a question by citing this book and quoting example code does not require permission. Incorporating a significant amount of example code from this book into your product's documentation does require permission.

We appreciate, but do not require, attribution. An attribution usually includes the title, author, publisher, and ISBN. For example: "*MySQL Troubleshooting* by Sveta Smirnova (O'Reilly). Copyright 2012 Sveta Smirnova, 978-1-449-31200-8."

If you feel your use of code examples falls outside fair use or the permission given here, feel free to contact us at *permissions@oreilly.com*.

Safari® Books Online

 Safari Books Online is an on-demand digital library that lets you easily search over 7,500 technology and creative reference books and videos to find the answers you need quickly.

With a subscription, you can read any page and watch any video from our library online. Read books on your cell phone and mobile devices. Access new titles before they are available for print, get exclusive access to manuscripts in development, and post feedback for the authors. Copy and paste code samples, organize your favorites, download chapters, bookmark key sections, create notes, print out pages, and benefit from tons of other time-saving features.

O'Reilly Media has uploaded this book to the Safari Books Online service. To have full digital access to this book and others on similar topics from O'Reilly and other publishers, sign up for free at *http://my.safaribooksonline.com*.

How to Contact Us

Please address comments and questions concerning this book to the publisher:

O'Reilly Media, Inc.
1005 Gravenstein Highway North
Sebastopol, CA 95472
800-998-9938 (in the United States or Canada)
707-829-0515 (international or local)
707-829-0104 (fax)

We have a web page for this book, where we list errata, examples, and any additional information. You can access this page at:

http://www.oreilly.com/catalog/9781449312008

To comment or ask technical questions about this book, send email to:

bookquestions@oreilly.com

For more information about our books, courses, conferences, and news, see our website at *http://www.oreilly.com.*

Find us on Facebook: *http://facebook.com/oreilly*

Follow us on Twitter: *http://twitter.com/oreillymedia*

Watch us on YouTube: *http://www.youtube.com/oreillymedia*

Acknowledgments

I want to say thank you to the people without whose help this book couldn't happen.

For a start, this includes my editor, Andy Oram, who did a great job making my English readable and who showed me gaps and places where I had not described information in enough detail. He also gave me insight into how prepared my readers would be, prompting me to add explanations for beginners and to remove trivial things known by everyone.

I also want to thank the whole MySQL Support Team. These folks share their expertise and support with every member of the team, and I learned a lot from them. I won't put names here, because I want to say "thank you" to all of the people with whom I've worked since joining in 2006, even those who have left and moved to server development or another company.

Thanks to Charles Bell, who helped me to start this book. He also did a review of the book and suggested a lot of improvements. Charles works in the MySQL Replication and Backup Team at Oracle and is the author of two books about MySQL. Therefore, his suggestions, both for content and style, were very helpful.

I would also like to thank the people who reviewed the book:

- Shane Bester, my colleague from the MySQL Support Group, who reviewed the part devoted to his Gypsy program and suggested how to improve the example.
- Alexander (Salle) Keremedarski, who reviewed the whole book and sent me a lot of great suggestions. Salle has provided MySQL support since its very early days, starting in the MySQL Support Team and now at SkySQL as Director of EMEA Support. His knowledge of common user misunderstandings helped me to find places where I explained things in too little detail, so that a troubleshooting situation could be read as a best practice when actually it is not.

- Tonci Grgin, who reviewed the parts about MySQL Connectors and suggested additions, explaining their behavior. Tonci used to work in the same group as me and now works in the MySQL Connectors Team. He is the first person I would ask about anything related to MySQL Connectors.

- Sinisa Milivojevic, who reviewed Chapters 3 and 4 and parts about the MyISAM check and repairing tools. Sinisa is another reviewer who has worked in MySQL Support since the very beginning. He was employee #2 in MySQL and still works in the MySQL Support Team at Oracle. His huge experience is fantastic, and one might even think he knows every little detail about the MySQL server. Sinisa gave me insights on some of the topics I discuss and suggested short but very significant improvements.

- Valeriy Kravchuk, who reviewed Chapters 2 and 4 and the section "InnoDB Monitors" on page 192. He also works in the MySQL Support Team. Valeriy found many deficiencies in the chapters he reviewed. His criticism forced me to improve these chapters, although there is always room for development.

- Mark Callaghan, who runs database servers at Facebook, reviewed the whole book. Mark suggested that I put more examples and further explanation in places that were not clear. He also suggested examples for Chapter 4 and pointed me to places where my suggestions can be wrong for certain installations, prompting me to explain both situations: when the original suggestions fit and when they don't. Thanks to Mark, I added more details about these arguable topics.

- Alexey Kopytov also reviewed the whole book. He is the author of the SysBench utility (which I describe in this book), worked in MySQL Development, and now works at Percona. Alexey sent me improvements for the SysBench part.

- Dimitri (dim) Kravtchuk, Principal Benchmark Engineer at Oracle, reviewed the whole book as well. He is also the author of the dim_STAT monitoring solution I describe in this book, the db_STRESS database benchmarking kit, and a famous blog where he posts articles about InnoDB performance and MySQL benchmarks. He suggested several improvements to sections where I describe InnoDB, Performance Schema, and hardware impacts.

Finally, thanks to my family:

- My mother, Yulia Ivanovna Ivanova, who showed me how fun engineering can be.
- My parents-in-law, Valentina Alekseevna Lasunova and Nikolay Nikolayevich Lasunov, who always helped us when we needed it.
- And last but not least, my husband, Sergey Lasunov, who supported me in all my initiatives.

## CHAPTER 1

Basics

When troubleshooting, you can generally save time by starting with the simplest possible causes and working your way to more complicated ones. I work dozens of trouble tickets at MySQL Support every month. For most of them, we start from trivial requests for information, and the final resolution may—as we'll see in some examples—be trivial as well, but sometimes we have quite an adventure in between. So it always pays to start with the basics.

The typical symptoms of a basic problem are running a query and getting unexpected results. The problem could manifest itself as results that are clearly wrong, getting no results back when you know there are matching rows, or odd behavior in the application. In short, this section depends on you having a good idea of what your application should be doing and what the query results should look like. Cases in which the source of wrong behavior is not so clear will be discussed later in this book.

We will always return to these basics, even with the trickiest errors or in situations when you would not know what caused the wrong behavior in your application. This process, which we'll discuss in depth in "Localizing the Problem (Minimizing the Test Case)" on page 205, can also be called *creating a minimal test case*.

Incorrect Syntax

This sounds absolutely trivial, but still can be tricky to find. I recommend you approach the possibility of incorrect SQL syntax very rigorously, like any other possible problem.

An error such as the following is easy to see:

```
SELECT * FRO t1 WHERE f1 IN (1,2,1);
```

In this case, it is clear that the user just forgot to type an "m", and the error message clearly reports this (I have broken the output lines to fit the page):

```
mysql> SELECT * FRO t1 WHERE f1 IN (1,2,1);
ERROR 1064 (42000): You have an error in your SQL syntax; check the manual that
corresponds to your MySQL server version for the right syntax to use near 'FRO
t1 WHERE f1 IN (1,2,1)' at line 1
```

Unfortunately, not all syntax errors are so trivial. I once worked on a trouble ticket concerning a query like this:

```
SELECT id FROM t1 WHERE accessible=1;
```

The problem was a migration issue; the query worked fine in version 5.0 but stopped working in version 5.1. The problem was that, in version 5.1, "accessible" is a reserved word. We added quotes (these can be backticks or double quotes, depending on your SQL mode), and the query started working again:

```
SELECT `id` FROM `t1` WHERE `accessible`=1;
```

The actual query looked a lot more complicated, with a large JOIN and a complex WHERE condition. So the simple error was hard to pick out among all the distractions. Our first task was to reduce the complex query to the simple one-line SELECT as just shown, which is an example of a minimal test case. Once we realized that the one-liner had the same bug as the big, original query, we quickly realized that the programmer had simply stumbled over a reserved word.

- The first lesson is to check your query for syntax errors as the first troubleshooting step.

But what do you do if you don't know the query? For example, suppose the query was built by an application. Even more fun is in store when it's a third-party library that dynamically builds queries.

Let's consider this PHP code:

```
$query = 'SELECT * FROM t4 WHERE f1 IN(';
for ($i = 1; $i < 101; $i ++)
$query .= "'row$i,";
$query = rtrim($query, ',');
$query .= ')';
$result = mysql_query($query);
```

Looking at the script, it is not easy to see where the error is. Fortunately, we can alter the code to print the query using an output function. In the case of PHP, this can be the echo operator. So we modify the code as follows:

```
...
echo $query;
//$result = mysql_query($query);
```

Once the program shows us the actual query it's trying to submit, the problem jumps right out:

```
$ php ex1.php
SELECT * FROM t4 WHERE f1 IN('row1,'row2,'row3,'row4,'row5,'row6,'row7,'row8,
'row9,'row10,'row11, 'row12,'row13,'row14,'row15,'row16,'row17,'row18,'row19,'row20)
```

If you still can't find the error, try running this query in the MySQL command-line client:

```
mysql> SELECT * FROM t4 WHERE f1 IN('row1,'row2,'row3,'row4,'row5,'row6,'row7,'row8,
'row9,'row10,'row11,'row12,'row13,'row14,'row15,'row16,'row17,'row18,'row19,'row20);
ERROR 1064 (42000): You have an error in your SQL syntax; check the manual that
corresponds to your MySQL server version for the right syntax to use near 'row2,
'row3,'row4,'row5,'row6,'row7,'row8,'row9,'row10,'row11, 'row12,'row13,'row' at
line 1
```

The problem is that the closing apostrophe is missing from each row. Going back to
the PHP code, I have to change:

```
$query .= "'row$i,";
```

to the following:

```
$query .= "'row$i',";
```

- An important debugging technique, therefore, consists of this: always try to view
  the query exactly as the MySQL server receives it. Don't debug only application
  code; get the query!

Unfortunately, you can't always use output functions. One possible reason, which I
mentioned before, is that you're using a third-party library written in a compiled
language to generate the SQL. Your application might also be using high-level abstrac-
tions, such as libraries that offer a CRUD (create, read, update, delete) interface. Or
you might be in a production environment where you don't want users to be able to
see the query while you are testing particular queries with specific parameters. In such
cases, check the MySQL general query log. Let's see how it works using a new example.

This is the PHP application where the problem exists:

```
private function create_query($columns, $table)
{
    $query = "insert into $table set ";
    foreach ($columns as $column) {
        $query .= $column['column_name'] . '=';
        $query .= $this->generate_for($column);
        $query .= ', ';
    }
    return rtrim($query, ',') . ';';
}

private function generate_for($column)
{
    switch ($column['data_type']) {
    case 'int':
        return rand();
    case 'varchar':
    case 'text':
      return "'" . str_pad(md5(rand()), rand(1,$column['character_maximum_length']),
      md5(rand()), STR_PAD_BOTH) . "'";
    default:
        return "''";
    }
}
```

This code updates a table defined in Example 1-1.

Example 1-1. Sample table of common troubleshooting situations

```
CREATE TABLE items(
    id INT NOT NULL AUTO_INCREMENT PRIMARY KEY,
    short_description VARCHAR(255),
    description TEXT,
    example TEXT,
    explanation TEXT,
    additional TEXT
) ENGINE=InnoDB DEFAULT CHARSET=utf8;
```

Now is time to start using the general query log. This log contains every single query the MySQL server receives. Many production applications don't want to use it on a day-to-day basis, because it grows extremely fast during a high load, and writing to it can take up MySQL server resources that are needed for more important purposes. Starting with version 5.1, you can turn the general query log on temporarily to record just the query you need:

```
mysql> SET GLOBAL general_log='on';
Query OK, 0 rows affected (0.00 sec)
```

You can also log into a table, which lets you easily sort logfile entries because you can query a log table like any other MySQL table:

```
mysql> SET GLOBAL log_output='table';
Query OK, 0 rows affected (0.00 sec)
```

Now let's run the application. After an iteration that executes the problem code, query the table containing the general log to find the problem query:

```
mysql> SELECT * FROM mysql.general_log\G
*************************** 1. row ***************************
  event_time: 2011-07-13 02:54:37
   user_host: root[root] @ localhost []
   thread_id: 27515
   server_id: 60
command_type: Connect
    argument: root@localhost on collaborate2011
*************************** 2. row ***************************
  event_time: 2011-07-13 02:54:37
   user_host: root[root] @ localhost []
   thread_id: 27515
   server_id: 60
command_type: Query
    argument: INSERT INTO items SET id=1908908263,
short_description='8786db20e5ada6cece1306d44436104c',
description='fc84e1dc075bca3fce13a95c41409764',
example='e4e385c3952c1b5d880078277c711c41',
explanation='ba0afe3fb0e7f5df1f2ed3f2303072fb',
additional='2208b81f320e0d704c11f167b597be85',
*************************** 3. row ***************************
  event_time: 2011-07-13 02:54:37
   user_host: root[root] @ localhost []
```

```
    thread_id: 27515
    server_id: 60
 command_type: Quit
     argument:
```

We are interested in the second row and query:

```
INSERT INTO items SET id=1908908263,
short_description='8786db20e5ada6cece1306d44436104c',
description='fc84e1dc075bca3fce13a95c41409764',
example='e4e385c3952c1b5d880078277c711c41',
explanation='ba0afe3fb0e7f5df1f2ed3f2303072fb',
additional='2208b81f320e0d704c11f167b597bc85',
```

The error again is trivial: a superfluous comma at the end of the query. The problem was generated in this part of the PHP code:

```
        $query .= ', ';
    }
    return rtrim($query, ',') . ';';
```

The rtrim function would work if the string actually ended with a comma because it could remove the trailing comma. But the line actually ends with a space character. So rtrim does not remove anything.

Now that we have the query that caused the error in our application, we can turn off the general query log:

```
mysql> SET GLOBAL general_log='off';
Query OK, 0 rows affected (0.08 sec)
```

In this section, we learned a few important things:

- Incorrect syntax can be the source of real-life problems.
- You should test exactly the same query that the MySQL server gets.
- Programming language output functions and the general query log can help you quickly find the query that the application sends to the MySQL server.

Wrong Results from a SELECT

This is another frequent problem reported by users of an application who don't see the updates they made, see them in the wrong order, or see something they don't expect.

There are two main reasons for getting wrong results: something is wrong with your SELECT query, or the data in database differs from what you expect. I'll start with the first case.

When I went over examples for this section, I had to either show some real-life examples or write my own toy cases. The real-life examples can be overwhelmingly large, but the toy cases wouldn't be much help to you, because nobody writes such code. So I've chosen to use some typical real-life examples, but simplified them dramatically.

The first example involves a common user mistake when using huge joins. We will use Example 1-1, described in the previous section. This table contains my collection of MySQL features that cause common usage mistakes I deal with in MySQL Support. Each mistake has a row in the `items` table. I have another table of `links` to resources for information. Because there's a many-to-many relationship between items and links, I also maintain an `items_links` table to tie them together. Here are the definitions of the `items` and `items_links` table (we don't need `links` in this example):

```
mysql> DESC items;
+-------------------+--------------+------+-----+---------+----------------+
| Field             | Type         | Null | Key | Default | Extra          |
+-------------------+--------------+------+-----+---------+----------------+
| id                | int(11)      | NO   | PRI | NULL    | auto_increment |
| short_description | varchar(255) | YES  |     | NULL    |                |
| description       | text         | YES  |     | NULL    |                |
| example           | text         | YES  |     | NULL    |                |
| explanation       | text         | YES  |     | NULL    |                |
| additional        | text         | YES  |     | NULL    |                |
+-------------------+--------------+------+-----+---------+----------------+
6 rows in set (0.30 sec)

mysql> DESC items_links;
+--------+---------+------+-----+---------+-------+
| Field  | Type    | Null | Key | Default | Extra |
+--------+---------+------+-----+---------+-------+
| iid    | int(11) | YES  | MUL | NULL    |       |
| linkid | int(11) | YES  | MUL | NULL    |       |
+--------+---------+------+-----+---------+-------+
2 rows in set (0.11 sec)
```

The first query I wrote worked fine and returned a reasonable result:

```
mysql> SELECT count(*) FROM items WHERE id IN (SELECT id FROM items_links);
+----------+
| count(*) |
+----------+
|       10 |
+----------+
1 row in set (0.12 sec)
```

...until I compared the number returned with the total number of links:

```
mysql> SELECT count(*) FROM items_links;
+----------+
| count(*) |
+----------+
|        6 |
+----------+
1 row in set (0.09 sec)
```

How could it be possible to have more links than associations?

Let's examine the query, which I made specially for this book, once more. It is simple and contains only two parts, a subquery:

```
SELECT id FROM items_links
```

and an outer query:

```
SELECT count(*) FROM items WHERE id IN ...
```

The subquery can be a good place to start troubleshooting because one should be able to execute it independently. Therefore, we can expect a compete result set:

```
mysql> SELECT id FROM items_links;
ERROR 1054 (42S22): Unknown column 'id' in 'field list'
```

Surprise! We have a typo, and actually there is no field named `id` in the `items_links` table; it says `iid` (for "items ID") instead. If we rewrite our query so that it uses the correct identifiers, it will work properly:

```
mysql> SELECT count(*) FROM items WHERE id IN (SELECT iid FROM items_links);
+----------+
| count(*) |
+----------+
|        4 |
+----------+
1 row in set (0.08 sec)
```

- We just learned a new debugging technique. If a SELECT query does not work as expected, split it into smaller chunks, and then analyze each part until you find the cause of the incorrect behavior.

 If you specify the full column name by using the format `table_name.column_name`, you can prevent the problems described here in the first place because you will get an error immediately:

```
mysql> SELECT count(*) FROM items WHERE items.id IN
    (SELECT items_links.id FROM items_links);
ERROR 1054 (42S22): Unknown column 'items_links.id' in 'field list'
```

A good tool for testing is the simple MySQL command-line client that comes with a MySQL installation. We will discuss the importance of this tool in Chapter 6.

But why didn't MySQL return the same error for the first query? We have a field named `id` in the `items` table, so MySQL thought we wanted to run a dependent subquery that actually selects `items.id` from `items_links`. A "dependent subquery" is one that refers to fields from the outer query.

We can also use EXPLAIN EXTENDED followed by SHOW WARNINGS to find the mistake. If we run these commands on the original query, we get:

```
mysql> EXPLAIN EXTENDED SELECT count(*) FROM items WHERE id IN
(SELECT id FROM items_links)\G
2 rows in set, 2 warnings (0.12 sec)
*************************** 1. row ***************************
           id: 1
  select_type: PRIMARY
        table: items
         type: index
```

```
   possible_keys: NULL
             key: PRIMARY
         key_len: 4
             ref: NULL
            rows: 10
        filtered: 100.00
           Extra: Using where; Using index
*************************** 2. row ***************************
              id: 2
     select_type: DEPENDENT SUBQUERY
           table: items_links
            type: index
   possible_keys: NULL
             key: iid_2
         key_len: 5
             ref: NULL
            rows: 6
        filtered: 100.00
           Extra: Using where; Using index
2 rows in set, 2 warnings (0.54 sec)

mysql> show warnings\G
*************************** 1. row ***************************
  Level: Note
   Code: 1276
Message: Field or reference 'collaborate2011.items.id' of SELECT #2 was resolved
in SELECT #1
*************************** 2. row ***************************
  Level: Note
   Code: 1003
Message: select count(0) AS `count(*)` from `collaborate2011`.`items` where
<in_optimizer7gt;(`collaborate2011`.`items`.`id`,<exists>(select 1 from
`collaborate2011`.`items_links` where
(<cache>(`collaborate2011`.`items`.`id`) =
`collaborate2011`.`items`.`id`)))
2 rows in set (0.00 sec)
```

Row 2 of the EXPLAIN EXTENDED output shows that the subquery is actually dependent: select_type is DEPENDENT SUBQUERY.

Before moving on from this example, I want to show one more technique that will help you avoid getting lost when your query contains lots of table references. It is easy to get lost if you join 10 or more tables in a single query, even when you know how they should be joined.

The interesting part of the previous example was the output of SHOW WARNINGS. The MySQL server does not always execute a query as it was typed, but invokes the optimizer to create a better execution plan so that the user usually gets the results faster. Following EXPLAIN EXTENDED, the SHOW WARNINGS command shows the optimized query.

In our example, the SHOW WARNINGS output contains two notes. The first is:

```
Field or reference 'collaborate2011.items.id' of SELECT #2 was resolved in SELECT #1
```

This note clearly shows that the server resolved the value of id in the subquery from the items table rather than from items_links.

The second note contains the optimized query:

```
select count(0) AS `count(*)` from `collaborate2011`.`items` where <in_optimizer>
(`collaborate2011`.`items`.`id`,<exists>
(select 1 from `collaborate2011`.`items_links` where
(<cache>(`collaborate2011`.`items`.`id`) = `collaborate2011`.`items`.`id`)))
```

This output also shows that the server takes the value of id from the items table.

Now let's compare the previous listing with the result of EXPLAIN EXTENDED on the correct query:

```
mysql> EXPLAIN EXTENDED SELECt count(*) FROM items WHERE id IN
(SELECT iid FROM items_links)\G
*************************** 1. row ***************************
           id: 1
  select_type: PRIMARY
        table: items
         type: index
possible_keys: NULL
          key: PRIMARY
      key_len: 4
          ref: NULL
         rows: 10
     filtered: 100.00
        Extra: Using where; Using index
*************************** 2. row ***************************
           id: 2
  select_type: DEPENDENT SUBQUERY
        table: items_links
         type: index_subquery
possible_keys: iid,iid_2
          key: iid
      key_len: 5
          ref: func
         rows: 1
     filtered: 100.00
        Extra: Using index; Using where
2 rows in set, 1 warning (0.03 sec)

mysql> show warnings\G
*************************** 1. row ***************************
  Level: Note
   Code: 1003
Message: select count(0) AS `count(*)` from `collaborate2011`.`items` where
<in_optimizer>(`collaborate2011`.`items`.`id`,<exists>
(<index_lookup>(<cache>(`collaborate2011`.`items`.`id`) in
items_links on iid where (<cache>(`collaborate2011`.`items`.`id`) =
`collaborate2011`.`items_links`.`iid`))))
1 row in set (0.00 sec)
```

The optimized query this time looks completely different, and really compares items.id with items_links.iid as we intended.

- We just learned another lesson: use EXPLAIN EXTENDED followed by SHOW WARNINGS to find how a query was optimized (and executed).

The value of select_type in the correct query is still DEPENDENT SUBQUERY. How can that be if we resolve the field name from the items_links table? The explanation starts with the part of the SHOW WARNINGS output that reads as follows:

```
where (<cache>(`collaborate2011`.`items`.`id`) =
`collaborate2011`.`items_links`.`iid`)
```

The subquery is still dependent because the id in clause of the outer query requires the subquery to check its rows against the value of iid in the inner query. This issue came up in the discussion of report #12106 (*http://bugs.mysql.com/bug.php?id=12106*) in the MySQL Community Bugs Database (*http://bugs.mysql.com*).

- I added a link to the bug report because it provides another important lesson: if you doubt the behavior of your query, use good sources to find information. The community bug database is one such source.

There can be many different reasons why a SELECT query behaves incorrectly, but the general method of investigation is always the same:

- Split the query into small chunks, and then execute them one by one until you see the cause of the problem.
- Use EXPLAIN EXTENDED followed by SHOW WARNINGS to get the query execution plan and information on how it was actually executed.
- If you don't understand the MySQL server behavior, use the Internet and good sources for information. The Appendix includes a list of useful resources.

When the Problem May Have Been a Previous Update

If a SELECT returns a result set you don't expect, this does not always mean something is wrong with the query itself. Perhaps you didn't insert, update, or delete data that you thought you had.

Before you investigate this possibility, you should faithfully carry out the investigation in the previous section, where we discussed a badly written SELECT statement. Here I examine the possibility that you have a good SELECT that is returning the values you asked for, and that the problem is your data itself. To make sure the problem is in the data and not the SELECT, try to reduce it to a simple query on a single table. If the table is small, go ahead and remove all the WHERE clauses, as well as any GROUP BY clauses, and examine the full data set with a brute-force SELECT * FROM *table_name*. For a larger table, judiciously use WHERE to cull the values you want to examine, and consider COUNT(*) if you just want to make sure the number of rows matching the query is what you expect.

Once you are sure the SELECT works fine, this means the data is inconsistent and you need to find where it is broken. There can be a lot of reasons: a badly applied backup, an incorrect UPDATE statement, or a slave getting out of sync with the master, just to name the most common. In this section, we'll look at some examples where a bad DELETE or UPDATE isn't revealed until a later SELECT. In a later section, we'll address those puzzling cases where the problem turns up long after it was triggered, and show you how to work backward to find the error. This section does not deal directly with problems in transactions, which are discussed in Chapter 2. Here I show cases where data in the database is stable, i.e., all transactions, if used, were completed. I will continue using examples reduced down from real cases.

Let's start from the best possible case, when data inconsistency was noticed right after the error was made. We will use the following initial data set:

```
mysql> CREATE TEMPORARY TABLE t1(f1 INT);
Query OK, 0 rows affected (0.01 sec)
mysql> CREATE TEMPORARY TABLE t2(f2 INT);
Query OK, 0 rows affected (0.08 sec)
mysql> INSERT INTO t1 VALUES(1);
Query OK, 1 row affected (0.01 sec)

mysql> SELECT * FROM t1;
+------+
| f1   |
+------+
|    1 |
+------+
1 row in set (0.00 sec)
```

In the application, the tables shown were temporary tables containing partial result sets selected from the main log table. This is a common technique frequently used in stored routines when only a small set of data from the main table is needed but the user doesn't want to change the data in the main table or lock the table.

So in this example, after finishing with a result set, the user wanted to delete rows from both tables. It always looks amazing when you can do things in a single query. But real life can work out differently from your plans, and you can get unexpected results or side effects:

```
mysql> DELETE FROM t1, t2 USING t1, t2;
Query OK, 0 rows affected (0.00 sec)
```

If the user paid attention to the string printed in response to the DELETE, he would realize right away that something had gone wrong. No rows were affected by the DELETE, meaning that it did nothing. The output from a statement is often not so obvious, however, and sometimes it is never seen, because the SQL statement is run within a program or script with no human being to watch over the results. In general, you should always check information returned by a statement execution to learn how many rows were affected and whether this value is same as you expect. In an application, you must explicitly check information functions.

Let's continue. If you run SELECT immediately, you could be surprised, thinking that the query was incorrect or even that the query cache had not been cleared:

```
mysql> SELECT * FROM t1;
+------+
| f1   |
+------+
|    1 |
+------+
1 row in set (0.00 sec)
```

You can be sure this is not a cache or some other problem if you convert the SELECT to ask for the number of rows. This easy example shows how we can use different ways to query a table to be sure the data is consistent:

```
mysql> SELECT count(*) FROM t1;
+----------+
| count(*) |
+----------+
|        1 |
+----------+
1 row in set (0.00 sec)
```

COUNT(*) still returns a positive number here, which shows the table is not empty as desired. As an attentive user would have seen, the DELETE didn't actually remove any rows. To find out why, we can convert the DELETE to the corresponding SELECT. This will show us which rows satisfy the condition for the delete.

Although our simple example had no WHERE clause, the technique is certainly useful to check the impact of a WHERE clause in a delete or update. The rows returned by a SELECT are the ones that DELETE would delete or that UPDATE would change:

```
mysql> SELECT * FROM t1, t2;
Empty set (0.00 sec)
```

Consistent with previous results, this returns an empty set. That's why no rows were removed! It still might not be clear why this happens, but now that we have a SELECT, we can use familiar techniques from the previous section. For this case, our best choice is to run SELECT followed by EXPLAIN and analyze its output:

```
mysql> \W
Show warnings enabled.

mysql> EXPLAIN EXTENDED SELECT * FROM t1, t2\G
*************************** 1. row ***************************
           id: 1
  select_type: SIMPLE
        table: t1
         type: system
possible_keys: NULL
          key: NULL
      key_len: NULL
          ref: NULL
         rows: 1
     filtered: 100.00
        Extra:
*************************** 2. row ***************************
           id: 2
```

```
   select_type: SIMPLE SUBQUERY
          table: t2
           type: system
  possible_keys: NULL
            key: NULL
        key_len: NULL
            ref: NULL
           rows: 0
       filtered: 0.00
          Extra: const row not found
2 rows in set, 1 warning (0.03 sec)
```

Note (Code 1003): select '1' AS `f1`,'0' AS `f2` from `test`.`t1` join `test`.`t2`

The final note in the output shows that the query was modified to an (inner) JOIN, which can return rows from each table only if there are matching rows in the other table. For each row in table t1, there should be at least one row in table t2 with a matching value in a matching row. In this case, because table t2 is empty, naturally the join returns an empty set.

- We just learned another important technique that helps us find out what is wrong with an UPDATE or DELETE: convert it to a SELECT with the same JOIN and WHERE conditions. With a SELECT, you can use EXPLAIN EXTENDED[1] to get the actual execution plan, as well as to manipulate the result set without the risk of modifying the wrong rows.

Here's a more complex example using UPDATE. We will use the items table again:

```
mysql> SELECT SUBSTR(description, 1, 20), additional IS NULL FROM items;
+----------------------------+--------------------+
| substr(description, 1, 20) | additional IS NULL |
+----------------------------+--------------------+
| NULL                       |                  1 |
| NULL                       |                  1 |
| One who has TRIGGER        |                  1 |
| mysql> revoke insert       |                  1 |
| NULL                       |                  0 |
+----------------------------+--------------------+
5 rows in set (0.00 sec)

mysql> SELECT description IS NULL, additional IS NULL FROM items;
+--------------------+--------------------+
| description IS NULL | additional IS NULL |
+--------------------+--------------------+
|                  1 |                  1 |
|                  1 |                  1 |
|                  0 |                  1 |
|                  0 |                  1 |
```

1. Since version 5.6.3, you can use EXPLAIN with UPDATE and DELETE as well, but converting such a query into SELECT still makes sense because it is easier to examine an actual result set and manipulate it than to just use EXPLAIN. This is especially true for complicated JOINs when EXPLAIN shows it examined more rows than were actually updated.

```
|                    1 |                    0 |
+----------------------+----------------------+
5 rows in set (0.00 sec)
```

The `description` and `additional` fields are of type TEXT. In this example, we will use an erroneous query that is supposed to replace NULL values with more descriptive text ("no description" for one table and "no additional comments" for the other):

```
mysql> UPDATE items SET description = 'no description' AND
additional = 'no additional comments' WHERE description IS NULL;
Query OK, 3 rows affected, 3 warnings (0.13 sec)
Rows matched: 3  Changed: 3  Warnings: 3
```

This query updates some data ("3 rows affected"), but let's check whether we have the proper values in the table now:

```
mysql> SELECT SUBSTR(description, 1, 20), additional IS NULL FROM items;
+----------------------------+--------------------+
| substr(description, 1, 20) | additional IS NULL |
+----------------------------+--------------------+
| 0                          |                  1 |
| 0                          |                  1 |
| One who has TRIGGER        |                  1 |
| mysql> revoke insert       |                  1 |
| 0                          |                  0 |
+----------------------------+--------------------+
5 rows in set (0.09 sec)
```

As we see, three rows changed their values in the `description` field, but 0 is different from the "no description" string we thought we were setting. Furthermore, the values in the `additional` field have not changed at all. To find out why this happened, we should check warnings. Notice in these statements returned by the server that we see a warnings count of three:

```
Query OK, 3 rows affected, 3 warnings (0.13 sec)
Rows matched: 3  Changed: 3  Warnings: 3

mysql> SHOW WARNINGS;
+---------+------+---------------------------------------------------------+
| Level   | Code | Message                                                 |
+---------+------+---------------------------------------------------------+
| Warning | 1292 | Truncated incorrect DOUBLE value: 'no description'      |
| Warning | 1292 | Truncated incorrect DOUBLE value: 'no description'      |
| Warning | 1292 | Truncated incorrect DOUBLE value: 'no description'      |
+---------+------+---------------------------------------------------------+
3 rows in set (0.00 sec)
```

The message looks strange. Why does it complain about a DOUBLE when `description` and `additional` are TEXT fields, as the following queries prove?

```
mysql> SHOW FIELDS FROM items LIKE 'description';
+-------------+------+------+-----+---------+-------+
| Field       | Type | Null | Key | Default | Extra |
+-------------+------+------+-----+---------+-------+
```

```
| description | text | YES |     | NULL    |       |
+-------------+------+------+-----+---------+-------+
1 row in set (0.13 sec)

mysql> SHOW FIELDS FROM items LIKE 'additional';
+------------+------+------+-----+---------+-------+
| Field      | Type | Null | Key | Default | Extra |
+------------+------+------+-----+---------+-------+
| additional | text | YES  |     | NULL    |       |
+------------+------+------+-----+---------+-------+
1 row in set (0.13 sec)
```

We also want to know why we did not get any warning about the `additional` field, when it was not changed at all.

Let's split the query in chunks and examine what it going in each of them:

```
UPDATE items
```

This is a common start for an `UPDATE`, and nothing's wrong with it:

```
SET description = 'no description' AND additional = 'no additional comments'
```

That used a `SET` statement. Let's examine what it is actually doing. What does the keyword `AND` mean in this case? Let me add parentheses to the query to underline operator precedence:

```
SET description = ('no description' AND additional = 'no additional comments')
```

So actually, the statement calculates the expression:

```
'no description' and additional = 'no additional comments'
```

and then assigns it to `description`. Evaluating the equal sign produces a Boolean result as a `LONGLONG` value. To prove this, start the MySQL command line client with the `--column-type-info` option and run the `SELECT` again:

```
$ mysql --column-type-info
mysql> SELECT 'no description' AND additional = 'no additional comments' FROM items;
Field     1:  `'no description' AND additional = 'no additional comments'`
Catalog:     `def`
Database:    ``
Table:       ``
Org_table:   ``
Type:        LONGLONG
Collation:   binary (63)
Length:      1
Max_length:  1
Decimals:    0
Flags:       BINARY NUM


+-----------------------------------------------------------+
| 'no description' AND additional = 'no additional comments' |
+-----------------------------------------------------------+
|                                                         0 |
|                                                         0 |
```

```
|                                                           0 |
|                                                           0 |
|                                                           0 |
+-----------------------------------------------------------+
 5 rows in set, 5 warnings (0.09 sec)
```

We clearly see that the result of the expression is 0, which was inserted into the description field. And because our update to the `additional` field got buried inside the absurd expression, nothing was inserted into the field, nor did the server see any reason to comment about the field.

Now you can rewrite the query without logic errors:

```
UPDATE items SET description = 'no description',
additional = 'no additional comments' WHERE description IS NULL;
```

You can examine the `WHERE` clause if you want, but in this case it has no error.

This example shows the importance of return values and information about query execution. Let's discuss them a bit more.

Getting Information About a Query

As we saw in the previous section, the server returns some important information about each query, displaying some of it directly in the MySQL client and making some of it easy to obtain through commands such as `SHOW WARNINGS`. When SQL is called from an application, it's just as important to retrieve this information and check to make sure nothing suspicious is going on. All programming APIs for MySQL support functions that retrieve the query information returned by the server. In this section, we will discuss these functions. I refer just to the C API because I had to choose one language, and most of the other APIs are based on the C API.[2]

Number of rows affected

Let's start with the simple output we saw earlier, which is displayed after each insert, update, or delete and shows how many rows were inserted, updated, or deleted:

```
Query OK, N rows affected
```

This means the query executed fine and changed *N* rows.

To get the same information in an application, use the call:

```
mysql_affected_rows()
```

This returns a positive number of rows if there were changes, 0 if nothing changed, or −1 in case of error.

---

2. You can find a detailed description of the C API syntax at *http://dev.mysql.com/doc/refman/5.5/en/c.html*.

For UPDATE statements, if the client flag CLIENT_FOUND_ROWS was set, this function returns the number of rows that matched the WHERE condition, which is not always the same as those that were actually changed.

 Using affected rows is turned off by default in Connector/J because this feature is not JDBC-compliant and will break most applications that rely on found (matched) rows instead of affected rows for DML statements. But it does cause correct update counts from INSERT ... ON DUPLICATE KEY UPDATE statements to be returned by the server. The useAffectedRows connection string property tells Connector/J whether to set the CLIENT_FOUND_ROWS flag when connecting to the server.

Number of matched rows

The string in the output that indicates this is:

```
Rows matched: M
```

which shows how many rows satisfy the WHERE conditions.

The following C function:

```
mysql_info()
```

returns additional information about the most recent query in the string format. For an UPDATE, it returns a string like:

```
Rows matched: # Changed: # Warnings: #
```

where each # represents the number of matched rows, changed rows, and warnings, correspondingly. You should parse the line for "matched: #" to find out how many corresponding rows were found.

Number of changed rows

The string in the output that indicates this is:

```
Changed: P
```

which shows how many rows were actually changed. Note that M (rows matched) and P (rows changed) can be different. Perhaps the columns you wanted to change already contained the values you specified; in that case, the columns appear in the "Matched" value but not the "Changed" value.

In an application, retrieve this information using mysql_info() as before, but in this case, parse for "Changed: #."

Warnings: number and message

The string in the output that indicates this is:

```
Warnings: R
```

You get warnings if the server detected something unusual and worth reporting during the query, but the query could still be executed and the rows could be modified. Be sure to check for warnings anyway, because they will let you know about potential problems.

In your application, you can retrieve warnings in a few different ways. You can use `mysql_info()` again and parse for "Warnings: #". You can also issue:

```
mysql_warning_count()
```

If there are warnings, run a `SHOW WARNINGS` query to get the text message that describes what happened. Another option is:

```
mysql_sqlstate()
```

This retrieves the most recent `SQLSTATE`. For example, "42000" means a syntax error. "00000" means 0 errors and 0 warnings.

> A value called `SQLSTATE` is defined by the ANSI SQL standard to indicate the status of a statement. The states are set to status codes, defined in the standard, that indicate whether a call completed successfully or returned an exception. The `SQLSTATE` is returned as a character string. To find out which values the MySQL server can return, refer to "Server Error Codes and Messages" (*http://dev .mysql.com/doc/refman/5.5/en/error-messages-server.html*) in the MySQL Reference Manual.

Errors

It is also always useful to check for errors. The following functions report the error value for the most recent SQL statement:

`mysql_errno()`

This returns the MySQL number of the latest error. For instance, a syntax error will generate the number 1064, whereas 0 means no error.

`mysql_error()`

This returns a text representation of the latest error. For a syntax error, it would be something like:

```
You have an error in your SQL syntax; check the manual that
corresponds to your MySQL server version for the right syntax
to use near 'FRO t1 WHERE f1 IN (1,2,1)' at line 1
```

This can be convenient for storing messages in a separate logfile that you can examine at any time.

> The official MySQL documentation contains a list of errors that the MySQL server can return (*http://dev.mysql.com/doc/refman/5.5/en/error -messages-server.html*) and a list of client errors (*http://dev.mysql.com/ doc/refman/5.5/en/error-messages-client.html*).

Tracing Back Errors in Data

If you rigorously check the results of your queries and updates, you'll catch many of the problems that could otherwise go undetected for weeks and cause a lot of grief when the problems finally grow too large to miss. But problems do creep up on you. Sometimes a SELECT suddenly starts returning wrong results, but your experiments with the query just confirm there is nothing wrong with it.

In this case, you need to imitate user actions, but in reverse order, until you find the source of the error. If you are lucky, you will catch the problem in a single step. Usually it will take multiple steps, and sometimes a very long time.

A lot of these issues happen because the data is different on the master and slave in a replication environment. One common problem is duplicate values where they are supposed to be unique (e.g., if a user relies on an INSERT ON DUPLICATE KEY UPDATE statement but a table has a different structure on the master and slave). For such setups, the user usually notices the problem later when SELECT statements query the slave, instead of noticing them when the INSERT takes place. Things become even worse when this happens during circular replication.

To illustrate this problem, we'll work with a stored procedure that inserts into a table from a temporary table that was created to hold the results of other selects. This is another example of a common technique when a user wants to handle data from large tables without the risk of modifying data inadvertently or blocking other applications that are using the large tables.

Let's create our table and populate it with temporary values. In a real application, the temporary table would hold a result set from some calculation that is waiting to be stored in the main table:

```
CREATE TABLE t1(f1 INT) ENGINE=InnoDB;
CREATE TEMPORARY TABLE t2(f1 INT) ENGINE=InnoDB;
```

Now create values in the temporary table:

```
INSERT INTO t2 VALUES(1),(2),(3);
```

The stored routine moves data from the temporary table into the main table. It checks first to make sure something is in the temporary table before doing the move. Our version looks like this:

```
CREATE PROCEDURE p1()
BEGIN
DECLARE m INT UNSIGNED DEFAULT NULL;
CREATE TEMPORARY TABLE IF NOT EXISTS t2(f1 INT) ENGINE=InnoDB;
SELECT MAX(f1) INTO m FROM t2;
IF m IS NOT NULL
THEN
   INSERT INTO t1(f1) SELECT f1 FROM t2;
END IF;
END
|
```

This routine creates the temporary table if it does not exist when the routine is called. This prevents errors that would be caused if the temporary table does not exist, but at the same time leads to new issues, as we will see.

> The example uses the MAX function just to check whether there is at least one row in the table. I prefer MAX to COUNT because InnoDB tables do not store the number of rows they contain, but calculate this value every time the COUNT function is called. Therefore, MAX(indexed_field) is faster than COUNT.

If a slave restarted after the first insert but before the stored procedure call, the temporary table on the slave would be empty and the main table on the slave would have no data. In that case, we will get the following on the master:

```
mysql> SELECT * FROM t1;
+------+
| f1   |
+------+
|    1 |
|    2 |
|    3 |
```

```
+------+
3 rows in set (0.03 sec)
```

Whereas on the slave we get:

```
mysql> SELECT * FROM t1;
Empty set (0.00 sec)
```

Even worse, if we insert into t1 after the stored procedure call runs, we will have a total mess in the slave's data.

Suppose we notice the error in an application that reads data from the main table. We now need to find out how data has been inserted into the slave table: was it a direct update on the slave, or was data replicated from the master?

 MySQL replication does not check data consistency for you, so updates of the same objects using both the SQL replication thread and the user thread on the slave leave the data different from the master, which in turn can lead to failure during later replicated events.

Because we imitated this situation in our example, we know at this point why data corruption happened: the slave was restarted after the first insert but before the stored procedure call. In a real-life situation, issues tend to be noticed later when a user issues a select:

```
mysql> SELECT * FROM t1;
Empty set (0.00 sec)
```

When you see unexpected results from SELECT, you need to find out whether this is caused by the query itself or by something that went wrong earlier. The query just shown is so simple that it couldn't produce errors unless the table was corrupted, so we must try to go back to see how the table was modified.

Our generic example is in a replicated environment with a read-only slave, so we can be sure that the wrong data arose in one of two ways: either the master inserted the wrong data, or the data was corrupted during replication.

So check first whether the master has the wrong data:

```
master> SELECT * FROM t1;
+------+
| f1   |
+------+
|    1 |
|    2 |
|    3 |
+------+
3 rows in set (0.03 sec)
```

The master's data is correct, so the source of the problem lies in the replication layer.

But why did it happen? Replication seems to be running fine,[3] so we suspect a logic error on the master. Having discovered a possible source of the problem, you need to analyze the stored procedure and the calls on the master to find a fix.

As I said before, the slave server was restarted after events that insert data into the temporary table were replicated and emptied the temporary table, but before the stored procedure call that selects and inserts data into the main table. So the slave just re-created an empty temporary table and inserted no data.

In this case, you can either switch to row-based replication or rewrite the procedure so it does not rely on the existence of the temporary table. Another approach is to truncate and then refill the table so that a sudden restart will not leave the slave without data.

One might think that this example is very artificial and that you can't predict when a server will suddenly restart. This is correct, but restarts are sure to happen from time to time. Therefore, you need to worry about such errors.

Actually, a slave replicates binary log events one by one, and when data is created within an atomic event (e.g., a transaction or stored procedure call), the slave would not be affected by this issue. But again, this example was just a simple one to show the concept behind events that do happen in real life.

- When you experience a problem on a statement that you know is correct, check what your application did before you saw the problem.

More details on replication errors are in Chapter 5.

Single Server Example

I once worked on a web application that stored measurements made in different cutting systems. The user could add a system, then edit the rules about how it saved its measurements.

The first time I met the error, I tested a web page with a list of systems:

```
Existing systems

* System 1
* Test
* test2
* test2
* test2

Enter name of new system:
<>
Description:
<>

<Go!>
```

---

3. We will discuss in great detail how to troubleshoot replication failures in Chapter 5, so I'm skipping the explanation here.

The list should not contain duplicate systems, because there is no sense in describing the same rule twice. So I was very surprised to see several items with the same name.

The code that printed the data used objects, and I could not see what statements were sent to the MySQL server just by reading the code:

```
return $this->addParameters(array(Field::ITEMS => DAO::system()->getPlainList()));
```

I used logging to get a real query. It happened to be correct:

```
SELECT `system`.`id`, `system`.`name`, `system`.`description` FROM `system`
```

Next I examined the contents of the table:

```
mysql> SELECT * FROM system;
+----+----------+-------------------------------------------------+
| id | name     | description                                     |
+----+----------+-------------------------------------------------+
|  1 | System 1 | Man and woman clothing construction             |
|  2 | Test     | Testing Geometric set                           |
|  3 | test2    | New test                                        |
|  4 | test2    | foobar                                          |
|  8 | test2    |                                                 |
+----+----------+-------------------------------------------------+
5 rows in set (0.00 sec)
```

So the SELECT was accurately returning the data set that existed in the table. I switched to checking the code that updated the table:

```
$system = System::factory()
->setName($this->form->get(Field::NAME))
->setDescription(
$this->form->get(Field::DESCRIPTION)
);
DAO::system()->take($system);
```

Again I used logging to get the query:

```
INSERT INTO `system` (`id`, `name`, `description`) VALUES ('', 'test2', '')
```

The query was right too! id seemed to be an auto-incremented field that got set automatically.

But at the same time, the query hints at the potential problem: it must be running repeatedly with no check for uniqueness. Making this guess, I decided to check the table definition:

```
mysql> SHOW CREATE TABLE system\G
*************************** 1. row ***************************
       Table: system
Create Table: CREATE TABLE `system` (
  `id` int(11) NOT NULL AUTO_INCREMENT,
  `name` varchar(255) NOT NULL,
  `description` tinytext NOT NULL,
  PRIMARY KEY (`id`)
) ENGINE=InnoDB AUTO_INCREMENT=9 DEFAULT CHARSET=utf8
1 row in set (0.09 sec)
```

And this clearly showed the source of the problem: the name field is not defined as UNIQUE. When creating the table, I probably was planning to use id as a unique identifier, but because I also use MySQL's ability to generate an auto-incremented value for `id` in the `INSERT`, nothing prevented me from using the same name repeatedly.

To solve the problem, I manually removed the superfluous rows and added a `UNIQUE` index:

```
ALTER TABLE system ADD UNIQUE(name)
```

We're done for now with problems related to wrong results. Next we'll turn to some other problems that occur frequently.

Slow Queries

One common issue with SQL applications is performance regression. In this section, I'll describe some basic actions to take when you hit performance problems. Don't worry about the details; just pick up the essential ideas. As your knowledge deepens, you'll find yourself using them in a more educated and therefore more effective manner.

When I considered which problems to include in this chapter, I questioned whether I should mention performance problems at all. There are a lot of sources describing performance issues in detail, starting with the wonderful "Optimization" chapter in the MySQL Reference Manual and extending to books published by O'Reilly. I will add a short overview of useful sources at the end of this book. One can easily spend one's career on this subject or drown in the flood of available information.

I will be speaking here mostly about `SELECT` queries. At the end of this section, I briefly address how to deal with a slow query that modifies data.

Three main techniques will help you work on slow queries: tuning the query itself, tuning your tables (including adding indexes), and tuning the server. Let's look at them in detail.

Tuning a Query with Information from EXPLAIN

The most powerful tool for query tuning is our old acquaintance `EXPLAIN`. This statement provides information about how the server actually executes a query. Details of MySQL `EXPLAIN` are covered quite well in the MySQL Reference Manual (*http://dev .mysql.com/doc/refman/5.5/en/explain-output.html*), and I will not repeat that information here. Rather, I'll pick out what I've found to be the most important and useful elements of the output.

The first lines you should look at are `type`, which actually shows the type of join performed, and `rows`, which shows an estimate of how many rows were examined during the query. (For instance, if the query had to scan the whole table, the number of rows would equal the number of rows in the table.) Multitable joins have to examine a Cartesian product of the number of rows examined in each table. Thus, if the query examines 20 rows in one table and 30 in another, the join performs a total of 600 examinations. EXPLAIN will contain a row for each table in the JOIN. We will see this in the following examples.

EXPLAIN reports a join even when you operate on a single table. This may sound a bit strange, but the MySQL optimizer internally treats any query as a join, even if it's a join on one table.

Let's look into the EXPLAIN output from the previous section again:

```
mysql> EXPLAIN EXTENDED SELECT count(*) FROM items WHERE id IN
(SELECT iid FROM items_links)\G
*************************** 1. row ***************************
           id: 1
  select_type: PRIMARY
        table: items
         type: index
possible_keys: NULL
          key: PRIMARY
      key_len: 4
          ref: NULL
         rows: 10
     filtered: 100.00
        Extra: Using where; Using index
*************************** 2. row ***************************
           id: 2
  select_type: DEPENDENT SUBQUERY
        table: items_links
         type: index_subquery
possible_keys: iid,iid_2
          key: iid
      key_len: 5
          ref: func
         rows: 1
     filtered: 100.00
        Extra: Using index; Using where
2 rows in set, 1 warning (0.48 sec)
```

The number of examined rows is 10 times 1 because the subquery executes once for every row in the outer query. The type of the first query is index, which means that the whole index will be read. The type of the second query is index_subquery. This is an index lookup function that works similar to the ref type. So, in this example, the optimizer will read all index entries from the items table and one row from the items_links table for each of the ten matching rows found from items.

How can we find out if this is a good plan for the query? First, let's repeat the query results and check how long the query actually took:

```
mysql> SELECT count(*) FROM items WHERE id IN (SELECT iid FROM items_links);
+----------+
| count(*) |
+----------+
|        4 |
+----------+
1 row in set (0.08 sec)
```

The MySQL server examined 10 rows and returned 4. How fast is it? To answer this question, let's count the number of rows in both tables:

```
mysql> SELECT count(*) FROM items;
+----------+
| count(*) |
+----------+
|       10 |
+----------+
1 row in set (0.11 sec)

mysql> SELECT count(*) FROM items_links;
+----------+
| count(*) |
+----------+
|        6 |
+----------+
1 row in set (0.00 sec)
```

We have 10 rows in the items table, each with a unique ID. The items_links table has 6 rows with nonunique IDs (iid). For the current amount of rows, the plan looks good, but at the same time, it shows a potential problem. Right now we have fewer links than items. Currently the difference in these numbers is not high, but it will be more noticeable if their numbers diverge.

To test this guess and to show you an example of query tuning, I will insert a few rows into the items table. The id is defined as INT NOT NULL AUTO_INCREMENT PRIMARY KEY, so we are guaranteed that no existing link will refer to a newly inserted row. This allows us to imitate a realistic situation that arises when a user needs to get a small number of links (six in our case) from a large table. The following statements are just a quick hack to create a lot of rows by repeatedly selecting all the rows in the table and inserting more:

```
mysql> INSERT INTO items( short_description , description,
example, explanation, additional) SELECT  short_description , description,
example, explanation, additional FROM items;
Query OK, 10 rows affected (0.17 sec)
Records: 10  Duplicates: 0  Warnings: 0
<Repeat this query few times>
mysql> INSERT INTO items( short_description , description,
example, explanation, additional) SELECT  short_description , description,
example, explanation, additional FROM items;
Query OK, 2560 rows affected (3.77 sec)
Records: 2560  Duplicates: 0  Warnings: 0
```

Now let's see whether our query plan changed:

```
mysql> EXPLAIN EXTENDED SELECT count(*) FROM items WHERE id IN
    -> (SELECT iid FROM items_links)\G
*************************** 1. row ***************************
           id: 1
  select_type: PRIMARY
        table: items
         type: index
possible_keys: NULL
```

```
          key: PRIMARY
      key_len: 4
          ref: NULL
         rows: 5136
     filtered: 100.00
        Extra: Using where; Using index
*************************** 2. row ***************************
           id: 2
  select_type: DEPENDENT SUBQUERY
        table: items_links
         type: index_subquery
possible_keys: iid,iid_2
          key: iid
      key_len: 5
          ref: func
         rows: 1
     filtered: 100.00
        Extra: Using index; Using where
2 rows in set, 1 warning (0.09 sec)
```

The query execution plan is the same—and it is going to examine 5,136 rows for just
six links! Is there any way to rewrite the query so it will execute faster?

The type of subquery is index_subquery. This means that the optimizer uses an index
lookup function that replaces the subquery completely. The output from SHOW
WARNINGS shows how the query has been rewritten:

```
mysql> SHOW WARNINGS\G
*************************** 1. row ***************************
  Level: Note
   Code: 1003
Message: select count(0) AS `count(*)` from `collaborate2011`.`items` where
<in_optimizer>(`collaborate2011`.`items`.`id`,<exists>
(<index_lookup>(<cache>(`collaborate2011`.`items`.`id`) in
items_links on iid where (<cache>(`collaborate2011`.`items`.`id`) =
`collaborate2011`.`items_links`.`iid`))))
1 row in set (0.00 sec)
```

The output is intimidating, but at least we can see some kind of join here. What if we
rewrite the query to be more explicit about the columns on which the join is performed?
We will also rewrite the subquery into an explicit JOIN; with current versions of MySQL,
this method can dramatically improve performance:

```
mysql> \W
Show warnings enabled.
mysql> EXPLAIN EXTENDED SELECT count(*) FROM items JOIN
items_links ON (items.id=items_links.iid)\G
*************************** 1. row ***************************
           id: 1
  select_type: SIMPLE
        table: items_links
         type: index
possible_keys: iid,iid_2
          key: iid_2
      key_len: 5
```

```
            ref: NULL
           rows: 6
       filtered: 100.00
          Extra: Using index
*************************** 2. row ***************************
             id: 1
    select_type: SIMPLE
          table: items
           type: eq_ref
  possible_keys: PRIMARY
            key: PRIMARY
        key_len: 4
            ref: collaborate2011.items_links.iid
           rows: 1
       filtered: 100.00
          Extra: Using index
2 rows in set, 1 warning (0.05 sec)

Note (Code 1003): select count(0) AS `count(*)` from `collaborate2011`.`items`
join `collaborate2011`.`items_links` where (`collaborate2011`.`items`.`id` =
`collaborate2011`.`items_links`.`iid`)
```

The result looks encouraging because it does not scan all the rows from the items table. But does the query work correctly?

```
mysql> SELECT count(*) FROM items JOIN items_links ON
(items.id=items_links.iid);
+----------+
| count(*) |
+----------+
|        6 |
+----------+
1 row in set (0.10 sec)
```

We get six rows instead of four. This is because we asked the query to return all matches, even when the same link was in two matches. We can fix this by adding the DISTINCT keyword:

```
mysql> SELECT count(distinct items.id) FROM items JOIN items_links ON
(items.id=items_links.iid);
+--------------------------+
| count(distinct items.id) |
+--------------------------+
|                        4 |
+--------------------------+
1 row in set (0.12 sec)
```

 You can use a query rewriting technique to confirm that DISTINCT is needed. Just replace count(*) with items.id to see the duplicate values.

With DISTINCT, is the query still fast? Let's try EXPLAIN once again:

```
mysql> EXPLAIN EXTENDED SELECT count(distinct items.id) FROM items
JOIN items_links ON (items.id=items_links.iid)\G
*************************** 1. row ***************************
           id: 1
  select_type: SIMPLE
        table: items_links
         type: index
possible_keys: iid,iid_2
          key: iid_2
      key_len: 5
          ref: NULL
         rows: 6
     filtered: 100.00
        Extra: Using index
*************************** 2. row ***************************
           id: 1
  select_type: SIMPLE
        table: items
         type: eq_ref
possible_keys: PRIMARY
          key: PRIMARY
      key_len: 4
          ref: collaborate2011.items_links.iid
         rows: 1
     filtered: 100.00
        Extra: Using index
2 rows in set, 1 warning (0.00 sec)

Note (Code 1003): select count(distinct `collaborate2011`.`items`.`id`) AS
`count(distinct items.id)` from `collaborate2011`.`items` join
`collaborate2011`.`items_links` where (`collaborate2011`.`items`.`id` =
`collaborate2011`.`items_links`.`iid`)
```

It still examines six rows. So we can consider the query to be optimized for this particular data set. I will explain later in this chapter why the structure of the data and its size matter.

In our example, the data set was small, so I could not make it run really slowly, even on my laptop. Still, the execution times of the original and optimized queries differ substantially. This was the original query:

```
mysql> SELECT count(*) FROM items  WHERE id IN (SELECT iid FROM
items_links );
+----------+
| count(*) |
+----------+
|        4 |
+----------+
1 row in set (0.21 sec)
```

And here is the optimized query:

```
mysql> SELECT count(distinct items.id) FROM items JOIN items_links
ON (items.id=items_links.iid);
+--------------------------+
| count(distinct items.id) |
```

```
+-------------------------+
|                       4 |
+-------------------------+
1 row in set (0.10 sec)
```

We achieved a two-fold improvement, even for such a small data set! For our test, this is just 0.11 sec, but for millions of rows, the improvement can be way better.

- You just learned a basic query tuning technique with the help of EXPLAIN: reading information about what currently happens and comparing it to what you wish to reach. A similar process can tune any query, from the simplest to the most complex.

Table Tuning and Indexes

In the previous section, we introduced the process of tuning queries. In all the examples, EXPLAIN output contained information about indexes. But what if a table has no index at all? Or if the indexes are not being used? How should you choose when, where, and which index to add?

The MySQL server uses indexes when results can be limited. Therefore, having indexes on columns listed in WHERE, JOIN, and GROUP BY can speed up queries. Having an index on the column in an ORDER BY clause can make sense as well because it will allow the server to do more effective sorting.

With those principles in mind, adding indexes becomes a simple task. Consider tables from the previous example, but without any indexes:

```
mysql> CREATE TEMPORARY TABLE items SELECT * FROM items;
Query OK, 5120 rows affected (6.97 sec)
Records: 5120  Duplicates: 0  Warnings: 0

mysql> CREATE TEMPORARY TABLE items_links SELECT * FROM items_links;
Query OK, 6 rows affected (0.36 sec)
Records: 6  Duplicates: 0  Warnings: 0

mysql> SHOW CREATE TABLE items;
+-------+--------------------------------------------------------------------+
| Table | Create Table                                                       |
+-------+--------------------------------------------------------------------+
| items | CREATE TEMPORARY TABLE `items` (
  `id` int(11) NOT NULL DEFAULT '0',
  `short_description` varchar(255) DEFAULT NULL,
  `description` text,
  `example` text,
  `explanation` text,
  `additional` text
) ENGINE=InnoDB DEFAULT CHARSET=utf8 |
+-------+--------------------------------------------------------------------+
1 row in set (0.10 sec)

mysql> SHOW CREATE TABLE items_links;
+-------------+--------------------------------------------------------------+
| Table       | Create Table                                                 |
+-------------+--------------------------------------------------------------+
| Table       | Create Table                                                 |
```

```
+-------------+------------------------------------------------------------------+
| items_links | CREATE TEMPORARY TABLE `items_links` (
  `iid` int(11) DEFAULT NULL,
  `linkid` int(11) DEFAULT NULL
) ENGINE=InnoDB DEFAULT CHARSET=utf8 |
+-------------+------------------------------------------------------------------+
1 row in set (0.00 sec)
```

As you can see, no index is specified. Let's try an unoptimized query on these tables, and then improve it:

```
mysql> EXPLAIN EXTENDED SELECT count(distinct items.id) FROM items JOIN
items_links ON (items.id=items_links.iid)\G
*************************** 1. row ***************************
           id: 1
  select_type: SIMPLE
        table: items_links
         type: ALL
possible_keys: NULL
          key: NULL
      key_len: NULL
          ref: NULL
         rows: 6
     filtered: 100.00
        Extra:
*************************** 2. row ***************************
           id: 1
  select_type: SIMPLE
        table: items
         type: ALL
possible_keys: NULL
          key: NULL
      key_len: NULL
          ref: NULL
         rows: 5137
     filtered: 100.00
        Extra: Using where; Using join buffer
2 rows in set, 1 warning (0.00 sec)

Note (Code 1003): select count(distinct `collaborate2011`.`items`.`id`) AS
`count(distinct items.id)` from `collaborate2011`.`items` join
`collaborate2011`.`items_links` where (`collaborate2011`.`items`.`id` =
`collaborate2011`.`items_links`.`iid`)
```

The type became ALL, the most expensive type, because it means all rows will be read. The query is examining 6*5,137 = 30,822 rows now. This is even worse than the query we considered to be slow in our earlier example.

Let's examine the query in detail:

```
SELECT count(distinct items.id)...
```

This query returns the number of unique not-null values in the result set. It would make sense to add an index on items.id, so that this search could use it.

Another part of the same query:

```
...FROM items JOIN items_links ON (items.id=items_links.iid)
```

The join refers to the `id` column from `items` and the `iid` column from `items_links`. So it makes sense to add indexes to both of those columns.

```
mysql> ALTER TABLE items ADD INDEX(id);
Query OK, 5120 rows affected (4.78 sec)
Records: 5120  Duplicates: 0  Warnings: 0

mysql> ALTER TABLE items_links ADD INDEX(iid);
Query OK, 6 rows affected (0.04 sec)
Records: 6  Duplicates: 0  Warnings: 0
```

Now we can see how this affects the query plan:

```
mysql> EXPLAIN EXTENDED SELECT count(distinct items.id) FROM items
JOIN items_links ON (items.id=items_links.iid)\G
*************************** 1. row ***************************
           id: 1
  select_type: SIMPLE
        table: items_links
         type: index
possible_keys: iid
          key: iid
      key_len: 5
          ref: NULL
         rows: 6
     filtered: 100.00
        Extra: Using index
*************************** 2. row ***************************
           id: 1
  select_type: SIMPLE
        table: items
         type: ref
possible_keys: id
          key: id
      key_len: 4
          ref: collaborate2011.items_links.iid
         rows: 1
     filtered: 100.00
        Extra: Using index
2 rows in set, 1 warning (0.00 sec)

Note (Code 1003): select count(distinct `collaborate2011`.`items`.`id`) AS
`count(distinct items.id)` from `collaborate2011`.`items` join
`collaborate2011`.`items_links` where (`collaborate2011`.`items`.`id` =
`collaborate2011`.`items_links`.`iid`)
```

This looks much better than before, with a single exception: the `ref` type for table items is worse than the `eq_ref` we got in the previous section. This type is used because we added a simple index, whereas the original table had a unique index on the same column. We can easily change the temporary table too, because IDs are unique and are supposed to be so:

```
mysql> EXPLAIN EXTENDED SELECT count(distinct items.id) FROM items
JOIN items_links ON (items.id=items_links.iid)\G
```

```
*************************** 1. row ***************************
           id: 1
  select_type: SIMPLE
        table: items_links
         type: index
possible_keys: iid
          key: iid
      key_len: 5
          ref: NULL
         rows: 6
     filtered: 100.00
        Extra: Using index
*************************** 2. row ***************************
           id: 1
  select_type: SIMPLE
        table: items
         type: eq_ref
possible_keys: id_2,id
          key: id_2
      key_len: 4
          ref: collaborate2011.items_links.iid
         rows: 1
     filtered: 100.00
        Extra: Using index
2 rows in set, 1 warning (0.00 sec)

Note (Code 1003): select count(distinct `collaborate2011`.`items`.`id`) AS
`count(distinct items.id)` from `collaborate2011`.`items` join
`collaborate2011`.`items_links` where (`collaborate2011`.`items`.`id` =
`collaborate2011`.`items_links`.`iid`)
```

Now, when the faster-executing type eq_ref is used, we can drop the redundant index on items.id. This is especially important if you care about the speed of queries that modify data because updating each index takes time. We will discuss when query tuning should be stopped in following section.

You just learned how indexes affect query execution and when it makes sense to add them.

Choosing Your Own Execution Plan

There are cases when an index actually slows down a query. In this case, you can drop the index or use an IGNORE INDEX clause if you need the index for other queries. You can also use FORCE INDEX to let the optimizer know which index you want to use. These clauses can also be very useful for query tuning when you want to see how a particular index can affect performance. Just try EXPLAIN using the clauses, and analyze the output.

Although use of IGNORE INDEX and FORCE INDEX may sound appealing, you should avoid using them in production when possible, unless you are ready to examine every query with such a clause during each following upgrade.

This is required because the optimizer always tries to choose the best plan for execution. Improving from version to version, it can create different plans for the same JOINs.

When you don't force or ignore an index, it will just create a plan as best as it can. But if you explicitly specify how it should use indexes in one of the tables from a multitable JOIN, such a rule can affect others, and the final execution plan could change in the new version to something worse than it was before.

Using IGNORE INDEX and FORCE INDEX in queries that access only one table is relatively safe. In all other cases, you must check to make sure the query execution plan was not changed during the upgrade.

Another problem with using IGNORE INDEX and FORCE INDEX in production is that the best execution plan for particular tables depends on the data they store. In normal operation, the optimizer checks table statistics and adjusts the plan as necessary, which it can't do when you use IGNORE INDEX and FORCE INDEX. If you use these clauses, you must regularly check whether they are still effective throughout the application's life.

When to Stop Optimizing

The previous sections discussed simple queries. Even there we found ways to improve the queries, sometimes with increasingly better results over several iterations of tuning. When you work with complicated queries with a lot of JOIN conditions, a lot of columns in WHERE clauses, and GROUP BY clauses, you have even more choices. It's possible to imagine that you could always find a way to make performance even faster and that these improvements can continue forever. So the question is when to consider a query properly optimized and put a stop to the research.

An in-depth knowledge of performance techniques could help you choose the proper solution. But there are still basic considerations that can help you to stop, even if you don't consider yourself an expert.

First, you need to find out what the query does. For example, the following query:

```
SELECT * FROM contacts
```

always returns all columns and rows from the table, and no optimization can be applied to it.

But even if you extract all columns, adding a JOIN can change the situation:

```
SELECT * FROM child JOIN parent ON (child.pid=parent.id)
```

This can be optimized because the ON condition limits the result set. The same analysis can be applied to queries with WHERE and GROUP BY conditions.

The second thing you need to look at is the join type from the EXPLAIN output. Although you will be trying to get the best possible JOIN types, keep in mind the limitations of your data. For example, a condition on a nonunique row can never lead to types eq_ref or better.

Your data is very important when you optimize queries. Differences in data can lead to completely different results for the same execution plan. The most trivial example is to compare results for a single row in a table to results for a table where more than 50% of the rows have the same value. In these cases, using indexes can decrease performance rather than increase it.

- Here is another rule: do not rely only on the EXPLAIN output; make sure to measure the actual query execution time.

Another thing you should keep in mind is the effect of indexes on changes to the table. Although indexes usually improve the speed of SELECT queries, they slightly decrease the speed of queries that modify data, especially INSERT statements. Therefore, it can sometimes be sensible to live with slow SELECT queries if it speeds up the execution of inserts. Always keep in mind the overall performance of your application, not just a single query.

Effects of Options

Suppose you have completely optimized your query and can't find any ways to tune it better, but it's still slow. Can you do anything to improve its performance? Yes. There are server options that allow you to tune factors affecting the query, such as the size of temporary tables in memory, buffers for sorting, and so on. Some options specific to a particular storage engine, such as InnoDB, can also be useful for query optimizing.

I will describe these configuration options in more detail in Chapter 3. Here I'll give an overview of how to use them to improve performance.

Tuning server options is a somewhat global activity because a change can potentially affect every query on the server (or in the case of engine-specific options, every query that refers to a table using that storage engine). But some options are used for particular kinds of optimization, and if your query does not meet the right conditions, it remains unaffected.

The first options to check are buffer sizes. Each memory buffer is allocated for specific reasons. The general rule is that large buffers mean higher performance—but only if the query can use the larger size for the particular role played by that buffer.

And of course there are trade-offs when you increase buffer sizes. Here are some of the issues large buffers can cause. I don't want to dissuade you from setting large buffers, because under the right circumstances it's a great way to improve performance significantly. You just need to keep the following issues in mind and adjust sizes reasonably.

Swapping
    A large buffer may lead to swapping at the operating-system level and therefore slow performance, depending on the size of RAM on your system. In general, the MySQL server works fast if all the memory it needs sits in physical RAM. When it starts swapping, performance degrades dramatically.

    Swapping can happen when you allocate more memory to buffers than your server has physically in RAM. Please note that some buffers are allocated for each user thread. To determine how much memory the server allocates for such buffers, use the formula *max_connections * buffer_size*. Calculate the sum of this product for all buffers, and make sure it is less than the amount of memory the *mysqld* server can use. This calculation is not decisive, because *mysqld* can actually allocate more memory than you explicitly specify.

Startup time
> The more memory *mysqld* needs to allocate, the longer it takes to start.

Stale data
> There are also scaling issues, mostly for caches shared between threads. Scaling the buffers that do the caching in these cases can lead to memory fragmentation. You will generally notice the fragmentation problem after hours of running the server, when old data needs to be removed from the buffer in order to make room for new data. This can cause a fast server to suddenly slow down. I show this in an example in Chapter 3.

After finishing with buffers, consider other options discussed in Chapter 3. Pay attention not only to options explicitly designated for performance tuning, such as optimizer options, but also to options that control high availability. The safer you make a transaction, the more checks are needed and the more slowly the query executes. But be careful with such options; tune them when and only when you can sacrifice safety for performance.

When you tune options, it is especially important to consider performance as a whole, because every option affects the whole server. For example, there is no sense in tuning engine-specific options if you don't use that engine. This might appear too obvious, but I have seen way too many installations where MyISAM options were huge when only the InnoDB storage engine was used, or vice versa. This is especially important to remember if you take some generic configuration as a template.

The MySQL server allows you to change most of its configuration dynamically. This is valuable for performance testing. Change options and rerun queries to make sure you get good results before applying the changes in the configuration file. It is also always a good idea to apply changes step by step, so that you can attribute bad effects to the right option and easily go back. We will discuss this technique in detail in Chapter 6.

Queries That Modify Data

We discussed effects on the performance of SELECT queries, and in this section, we turn to tuning queries that modify data. UPDATE and DELETE queries can use the same conditions as SELECT to limit the number of rows affected. Therefore, the same rules for tuning can be applied to these queries.

We saw in "When the Problem May Have Been a Previous Update" on page 10 how to convert UPDATE and DELETE queries to SELECT queries and run EXPLAIN on them. You can use this technique to troubleshoot performance issues on versions prior to 5.6.3, which introduced EXPLAIN for INSERT, UPDATE, and DELETE queries, but remember that UPDATE and DELETE are sometimes executed slightly differently from the corresponding SELECT.

Check whether indexes were used by querying the Handler_% status variables before and after query execution:

```
mysql> SHOW STATUS LIKE 'Handler_%'; ❶
+----------------------------+-------+
| Variable_name              | Value |
+----------------------------+-------+
| Handler_commit             | 0     |
| Handler_delete             | 0     |
| Handler_discover           | 0     |
| Handler_prepare            | 0     |
| Handler_read_first         | 0     |
| Handler_read_key           | 0     |
| Handler_read_last          | 0     |
| Handler_read_next          | 0     |
| Handler_read_prev          | 0     |
| Handler_read_rnd           | 0     |
| Handler_read_rnd_next      | 19    |
| Handler_rollback           | 0     |
| Handler_savepoint          | 0     |
| Handler_savepoint_rollback | 0     |
| Handler_update             | 0     |
| Handler_write              | 17    |
+----------------------------+-------+
16 rows in set (0.00 sec)
```

❶ Here I used SHOW STATUS, which is a synonym of SHOW SESSION STATUS and shows the status variables for the current session.

 It is convenient to reset these variables before testing using a FLUSH STATUS query.

We'll talk about particular variables in the preceding list as we continue. You should be aware, though, that these are cumulative values, so they increase as you issue each query. Now let's tune our example query from "When the Problem May Have Been a Previous Update" on page 10 so that it will update null-able columns:

```
mysql> UPDATE items SET description = 'no description', additional
= 'no additional comments' WHERE description IS NULL;
Query OK, 0 rows affected (6.95 sec)
Rows matched: 0  Changed: 0  Warnings: 0
```

This changed no rows because we corrupted the data in an earlier step: we have 0 in each field instead of NULL now. But the query runs very slowly. Let's look at the handler variables:

```
mysql> show status like 'Handler_%';
+----------------------------+-------+
```

```
| Variable_name              | Value |
+----------------------------+-------+
| Handler_commit             | 1     |
| Handler_delete             | 0     |
| Handler_discover           | 0     |
| Handler_prepare            | 0     |
| Handler_read_first         | 1     |
| Handler_read_key           | 2     |
| Handler_read_last          | 0     |
| Handler_read_next          | 0     |
| Handler_read_prev          | 0     |
| Handler_read_rnd           | 0     |
| Handler_read_rnd_next      | 5140  |
| Handler_rollback           | 0     |
| Handler_savepoint          | 0     |
| Handler_savepoint_rollback | 0     |
| Handler_update             | 0     |
| Handler_write              | 17    |
+----------------------------+-------+
16 rows in set (0.01 sec)
```

What jumps out is the high value of `Handler_read_rnd_next`, which shows how often the next row in a datafile was read. A high value typically means that a table scan was used, which is not good for performance. `Handler_read_key` is a related variable showing the number of index read requests. It shouldn't be so low in relation to `Handler_read_rnd_next`, because that means a lot of rows were read instead of using an index. In addition, the values of `Handler_commit` and `Handler_read_first` have increased slightly. These refer respectively to the number of commits and the number of times the first entry in an index was read. Finally, the unobtrusive 1 in `Handler_read_first` shows that we asked the server to read a first entry in the index, which can be a symptom of a full index scan.

Hopefully, this run-through of a few `Handler_%` status variables has shown you how they can be used to check how queries are running. I'll leave the question of whether the speed of this query can be improved as homework for you.

I'll just spend a little space on `INSERT` queries. They have no conditions that limit the set of rows affected, so the presence of indexes in a table merely slows them down because each insert has to update the indexes. The performance of inserts should be tuned using server options. Here especially, the options offered by the InnoDB storage engine can be helpful.

One way to speed up inserts is to combine many of them in one statement, also called "bulk insert":

```
insert into t1 (f1, f2, f3, ...) values (v1, v2, v3, ...), (v1, v2, v3, ...), ...
```

But please note that inserts block table rows or even whole tables, so other queries are denied access while the insert runs. So I'll end this section by repeating the general rule:

- Keep the performance of the whole application in mind while tuning any single query.

No Silver Bullet

We just learned how tuning server options can dramatically improve performance. We've also seen in this chapter how to tune a particular query so it runs really fast. Tuning a query and tuning a server are often alternative solutions to performance problems. Is there any general rule about which kind of tuning you should start with?

I am afraid not. Tuning server options looks so promising that many people think finding and changing the right option will make *mysqld* run like a rocket. If you believe that too, I have to disappoint you: badly written queries will still be a drain on server resources. And you may enjoy good performance for a few hours after restarting the server only to see it decrease again, because every query will need a lot of resources and your caches will fill up. At times, the server will be inundated with millions of queries that want more and more resources.

However, tuning every single query might not be an option. Some of them are called rarely, so there is no need to spend human resources on them. Others may query all the rows in a table, which defeats attempts to optimize them.

I usually advocate some kind of "mixed" mode. Tune server options first, paying particular attention to options specific to your storage engine, then tune queries. After the important queries are tuned, go back to the server options and consider what you can tune more, then back to the rest of the queries, and so on, until you are happy with performance.

You can also start with the slowest queries in your application or find ones that can obviously benefit from trivial optimizations, then turn to server options. Consult the status variables, as shown earlier. I will describe them in more detail in Chapter 6.

Last but not least: use numerous information sources on performance tuning to create your own strategy.

When the Server Does Not Answer

Occasionally a MySQL client gets the catastrophic message "Lost connection to server during query" or "Server has gone away." Although I hope you will never face this problem, it's good to be prepared in case it happens. There are two main reasons for this problem caused by the MySQL installation itself: server issues (most likely a crash) or the misuse of connection options (usually timeout options or max_allowed_packet).

We will discuss the configuration of connections in Chapter 3. Problems caused by hardware and third-party software will be touched on in Chapter 4. Here I want to briefly describe what to do if the server crashes.

First, determine whether you really had a server crash. You can do this with the help of process status monitors. If you run *mysqld_safe* or another daemon that restarts the server after a failure, the error log will contain a message indicating the server has been restarted. When *mysqld* starts, it always prints something like this to the error logfile:

```
110716 14:01:44 [Note] /apps/mysql-5.1/libexec/mysqld: ready for connections.
Version: '5.1.59-debug'  socket: '/tmp/mysql51.sock'  port: 3351  Source distribution
```

So if you find such a message, the server has been restarted. If there is no message and the server is up and running, a lost connection is most likely caused by the misuse of connection options, which will be discussed in Chapter 3.

 If you remember when your MySQL server was originally started, you can use the status variable `uptime`, which shows the number of seconds since the server started:

```
mysql> SHOW GLOBAL STATUS LIKE 'uptime';
+---------------+-------+
| Variable_name | Value |
+---------------+-------+
| Uptime        | 10447 |
+---------------+-------+
1 row in set (0.00 sec)
```

This information will also help when you want to check whether *mysqld* failure was not caused by an operating system restart. Just compare the value of this variable with the operating system uptime.

The reason why I rely on error logfiles comes from my job experience with cases when customers notice a problem hours after a server crash and even some time after a planned *mysqld* restart.

If you confirm that the server has restarted, you should examine the error log again and look for information about the crash itself. Usually you can derive enough information about the crash from the error log to avoid the same situation in the future. We'll discuss how to investigate the small number of difficult cases you may encounter in Chapter 6. Now let's go back to the error logfile and see examples of its typical contents in case of a server crash. I'll list a large extract here:

```
Version: '5.1.39' socket: '/tmp/mysql_sandbox5139.sock' port: 5139
MySQL Community Server (GPL)
091002 14:56:54 - mysqld got signal 11 ;
This could be because you hit a bug. It is also possible that this binary
or one of the libraries it was linked against is corrupt, improperly built,
or misconfigured. This error can also be caused by malfunctioning hardware.
We will try our best to scrape up some info that will hopefully help diagnose
the problem, but since we have already crashed, something is definitely wrong
and this may fail.
key_buffer_size=8384512
read_buffer_size=131072
max_used_connections=1
max_threads=151
threads_connected=1

It is possible that mysqld could use up to
```

```
key_buffer_size + (read_buffer_size + sort_buffer_size)*max_threads = 338301 K
bytes of memory
Hope that's ok; if not, decrease some variables in the equation.
thd: 0x69e1b00
Attempting backtrace. You can use the following information to find out
where mysqld died. If you see no messages after this, something went
terribly wrong...
stack_bottom = 0x450890f0 thread_stack 0x40000
/users/ssmirnova/blade12/5.1.39/bin/mysqld(my_print_stacktrace+0x2e)[0x8ac81e]
/users/ssmirnova/blade12/5.1.39/bin/mysqld(handle_segfault+0x322)[0x5df502]
/lib64/libpthread.so.0[0x3429e0dd40]
/users/ssmirnova/blade12/5.1.39/bin/mysqld(_ZN6String4copyERKS_+0x16)[0x5d9876]
/users/ssmirnova/blade12/5.1.39/bin/mysqld(_ZN14Item_cache_str5storeEP4Item+0xc9)
[0x52ddd9]
/users/ssmirnova/blade12/5.1.39/bin/mysqld(_ZN26select_singlerow_subselect9send_
dataER4ListI4ItemE+0x45)
[0x5ca145]
/users/ssmirnova/blade12/5.1.39/bin/mysqld[0x6386d1]
/users/ssmirnova/blade12/5.1.39/bin/mysqld[0x64236a]
/users/ssmirnova/blade12/5.1.39/bin/mysqld(_ZN4JOIN4execEv+0x949)[0x658869]
/users/ssmirnova/blade12/5.1.39/bin/mysqld(_ZN30subselect_single_select_
engine4execEv+0x36c)[0x596f3c]
/users/ssmirnova/blade12/5.1.39/bin/mysqld(_ZN14Item_subselect4execEv+0x26)[0x595d96]
/users/ssmirnova/blade12/5.1.39/bin/mysqld(_ZN24Item_singlerow_subselect8val_
realEv+0xd)[0x595fbd]
/users/ssmirnova/blade12/5.1.39/bin/mysqld(_ZN14Arg_comparator18compare_real_
fixedEv+0x39)[0x561b89]
/users/ssmirnova/blade12/5.1.39/bin/mysqld(_ZN12Item_func_ne7val_intEv+0x23)[0x568fb3]
/users/ssmirnova/blade12/5.1.39/bin/mysqld(_ZN4JOIN8optimizeEv+0x12ef)[0x65208f]
/users/ssmirnova/blade12/5.1.39/bin/mysqld(_Z12mysql_selectP3THDPPP4ItemP10TABLE_
LISTjR4ListIS1_ES2_jP8
st_orderSB_S2_SB_yP13select_resultP18st_select_lex_unitP13st_select_lex+0xa0)
[0x654850]
/users/ssmirnova/blade12/5.1.39/bin/mysqld(_Z13handle_selectP3THDP6st_lexP13select_
resultm+0x16c)
[0x65a1cc]
/users/ssmirnova/blade12/5.1.39/bin/mysqld[0x5ecbda]
/users/ssmirnova/blade12/5.1.39/bin/mysqld(_Z21mysql_execute_commandP3THD+0x602)
[0x5efdd2]
/users/ssmirnova/blade12/5.1.39/bin/mysqld(_Z11mysql_parseP3THDPKcjPS2_+0x357)
[0x5f52f7]
/users/ssmirnova/blade12/5.1.39/bin/mysqld(_Z16dispatch_command19enum_server_
commandP3THDPcj+0xe93)
[0x5f6193]
/users/ssmirnova/blade12/5.1.39/bin/mysqld(_Z10do_commandP3THD+0xe6)[0x5f6a56]
/users/ssmirnova/blade12/5.1.39/bin/mysqld(handle_one_connection+0x246)[0x5e93f6]
/lib64/libpthread.so.0[0x3429e061b5]
/lib64/libc.so.6(clone+0x6d)[0x34292cd39d]`)
Trying to get some variables.
Some pointers may be invalid and cause the dump to abort...
thd->query at 0x6a39e60 = select 1 from `t1` where `c0` <>
(select geometrycollectionfromwkb(`c3`) from `t1`)
thd->thread_id=2
thd->killed=NOT_KILLED
```

```
The manual page at http://dev.mysql.com/doc/mysql/en/crashing.html contains
information that should help you find out what
```

The key line indicating the reason for the crash is:

```
091002 14:56:54 - mysqld got signal 11 ;
```

This means the MySQL server was killed after it asked the operating system for a
resource (e.g., access to a file or RAM), getting an error with code 11. In most operating
systems, this signal refers to a segmentation fault. You can find more detailed information in the user manual for your operating system. Run `man signal` for Unix and
Linux. In Windows, similar cases will usually generate a log message like "mysqld got
exception 0xc0000005." Search the Windows user manual for the meanings of these
exception codes.

The following is the excerpt from the log about a query that was running in the thread
that crashed the server:

```
Trying to get some variables.
Some pointers may be invalid and cause the dump to abort...
thd->query at 0x6a39e60 = SELECT 1 FROM `t1` WHERE `c0` <>
(SELECT geometrycollectionfromwkb(`c3`) FROM `t1`)
thd->thread_id=2
thd->killed=NOT_KILLED
```

To diagnose, rerun the query to see whether it was the cause of the crash:

```
mysql> SELECT 1 FROM `t1` WHERE `c0` <> (SELECT
geometrycollectionfromwkb(`c3`) FROM `t1`);
ERROR 2013 (HY000): Lost connection to MySQL server during query
```

 When I recommend repeating problems, I assume you will use the
development server and not your production server. We will discuss
how to safely troubleshoot in an environment dedicated to this purpose
in "Sandboxes" on page 181. Please don't try to repeat this example; it
is based on a known bug #47780 (*http://bugs.mysql.com/bug.php?id=
47780*) that's fixed in current versions. The fix exists since versions
5.0.88, 5.1.41, 5.5.0, and 6.0.14.

At this point, you have identified the source of the crash and confirmed this was really
the source, but you have to rewrite the query so it does not cause a crash next time.
Now we can get help from the backtrace that was printed in the log:

```
Attempting backtrace. You can use the following information to find out
where mysqld died. If you see no messages after this, something went
terribly wrong...
stack_bottom = 0x450890f0 thread_stack 0x40000
/users/ssmirnova/blade12/5.1.39/bin/mysqld(my_print_stacktrace+0x2e)[0x8ac81e]
/users/ssmirnova/blade12/5.1.39/bin/mysqld(handle_segfault+0x322)[0x5df502]
/lib64/libpthread.so.0[0x3429e0dd40]
/users/ssmirnova/blade12/5.1.39/bin/mysqld(_ZN6String4copyERKS_+0x16)[0x5d9876]
/users/ssmirnova/blade12/5.1.39/bin/mysqld(_ZN14Item_cache_str5storeEP4Item+0xc9)
```

```
[0x52ddd9]
/users/ssmirnova/blade12/5.1.39/bin/mysqld(_ZN26select_singlerow_subselect9
send_dataER4ListI4ItemE+0x45)
[0x5ca145]
/users/ssmirnova/blade12/5.1.39/bin/mysqld[0x6386d1]
/users/ssmirnova/blade12/5.1.39/bin/mysqld[0x64236a]
/users/ssmirnova/blade12/5.1.39/bin/mysqld(_ZN4JOIN4execEv+0x949)[0x658869]
/users/ssmirnova/blade12/5.1.39/bin/mysqld(_ZN30subselect_single_select_engine4execEv
+0x36c)[0x596f3c]
/users/ssmirnova/blade12/5.1.39/bin/mysqld(_ZN14Item_subselect4execEv+0x26)[0x595d96]
/users/ssmirnova/blade12/5.1.39/bin/mysqld(_ZN24Item_singlerow_subselect8val_realEv
+0xd)[0x595fbd]
/users/ssmirnova/blade12/5.1.39/bin/mysqld(_ZN14Arg_comparator18compare_real_fixedEv
+0x39)[0x561b89]
/users/ssmirnova/blade12/5.1.39/bin/mysqld(_ZN12Item_func_ne7val_intEv+0x23)[0x568fb3]
/users/ssmirnova/blade12/5.1.39/bin/mysqld(_ZN4JOIN8optimizeEv+0x12ef)[0x65208f]
/users/ssmirnova/blade12/5.1.39/bin/mysqld(_Z12mysql_selectP3THDPPP4ItemP10TABLE_
LISTjR4ListIS1_ES2_jP8
st_orderSB_S2_SB_yP13select_resultP18st_select_lex_unitP13st_select_lex+0xa0)
[0x654850]
/users/ssmirnova/blade12/5.1.39/bin/mysqld(_Z13handle_selectP3THDP6st_lexP13select_
resultm+0x16c)
[0x65a1cc]
/users/ssmirnova/blade12/5.1.39/bin/mysqld[0x5ecbda]
/users/ssmirnova/blade12/5.1.39/bin/mysqld(_Z21mysql_execute_commandP3THD+0x602)
[0x5efdd2]
/users/ssmirnova/blade12/5.1.39/bin/mysqld(_Z11mysql_parseP3THDPKcjPS2_+0x357)
[0x5f52f7]
/users/ssmirnova/blade12/5.1.39/bin/mysqld(_Z16dispatch_command19enum_server_
commandP3THDPcj+0xe93)
[0x5f6193]
/users/ssmirnova/blade12/5.1.39/bin/mysqld(_Z10do_commandP3THD+0xe6)[0x5f6a56]
/users/ssmirnova/blade12/5.1.39/bin/mysqld(handle_one_connection+0x246)[0x5e93f6]
/lib64/libpthread.so.0[0x3429e061b5]
/lib64/libc.so.6(clone+0x6d)[0x34292cd39d]`)
```

The relevant lines are the calls to Item_subselect and Item_singlerow_subselect:

```
/users/ssmirnova/blade12/5.1.39/bin/mysqld(_ZN14Item_subselect4execEv+0x26)[0x595d96]
/users/ssmirnova/blade12/5.1.39/bin/mysqld(_ZN24Item_singlerow_subselect8val_realEv
+0xd)[0x595fbd]
```

How did I decide these were the culprits? In this case, I recognized the calls from my previous troubleshooting. But a good rule of thumb is to start from the top. These first functions are usually operating system calls, which can be relevant, but are of no help in these circumstances, because you cannot do anything with them, and then follow calls to the MySQL library. Examine these from top to bottom to find which ones you can affect. You can't do anything with String4copy or Item_cache_str5store, for instance, but you can rewrite a subselect, so we'll start from there.

Here, even without looking into the source code for *mysqld*, we can play around to find the cause of the crash. It's a good guess that the use of a subquery is the problem because subqueries can be converted easily to JOIN. Let's try rewriting the query and testing it:

```
mysql> SELECT 1 FROM `t1` WHERE `c0` <> geometrycollectionfromwkb(`c3`);
Empty set (0.00 sec)
```

The new query does not crash, so all you need to do is change the query in the application to match.

- You just learned something important about MySQL troubleshooting: the first thing to check in case of an unknown error is the error logfile. Always have it turned on.

Here I want to add a note about bugs. When you are faced with a crash and identify the reason, check the MySQL bug database for similar problems. When you find a bug that looks like the one you hit, check whether it has been fixed, and if so, upgrade your server to the version where the bug was fixed (or a newer one). This can save you time because you won't have to fix the problematic query.

If you can't find a bug similar to one you hit, try downloading the latest version of the MySQL server and running your query. If the bug is reproducible there, report it. It's important to use the latest versions of stable general availability (GA) releases because they contain all current bug fixes and many old issues won't reappear. Chapter 6 discusses how to safely test crashes in sandbox environments.

Crashes can be caused not only by particular queries, but also by the environment in which the server runs. The most common reason is the lack of free RAM. This happens particularly when the user allocates huge buffers. As I noted before, *mysqld* always needs slightly more RAM than the sum of all buffers. Usually the error logfile contains a rough estimation of the RAM that can be used. It looks like this:

```
key_buffer_size=235929600
read_buffer_size=4190208
max_used_connections=17
max_connections=2048
threads_connected=13
It is possible that mysqld could use up to
key_buffer_size + (read_buffer_size + sort_buffer_size)*max_connections = 21193712 K
-----
21193712K ~= 20G
```

Such estimations are not precise, but still worth checking. The one just shown claims that *mysqld* can use up to 20G RAM! You can get powerful boxes nowadays, but it is worth checking whether you really have 20G RAM.

Another issue in the environment is other applications that run along with the MySQL server. It is always a good idea to dedicate a server for MySQL in production because other applications can use resources that you expect MySQL to use. We will describe how to debug the effects of other applications on *mysqld* in Chapter 4.

Issues with Solutions Specific to Storage Engines

Actually, any problem this book discusses could have specific nuances based on the storage engine you use. We will touch upon these aspects throughout the book. In this section, I want to show a few features of storage engines that are independent of other problems. We'll cover a few basic problems that use tools specific to MyISAM or InnoDB because these are the most popular and frequently used storage engines. If you use a third-party storage engine, consult its user manual for useful tools.

Errors related to a storage engine are either reported back to the client or recorded in the error logfile. Usually the name of the storage engine appears in the error message. In rare cases, you will get an error number not known by the *perror* utility. This is usually a symptom of an issue with a storage engine.

One common storage engine issue is corruption. This is not always the fault of the storage engine, but can have an external cause such as disk damage, a system crash, or a MySQL server crash. For example, if somebody runs `kill -9` on the server's process, she is almost asking for data corruption. We will discuss here what to do in case of MyISAM and InnoDB corruption. We will not discuss how to fix corruption of a third-party storage engine; consult its documentation for guidance. As a general recommendation, you can try `CHECK TABLE`, which many storage engines support. (`CHECK TABLE` for the MyISAM storage engine is explained in "Repairing a MyISAM table from SQL" on page 46.)

Corruption is a difficult problem to diagnose because the user might not notice it until the MySQL server accesses a corrupted table. The symptoms can also be misleading. In the best case, you will get an error message. However, the problem might be manifested by incorrect execution of queries or even a server shutdown. If problems crop up suddenly on a particular table, always check for corruption.

> Once you suspect corruption, you need to repair the corrupted table. It's always a good practice to back up table files before doing a repair so you can go back if something goes wrong.

MyISAM Corruption

MyISAM stores every table as a set of three files: *table_name.frm* contains the table structure (schema), *table_name.MYD* contains the data, and *table_name.MYI* contains the index. Corruption can damage the datafile, the index file, or both. In such cases, you will get an error like "`ERROR 126 (HY000): Incorrect key file for table './test/t1.MYI'; try to repair it`" or "`Table './test/t2' is marked as crashed and last (automatic?) repair failed`" when you access the table. The error message can vary, but check for the words "repair" or "crashed" as a clue that the table is corrupted.

The SQL statements CHECK TABLE and REPAIR TABLE troubleshoot corruption. From the operating system shell, you can also used the *myisamchk* utility for the same purpose. One advantage of *myisamchk* is that you can use it without access to a running MySQL server. For instance, you can try to repair a table after a crash before bringing up the server again.

Repairing a MyISAM table from SQL

CHECK TABLE without parameters shows the current table status:

```
mysql> CHECK TABLE t2;
+---------+-------+----------+-------------------------------------------------+
| Table   | Op    | Msg_type | Msg_text                                        |
+---------+-------+----------+-------------------------------------------------+
| test.t2 | check | warning  | Table is marked as crashed and last repair failed |
| test.t2 | check | warning  | Size of indexfile is: 1806336      Should be: 495616 |
| test.t2 | check | error    | Record-count is not ok; is 780   Should be: 208 |
| test.t2 | check | warning  | Found 780 key parts. Should be: 208             |
| test.t2 | check | error    | Corrupt                                         |
+---------+-------+----------+-------------------------------------------------+
5 rows in set (0.09 sec)
```

This is an example of output for a corrupted table. Your first resort is to run REPAIR TABLE without parameters:

```
mysql> REPAIR TABLE t2;
+---------+--------+----------+------------------------------------+
| Table   | Op     | Msg_type | Msg_text                           |
+---------+--------+----------+------------------------------------+
| test.t2 | repair | warning  | Number of rows changed from 208 to 780 |
| test.t2 | repair | status   | OK                                 |
+---------+--------+----------+------------------------------------+
2 rows in set (0.05 sec)
```

This time we were lucky and the table was repaired successfully. We can run CHECK TABLE again to confirm this:

```
mysql> CHECK TABLE t2;
+---------+-------+----------+----------+
| Table   | Op    | Msg_type | Msg_text |
+---------+-------+----------+----------+
| test.t2 | check | status   | OK       |
+---------+-------+----------+----------+
1 row in set (0.02 sec)
```

If a simple REPAIR TABLE run does not help, there are two more options. REPAIR TABLE EXTENDED works more slowly than the bare REPAIR TABLE, but can fix 99% of errors. As a last resort, run REPAIR TABLE USE_FRM, which does not trust the information in the index file. Instead, it drops and then recreates the index using the description from the *table_name.frm* file and fills the key with values from the *table_name.MYD* file.

For the very same purpose, you can use a utility named *mysqlcheck*. This program works by sending CHECK and REPAIR statements to the server. It also has very nice options, such as --all-databases, which can help you perform table maintenance effectively.

mysqlcheck connects to the MySQL server as any other client does, and thus can be used remotely.

Repairing a MyISAM table using myisamchk

All of these steps can also be performed using *myisamchk*, which has a lot of additional table maintenance options. I won't describe all the features of the utility here, but instead concentrate on those specific to table repair.

myisamchk directly accesses table files and does not require the MySQL server to be started. This can be very useful in some situations. At the same time, *myisamchk* requires exclusive access to table files, and you should avoid using it when the MySQL server is running.

If you have to use *myisamchk* while the server is running, issue the queries FLUSH TABLES and LOCK TABLE *table_name* WRITE, then wait until the latest query returns a command prompt, and then run *myisamchk* in a parallel session. If other processes besides *myisamchk* access the table while *myisamchk* is running, even worse corruption can occur.

A basic recovery command is:

```
$myisamchk --backup --recover t2
- recovering (with sort) MyISAM-table 't2'
Data records: 208
- Fixing index 1
- Fixing index 2
Data records: 780
```

The --backup option tells *myisamchk* to back up the datafile before trying to fix the table, and --recover does the actual repair. If this command is insufficient, you can use the --safe-recover option. The latter option uses a recovery method that has existed since very early versions of MySQL and can find issues that the simple --recover option cannot. An even more drastic option is --extend-check.

You can also use the option --sort-recover, which uses sorting to resolve the keys even when the temporary file is very large.

Among other options, which I recommend you study carefully, is the very useful --description option, which prints a description of the table. Taken together with -v or its synonym, --verbose, it will print additional information. You can specify the -v option twice or even three times to get more information.

InnoDB Corruption

InnoDB stores its data and indexes in shared tablespaces. If the server was started with the option `--innodb_file_per_table` at the moment of table creation, it also has its own datafile, but the table definition still exists in a shared tablespace. Understanding how table files are stored can help to effectively maintain the data directory and backups.

InnoDB is a transactional storage engine and has internal mechanisms that automatically fix most kinds of corruption. It does this recovery at server startup. The following excerpt from the error log, taken after a backup by MySQL Enterprise Backup (MEB) using the `mysqlbackup --copy-back` command, shows a typical recovery[4]:

```
InnoDB: The log file was created by ibbackup --apply-log at
InnoDB: ibbackup 110720 21:33:50
InnoDB: NOTE: the following crash recovery is part of a normal restore.
InnoDB: The log sequence number in ibdata files does not match
InnoDB: the log sequence number in the ib_logfiles!
110720 21:37:15  InnoDB: Database was not shut down normally!
InnoDB: Starting crash recovery.
InnoDB: Reading tablespace information from the .ibd files...
InnoDB: Restoring possible half-written data pages from the doublewrite
InnoDB: buffer...
InnoDB: Last MySQL binlog file position 0 98587529, file name ./blade12-bin.000002
110720 21:37:15 InnoDB Plugin 1.0.17 started; log sequence number 1940779532
110720 21:37:15 [Note] Event Scheduler: Loaded 0 events
110720 21:37:15 [Note] ./libexec/mysqld: ready for connections.
Version: '5.1.59-debug'  socket: '/tmp/mysql_ssmirnova.sock'  port: 33051
Source distribution
```

But sometimes corruption is extremely bad and InnoDB cannot repair it without user interaction. For such situations, the startup option `--innodb_force_recovery` exists. It can be set to any value from 0 to 6 (0 means no forced recovery, 1 is the lowest level, and 6 is the highest level). When recovery is successful, you can run certain types of queries against the table that was repaired, but you're prevented from issuing certain commands. You can't issue operations that modify data, but the option still allows certain SELECT select statements, as well as DROP statements. At level 6, for instance, you can run only queries of the form SELECT * FROM *table_name* with no qualifying condition—no WHERE, ORDER BY, or other clauses.

In case of corruption, try each level of `--innodb_force_recovery`, starting from 1 and increasing, until you are able to start the server and query the problem table. Your prior investigation should have uncovered which table is corrupted. Dump it to a file using SELECT INTO OUTFILE, then recreate it using DROP and CREATE. Finally, restart the server with `--innodb_force_recovery=0` and load the dump. If the problem persists, try to find other tables that are corrupted and go through the process until the server is fine again.

---

4. MySQL Enterprise Backup (MEB), formerly known as InnoDB HotBackup, is a tool that creates hot online backups of InnoDB tables and warm online backups of tables that use other storage engines. We will discuss backup methods in Chapter 7.

If you need to begin your repair of a database by using a positive value for
--innodb_force_recovery, the error log often mentions it explicitly through messages
such as this:

```
InnoDB: We intentionally generate a memory trap.
InnoDB: Submit a detailed bug report to http://bugs.mysql.com.
InnoDB: If you get repeated assertion failures or crashes, even
InnoDB: immediately after the mysqld startup, there may be
InnoDB: corruption in the InnoDB tablespace. Please refer to
InnoDB: http://dev.mysql.com/doc/refman/5.1/en/forcing-recovery.html
InnoDB: about forcing recovery.
```

You will also find information there about unsuccessful automatic recovery and startup
failure.

> InnoDB writes checksums for data, index, and log pages immediately
> before writing actual data, and confirms the checksums immediately
> after reading from the disk. This allows it to prevent a majority of prob-
> lems. Usually when you encounter InnoDB corruption, this means you
> have issues with either the disk or RAM.

Permission Issues

MySQL has a complex privilege scheme, allowing you to tune precisely which users
and hosts are allowed to perform one or another operation. Since version 5.5, MySQL
also has pluggable authentication.

Although it has advantages, this scheme is complicated. For example, having
user1@hostA different from user2@hostA and user1@hostB makes it easy to mix up their
privileges. It is even easier to do this when the username is the same and the host
changes.

MySQL allows you to tune access at the object and connection level. You can restrict
a user's access to a particular table, column, and so on.

Users usually experience two kinds of permission issues:

- Users who should be able to connect to the server find they cannot, or users who
  should not be able to connect find that they can.
- Users can connect to the server, but can't use objects to which they are supposed
  to have access, or can use objects to which they are not supposed to have access.

Before you start troubleshooting these problems, you need to find out whether you can
connect to the server.

After you succeed in connecting as the user you're troubleshooting (we will discuss the
case when connection is not possible a bit later in this chapter), run the query:

```
SELECT USER(), CURRENT_USER()
```

The USER() function returns the connection parameters used when the user connects. These are usually the username that was specified and the hostname of a box where the client is running. CURRENT_USER() returns the username and hostname pair of those privileges chosen from privilege tables. These are the username and hostname pairs used by *mysqld* to check access to database objects. By comparing the results of these functions, you can find out why *mysqld* uses privileges that are different from what you expected. A typical problem is trying to use a % wildcard for the hostname:

```
root> GRANT ALL ON book.* TO sveta@'%';
Query OK, 0 rows affected (0.00 sec)

root> GRANT SELECT ON book.* TO sveta@'localhost';
Query OK, 0 rows affected (0.00 sec)
```

If I now connect as sveta and try to create a table, I get an error:

```
$mysql -usveta book
Welcome to the MySQL monitor.  Commands end with ; or \g.
Your MySQL connection id is 30
Server version: 5.1.52 MySQL Community Server (GPL)

Copyright (c) 2000, 2011, Oracle and/or its affiliates. All rights reserved.

Oracle is a registered trademark of Oracle Corporation and/or its
affiliates. Other names may be trademarks of their respective
owners.

Type 'help;' or '\h' for help. Type '\c' to clear the current input statement.

mysql> CREATE TABLE t1(f1 INT);
ERROR 1142 (42000): CREATE command denied to user 'sveta'@'localhost' for table 't1'
```

The problem is that the MySQL server expands sveta to sveta@localhost, not to the wild card:

```
mysql> SELECT user(), current_user();
+----------------+----------------+
| user()         | current_user() |
+----------------+----------------+
| sveta@localhost | sveta@localhost |
+----------------+----------------+
1 row in set (0.00 sec)
```

If you don't understand why one or another host was chosen, run a query like this:

```
mysql> SELECT user, host FROM mysql.user WHERE user='sveta' ORDER
BY host DESC;
+-------+-----------+
| user  | host      |
+-------+-----------+
| sveta | localhost |
| sveta | %         |
+-------+-----------+
2 rows in set (0.00 sec)
```

MySQL sorts rows in this table from the most specific to the least specific host value and uses the first value found. Therefore, it connected me as the user account sveta@localhost, which does not have CREATE privileges.

- USER() and CURRENT_USER(), together with the query SELECT user, host FROM mysql.user ORDER BY host DESC, are the first resort in case of a permission issue.

Another issue with privileges arises when it is not possible to connect as the specified user. In this case, you can usually learn the reason from the error message, which looks similar to the following:

```
$mysql -usveta books
ERROR 1044 (42000): Access denied for user 'sveta'@'localhost' to database 'books'
```

After seeing this, you know the user credentials. Connect as the root superuser, and check whether such a user exists and has the required privileges:

```
mysql> SELECT user, host FROM mysql.user WHERE user='sveta' ORDER
BY host DESC;
+-------+-----------+
| user  | host      |
+-------+-----------+
| sveta | localhost |
| sveta | %         |
+-------+-----------+
2 rows in set (0.00 sec)

mysql> SHOW GRANTS FOR 'sveta'@'localhost';
+------------------------------------------------+
| Grants for sveta@localhost                     |
+------------------------------------------------+
| GRANT USAGE ON *.* TO 'sveta'@'localhost'      |
| GRANT SELECT ON `book`.* TO 'sveta'@'localhost' |
+------------------------------------------------+
2 rows in set (0.00 sec)

mysql> SHOW GRANTS FOR 'sveta'@'%';
+------------------------------------------------+
| Grants for sveta@%                             |
+------------------------------------------------+
| GRANT USAGE ON *.* TO 'sveta'@'%'              |
| GRANT ALL PRIVILEGES ON `book`.* TO 'sveta'@'%' |
+------------------------------------------------+
2 rows in set (0.00 sec)
```

In this output, you can see that user 'sveta'@'localhost' has privileges only on the database named book, but no privileges on the books database. Now you can fix the problem: give user sveta@localhost the necessary privileges.

The previous examples discussed users who lacked necessary privileges. Users who are granted superfluous privileges can be handled in the same way; you just need to revoke the unnecessary privileges.

MySQL privileges are detached from objects they control: this means *mysqld* does not check for the existence of an object when you grant a privilege on it and does not remove a privilege when all objects it grants access to are removed. This is both a great advantage, because it allows us to grant necessary privileges in advance, and a potential cause of an issue if used without care.

As a best practice, I recommend careful study of how MySQL privileges work. This is especially important if you grant privileges on the object level because you should understand how a grant on one level affects grants of others. The same considerations apply to revoking privileges, which can be even more critical because if you think you revoked a privilege and it is still present, this allows unwanted access.

## CHAPTER 2

You Are Not Alone: Concurrency Issues

MySQL is rarely deployed in a single-user environment. Usually it handles many connection threads doing different jobs for different people at the same time. These parallel connections can access the same databases and tables, so it is hard to know what the state of the database was when a particular connection had a problem.

This chapter describes issues caused by parallel execution. Unlike the troubleshooting scenarios shown in Chapter 1, this chapter covers more complex situations where you may experience problems without knowing which particular query caused them.

One of the symptoms of a concurrency issue is a sudden slowdown of a well-optimized query. The slowdown may not happen consistently, but even a few random occurrences should signal you to check for concurrency problems.

Concurrency can even affect the slave SQL thread. I explicitly mention this to correct a possible misconception. One might think that because the slave SQL is single-threaded,[1] it doesn't require any troubleshooting techniques related to concurrency. This is actually not so: replication can be affected by concurrency on both the master and the slave. This chapter therefore contains a section devoted to replication.

 Let's agree on some terms to start with. For each connected client, the MySQL server creates a separate thread. I will use the words *thread*, *connection*, or *connection thread* to refer a thread that serves a client connection. I will explicitly mention when the context requires another meaning of the word "thread." I use "thread" instead of "query," "statement," or "transaction" because when you are troubleshooting, you often have to isolate a problematic thread before you can deal with the particular statement that might cause the problem.

---

1. This will change in future: version 5.6.2 contains a preview of a multithreaded slave (*http://forge.mysql .com/wiki/ReplicationFeatures/ParallelSlave*).

Locks and Transactions

The MySQL server has internal mechanisms that prevent one user from damaging information inserted by another. Although these usually do their job silently and competently, being unaware of these safeguards can lead to problems for your own application as well as others. Therefore, I'm starting with a short overview of concurrency control mechanisms that the MySQL server uses.

The MySQL server uses locks and transactions to handle concurrent access to its tables. I will give a short overview of lock types and transaction processing first, then go on to troubleshooting techniques.

A lock is set when a thread requests a data set. In MySQL, this can be a table, a row, a page, or metadata. After a thread finishes working with a particular data set, its locks are released. I will describe the locks set by MySQL in detail in "Locks" on page 54 and "Metadata Locking Versus the Old Model" on page 75. I cover metadata locking in a separate section because this is a new feature that invented differences in how the MySQL server handles concurrency. If you are familiar with the old table-locking mechanism and not with metadata locking, the latter section can help you determine whether you hit a metadata lock in a particular situation.

Database transactions are units of work treated in a coherent and reliable way that allow a user to work without the risk of intervening with other transactions. The transaction's *isolation level* controls whether the transaction can see the changes made by concurrent operations, and if yes, which changes. We will discuss MySQL transactions in detail in "Transactions" on page 63.

Locks

Locks can be set both by the server and by an individual storage engine. Locks are usually set differently for read and write operations. Read, or shared, locks allow concurrent threads to read from the locked data, but prevent writes. In contrast, write, or exclusive, locks prevent other threads from either reading or writing. In a storage engine, the implementation of such locks can differ, but the rationale for these policies is solid and will be the same nearly everywhere.

Read locks are set when you SELECT from a table or explicitly lock it with LOCK TABLE … READ. Write locks are set when you either modify a table or lock it explicitly with LOCK TABLE … WRITE.

 InnoDB uses the shortcut S for read/shared locks and X for write/exclusive locks. You will see this notation in its debugging output.

As I mentioned before, MySQL has four kind of locks: table, row, page, and metadata. A table lock, as the name suggests, locks the whole table so that no one can access any row in the table until the locking thread unlocks the table. Row locking is much more fine-grained, locking just one row or whatever number of rows are being accessed by the thread, so other rows in the same table are available for access by concurrent threads. Page locks lock a page, but they are found only in the rarely used BDB storage engine, so I will say no more about it. However, general lock troubleshooting recommendations apply to this kind of lock as well.

Metadata locks are a new feature introduced in MySQL version 5.5. These locks apply only to the metadata for a table, and lock all the metadata for that table when a thread starts to use the table. Metadata is the information altered by DDL (Data Definition Language or Data Description Language) statements, the CREATE, DROP, and ALTER statements that modify schemes. The introduction of metadata locks solved a problem in earlier versions of MySQL, when a thread could modify a table definition or even drop it while another thread used the same table in a multistatement transaction.

In the following sections I describe table, row, and metadata locks and the issues they can cause in your application.

Table Locks

When a table lock is set, the whole table is locked. This means concurrent threads cannot use the table as defined by the lock, e.g., write access is not allowed if the READ lock is set, and both read and write access are forbidden if the WRITE lock is set. Table locks are set when you access a table using a storage engine that supports table locking, notably MyISAM. You also invoke a table lock for any engine when you run LOCK TABLES explicitly or issue DDL operations on a version of MySQL earlier than 5.5.

As I like to demonstrate concepts by example, here is one demonstrating the effects of table locking:

```
mysql> SELECT * FROM t;
+-----+
| a   |
+-----+
|   0 |
| 256 |
+-----+
2 rows in set (3 min 18.71 sec)
```

Three minutes to retrieve two rows? When I showed this example at a conference, I paused and asked whether anybody could figure out why. At that time, the netbook boom had just started, and the whole audience shouted, "It is running on an Atom CPU!" Actually, such a delay is way too much for any kind of modern processor. Let's look at the table definition and try the same query again:

```
mysql> SHOW CREATE TABLE t\G
*************** 1. row ***************
       Table: t
Create Table: CREATE TABLE `t` (
  `a` int(10) unsigned NOT NULL AUTO_INCREMENT,
  PRIMARY KEY (`a`)
) ENGINE=MyISAM AUTO_INCREMENT=257 DEFAULT CHARSET=utf8
1 row in set (0.00 sec)

mysql> SELECT * FROM t;
+-----+
| a   |
+-----+
|   0 |
| 256 |
+-----+
2 rows in set (0.00 sec)
```

Now it runs in almost zero time!

To find out what happened, we need to run SHOW PROCESSLIST during the time the query is running slowly.

 In an actual application environment, you would either need to manually run a diagnostic query during a busy time or schedule a job that will do it for you from time to time and save the results.

```
mysql> SHOW PROCESSLIST\G
******************* 1. row *******************
     Id: 1311
   User: root
   Host: localhost
     db: test
Command: Query
   Time: 35
  State: Locked
   Info: SELECT * FROM t
******************* 2. row *******************
     Id: 1312
   User: root
   Host: localhost
     db: test
Command: Query
   Time: 36
  State: User sleep
   Info: UPDATE t SET a=sleep(200) WHERE a=0
******************* 3. row *******************
     Id: 1314
   User: root
   Host: localhost
     db: NULL
Command: Query
   Time: 0
```

```
    State: NULL
     Info: SHOW PROCESSLIST
3 rows in set (0.00 sec)
```

The fields of the output are as follows:

Id
> The ID of the connection thread running in the MySQL server.

User, Host, *and* db
> The connection options specified by the client when connecting to the server.

Command
> The command currently executing in the thread.

Time
> The elapsed wall clock time since the thread started to execute the command.

State
> The internal state of the thread.

Info
> Shows what the thread is currently doing. It contains a query if one is executing and NULL if the thread is sleeping while waiting for the next user command.

To find out what happened with our query, we need to find a row where Info contains the text of the query, and then examine the query's state. At the top of the output, we can see that the state of our query is Locked, which means the query cannot proceed, because another thread holds the lock our thread is waiting for. The following row shows a query:

```
UPDATE t SET a=sleep(200) WHERE a=0
```

which accesses the same table t and has already run for 36 seconds. Because the table is the same and no other thread is using our table, we can conclude that this update is preventing our query from starting. In fact, our query will wait all 200 seconds until the other one is finished.

- You just learned an important new debugging technique: run SHOW PROCESSLIST when you suspect concurrent threads are affecting the query.

Row Locks

Row locks block a set of rows, not the whole table. Therefore, you can modify rows in the table that are not blocked by the lock.

Row locks are set at the storage engine level. InnoDB is the main storage engine that currently uses row locks.

To show the difference between table and row locks, we will use a slightly modified example from the previous section:

```
mysql>  CREATE TABLE `t` (
    ->   `a` INT(10) UNSIGNED NOT NULL AUTO_INCREMENT,
    ->   PRIMARY KEY (`a`)
    -> ) ENGINE=InnoDB DEFAULT CHARSET=utf8;
Query OK, 0 rows affected (1.29 sec)

mysql>  INSERT INTO t VALUES();
Query OK, 1 row affected (0.24 sec)

mysql>  INSERT INTO t SELECT NULL FROM t;
Query OK, 1 row affected (0.19 sec)
Records: 1  Duplicates: 0  Warnings: 0

mysql>  INSERT INTO t SELECT NULL FROM t;
Query OK, 2 rows affected (0.00 sec)
Records: 2  Duplicates: 0  Warnings: 0

mysql>  INSERT INTO t SELECT NULL FROM t;
Query OK, 4 rows affected (0.01 sec)
Records: 4  Duplicates: 0  Warnings: 0

mysql>  INSERT INTO t SELECT NULL FROM t;
Query OK, 8 rows affected (0.00 sec)
Records: 8  Duplicates: 0  Warnings: 0

mysql>  SELECT * FROM t;
+----+
| a  |
+----+
|  1 |
|  2 |
|  3 |
|  4 |
|  6 |
|  7 |
|  8 |
|  9 |
| 13 |
| 14 |
| 15 |
| 16 |
| 17 |
| 18 |
| 19 |
| 20 |
+----+
16 rows in set (0.00 sec)
```

Let's run the same sleeping UPDATE query as before to see the different effect of row locking compared to table locks:

```
mysql>  UPDATE t SET a=sleep(200) WHERE a=6;
```

While the sleeping query is running, we have enough time to try to select rows using another client:

```
mysql>  SELECT * FROM t;
+----+
| a  |
+----+
|  1 |
|  2 |
|  3 |
|  4 |
|  6 |
|  7 |
|  8 |
|  9 |
| 13 |
| 14 |
| 15 |
| 16 |
| 17 |
| 18 |
| 19 |
| 20 |
+----+
16 rows in set (0.00 sec)
```

We got results immediately. Now let's try to update a row:

```
mysql>  UPDATE t SET a=23 WHERE a=13;
Query OK, 1 row affected (0.00 sec)
Rows matched: 1  Changed: 1  Warnings: 0

mysql>  UPDATE t SET a=27 WHERE a=7;
Query OK, 1 row affected (0.09 sec)
Rows matched: 1  Changed: 1  Warnings: 0
```

Updates of rows that are not locked work fine too. Now let's see what happens if we try to update a row using the same WHERE condition as the blocking UPDATE:

```
mysql>  UPDATE t SET a=26 WHERE a=6;
ERROR 1205 (HY000): Lock wait timeout exceeded; try restarting transaction
```

Our new query waits for innodb_lock_wait_timeout seconds (the default value is 50), then dies with an error. We have the same result as table locks in terms of data consistency, but the InnoDB lock does not affect parallel threads until they try to access the exact row that is locked.

 Actually, row-level locking is more complicated than I have described. For example, if we tried to access a table using a WHERE condition that could not be resolved using a UNIQUE key, we could not update any row in parallel, because the storage engine could not determine whether the other thread was trying to update the same row. This is not the only detail I skipped in my discussion of row-level locks to save space for the troubleshooting techniques themselves. Consult the Appendix to find sources of information you can use to learn more about MySQL locks.

Now let's see how the process list output changed. I will use the table `INFORMATION_SCHEMA.PROCESSLIST` in this example. It actually has same information as `SHOW PROCESSLIST`, but because it is in the table you can sort the query results as you wish. This is especially convenient if you have dozens of parallel threads:

```
mysql> SELECT * FROM PROCESSLIST\G
*************************** 1. row ***************************
     ID: 4483
   USER: root
   HOST: localhost
     DB: NULL
COMMAND: Sleep
   TIME: 283
  STATE:
   INFO: NULL
*************************** 2. row ***************************
     ID: 4482
   USER: root
   HOST: localhost
     DB: information_schema
COMMAND: Query
   TIME: 0
  STATE: executing
   INFO: SELECT * FROM PROCESSLIST
*************************** 3. row ***************************
     ID: 4481
   USER: root
   HOST: localhost
     DB: test
COMMAND: Query
   TIME: 7
  STATE: Updating
   INFO: UPDATE t SET a=26 WHERE a=6
*************************** 4. row ***************************
     ID: 4480
   USER: root
   HOST: localhost
     DB: test
COMMAND: Query
   TIME: 123
  STATE: User sleep
   INFO: UPDATE t SET a=sleep(200) WHERE a=6
4 rows in set (0.09 sec)
```

Here you can see another difference from the previous example: the state of our query is `Updating`, not `Locked`.

To find out whether a query is blocked by a lock in InnoDB, you can run the query `SHOW ENGINE INNODB STATUS`, which is part of a mechanism called the InnoDB Monitor. This is especially helpful if you analyze the effect of parallel multistatement transactions, which we will discuss a bit later in this chapter. I will not print here the whole output of this great tool, just the part relevant to our current example. We will discuss this tool further in "SHOW ENGINE INNODB STATUS and InnoDB Monitors" on page 96 and in detail in Chapter 6:

```
mysql> SHOW ENGINE INNODB STATUS \G
*************************** 1. row ***************************
  Type: InnoDB
  Name:
Status:
=====================================
110802  2:03:45 INNODB MONITOR OUTPUT
=====================================
Per second averages calculated from the last 41 seconds
...
------------
TRANSACTIONS
------------
Trx id counter 0 26243828
Purge done for trx's n:o < 0 26243827 undo n:o < 0 0
History list length 25
LIST OF TRANSACTIONS FOR EACH SESSION:
---TRANSACTION 0 0, not started, OS thread id 101514240
MySQL thread id 4483, query id 25022097 localhost root
show engine innodb status
---TRANSACTION 0 26243827, ACTIVE 9 sec, OS thread id 101403136 starting index read
mysql tables in use 1, locked 1
LOCK WAIT 2 lock struct(s), heap size 320, 1 row lock(s)
MySQL thread id 4481, query id 25022095 localhost root Updating
update t set a=26 where a=6
------- TRX HAS BEEN WAITING 9 SEC FOR THIS LOCK TO BE GRANTED:
RECORD LOCKS space id 349 page no 3 n bits 88 index `PRIMARY` of table `test`.`t`
trx id 0 26243827 lock_mode X locks rec but not gap waiting
Record lock, heap no 6 PHYSICAL RECORD: n_fields 3; compact format; info bits 0
 0: len 4; hex 00000006; asc     ;; 1: len 6; hex 0000019072e3; asc    r ;; 2:
 len 7; hex 800000002d0110; asc   -  ;;

------------------
---TRANSACTION 0 26243821, ACTIVE 125 sec, OS thread id 101238272,
thread declared inside InnoDB 500
mysql tables in use 1, locked 1
2 lock struct(s), heap size 320, 1 row lock(s)
MySQL thread id 4480, query id 25022091 localhost root User sleep
update t set a=sleep(200) where a=6
```

The important part we need to pay attention to is:

```
---TRANSACTION 0 26243827, ACTIVE 9 sec, OS thread id 101403136 starting index read
mysql tables in use 1, locked 1
LOCK WAIT 2 lock struct(s), heap size 320, 1 row lock(s)
MySQL thread id 4481, query id 25022095 localhost root Updating
update t set a=26 where a=6
------- TRX HAS BEEN WAITING 9 SEC FOR THIS LOCK TO BE GRANTED:
```

This shows that a query is waiting for a lock.

Here are a few details about the preceding output, before we return to the lock:

TRANSACTION 0 26243827
:   This is the ID of the transaction.

ACTIVE 9 sec
:   Number of seconds the transaction was active for.

OS thread id 101403136
:   ID of the MySQL thread that is running the transaction.

starting index read
:   What the transaction is doing.

mysql tables in use 1, locked 1
:   How many tables are used and locked.

LOCK WAIT 2 lock struct(s), heap size 320, 1 row lock(s)
:   Information about the locks.

MySQL thread id 4481, query id 25022095 localhost root Updating
:   Information about the MySQL thread: ID, ID of the query, user credentials, and MySQL state.

update t set a=26 where a=6
:   Currently running query.

And here are details about the lock:

```
RECORD LOCKS space id 349 page no 3 n bits 88 index `PRIMARY` of table `test`.`t`
trx id 0 26243827 lock_mode X locks rec but not gap waiting
Record lock, heap no 6 PHYSICAL RECORD: n_fields 3; compact format; info bits 0
 0: len 4; hex 00000006; asc      ;; 1: len 6; hex 0000019072e3; asc     r ;; 2:
 len 7; hex 800000002d0110; asc    -  ;;
```

This shows the exact coordinates of the blocked transaction in the InnoDB tablespace, the type of the lock (exclusive, because we are going to do an update), and the binary content of the physical record.

Finally, let's look at the information about the transaction running the query that locks the rows:

```
---TRANSACTION 0 26243821, ACTIVE 125 sec, OS thread id 101238272,
thread declared inside InnoDB 500
mysql tables in use 1, locked 1
2 lock struct(s), heap size 320, 1 row lock(s)
MySQL thread id 4480, query id 25022091 localhost root User sleep
update t set a=sleep(200) where a=6
```

Now that the situation is clear, we can consider how to fix it.

- You just learned about another important troubleshooting instrument: InnoDB Monitor, which can be called with the help of SHOW ENGINE INNODB STATUS. I will add more details about InnoDB Monitors at the end of this chapter in "SHOW ENGINE INNODB STATUS and InnoDB Monitors" on page 96.

I need to point out one thing about the performance troubleshooting section in the previous chapter, "Slow Queries" on page 24. In that section, I wrote that indexes can decrease the performance of inserts because they need to update index files as well as insert data. But when row locks are in use, indexes can increase overall application performance, especially when an index is unique, because while updating such an indexed field, insert would not block access to the whole table.

Next, I take a short break from locks to describe transactions. Later, we will return to metadata locking. I decided to order the information in this way because we need to be acquainted with transactions before discussing metadata locks.

Transactions

MySQL supports transactions at the storage engine level. The most popular among the officially supported storage engines, InnoDB, provides transaction support. In this section, we discuss how to troubleshoot InnoDB transactions.

In MySQL, you can start a transaction using a `START TRANSACTION` or `BEGIN` statement. To commit a transaction, call `COMMIT`, and to roll it back (cancel it), call `ROLLBACK`.

An alternate way to start a multistatement transaction is to set the variable `autocommit` to zero. This will override the default MySQL behavior, which sends an implicit commit after each statement. With `autocommit` set to 0, you need to call `COMMIT` or `ROLLBACK` explicitly. After that, the next statement begins a new transaction automatically.

MySQL also provides `SAVEPOINT` and `XA` transaction interfaces. Although InnoDB supports both, I will not describe them in this book, because it would not offer any extra insight related to our troubleshooting techniques. In other words, the same techniques I describe can be applied to such transactions.

Hidden Queries

InnoDB treats every request for data as a transaction. It does not matter whether the transaction is a single statement or if it is multiple statements. With regard to troubleshooting, you can handle single-query transactions as described in "Row Locks" on page 57. You need to find out which queries run concurrently and which locks get in the way of each other.

Things change when you have transactions that consist of multiple statements. In this case, the transaction can lock rows even when you see no query in the `SHOW PROCESSLIST` output.

To illustrate this problem, let's modify our example one more time. Now we don't even need to call `sleep` to create a delay. Before running this example, I reverted the changed rows, so the table has the same values as in the initial test setup.

```
mysql1> BEGIN;
Query OK, 0 rows affected (0.00 sec)

mysql1> UPDATE t SET a=26 WHERE a=6;
Query OK, 1 row affected (0.00 sec)
Rows matched: 1  Changed: 1  Warnings: 0
```

Please note that the transaction is not closed. Let's start another from another connection:

```
mysql2> BEGIN;
Query OK, 0 rows affected (0.00 sec)

mysql2> UPDATE t SET a=36  WHERE a=6;
```

Now let's run SHOW PROCESSLIST. Our query is in the same Updating state as it was in our row locks example, but now it is not clear what is preventing the actual update:

```
mysql3> SHOW PROCESSLIST\G
*************************** 1. row ***************************
     Id: 4484
   User: root
   Host: localhost
     db: test
Command: Sleep
   Time: 104
  State:
   Info: NULL
*************************** 2. row ***************************
     Id: 4485
   User: root
   Host: localhost
     db: test
Command: Query
   Time: 2
  State: Updating
   Info: UPDATE t SET a=36  WHERE a=6
*************************** 3. row ***************************
     Id: 4486
   User: root
   Host: localhost
     db: test
Command: Query
   Time: 0
  State: NULL
   Info: SHOW PROCESSLIST
*************************** 4. row ***************************
     Id: 4487
   User: root
   Host: localhost
     db: NULL
Command: Sleep
   Time: 33
  State:
   Info: NULL
4 rows in set (0.09 sec)
```

Here is our sorted output from SHOW ENGINE INNODB STATUS:

```
mysql> SHOW ENGINE INNODB STATUS\G
*************************** 1. row ***************************
  Type: InnoDB
  Name:
Status:
=====================================
110802 14:35:28 INNODB MONITOR OUTPUT
=====================================
...
------------
TRANSACTIONS
------------
Trx id counter 0 26243837
Purge done for trx's n:o < 0 26243834 undo n:o < 0 0
History list length 2
LIST OF TRANSACTIONS FOR EACH SESSION:
---TRANSACTION 0 0, not started, OS thread id 101515264
MySQL thread id 4487, query id 25022139 localhost root
show engine innodb status
---TRANSACTION 0 26243836, ACTIVE 4 sec, OS thread id 101514240
starting index read
mysql tables in use 1, locked 1
LOCK WAIT 2 lock struct(s), heap size 320, 1 row lock(s)
MySQL thread id 4485, query id 25022137 localhost root Updating
update t set a=36  where a=6
------- TRX HAS BEEN WAITING 4 SEC FOR THIS LOCK TO BE GRANTED:
RECORD LOCKS space id 349 page no 3 n bits 88 index `PRIMARY` of table `test`.`t`
trx id 0 26243836 lock_mode X locks rec but not gap waiting
Record lock, heap no 6 PHYSICAL RECORD: n_fields 3; compact format; info bits 32
 0: len 4; hex 00000006; asc     ;; 1: len 6; hex 0000019072fb; asc     r ;; 2:
 len 7; hex 000000003202ca; asc    2  ;;

------------------
---TRANSACTION 0 26243835, ACTIVE 106 sec, OS thread id 100936704
2 lock struct(s), heap size 320, 1 row lock(s), undo log entries 2
MySQL thread id 4484, query id 25022125 localhost root
```

 The same recipe will work for MyISAM tables locked with LOCK TABLE query, and thus not necessarily visible in the SHOW PROCESSLIST output. InnoDB prints information about such tables in its status output:

```
------------
TRANSACTIONS
------------
Trx id counter B55
Purge done for trx's n:o < B27 undo n:o < 0
History list length 7
LIST OF TRANSACTIONS FOR EACH SESSION:
---TRANSACTION 0, not started
MySQL thread id 3, query id 124 localhost ::1 root
show engine innodb status

---TRANSACTION B53, not started
mysql tables in use 1, locked 1
```

```
MySQL thread id 1, query id 115 localhost ::1 root
--------
```

The lock information is similar to what we saw in "Row Locks" on page 57:

```
------- TRX HAS BEEN WAITING 4 SEC FOR THIS LOCK TO BE GRANTED:
RECORD LOCKS space id 349 page no 3 n bits 88 index `PRIMARY` of table `test`.`t`
trx id 0 26243836 lock_mode X locks rec but not gap waiting
Record lock, heap no 6 PHYSICAL RECORD: n_fields 3; compact format; info bits 32
 0: len 4; hex 00000006; asc      ;; 1: len 6; hex 0000019072fb; asc     r ;; 2:
 len 7; hex 000000003202ca; asc     2 ;;
```

This clearly shows that our transaction is waiting for the lock. From this listing, though, it is not clear what holds the lock. If you are using version 5.0 or use bundled InnoDB in 5.1, you have two choices: figure it out yourself, or use the InnoDB Lock monitor. In our example, we have only two transactions, so it's easy to see the answer, and "figuring it out" would work. But if you have dozens of connections using different rows of the same table, it would not be so easy. I will describe the InnoDB Lock monitor later in this chapter in "SHOW ENGINE INNODB STATUS and InnoDB Monitors" on page 96. Here we will use a third choice, available for the InnoDB Plugin only.

The InnoDB Plugin, in addition to monitors, has INFORMATION_SCHEMA tables named INNODB_LOCKS, INNODB_LOCK_WAITS (which holds information about acquired locks and waits for locks), and INNODB_TRX, which holds information about running transactions.

For our example, we can query these tables:

```
mysql> SELECT * FROM innodb_locks\G
*************************** 1. row ***************************
    lock_id: 3B86:1120:3:6
lock_trx_id: 3B86
  lock_mode: X
  lock_type: RECORD
 lock_table: `test`.`t`
 lock_index: `PRIMARY`
 lock_space: 1120
  lock_page: 3
   lock_rec: 6
  lock_data: 6
*************************** 2. row ***************************
    lock_id: 3B85:1120:3:6
lock_trx_id: 3B85
  lock_mode: X
  lock_type: RECORD
 lock_table: `test`.`t`
 lock_index: `PRIMARY`
 lock_space: 1120
  lock_page: 3
   lock_rec: 6
  lock_data: 6
2 rows in set (0.01 sec)
```

This shows information about locks. Both transactions have locks set on the same record, but the result does not give any idea as to which transaction holds the lock and which waits on it. More information about what is going on can be obtained from the table INNODB_LOCK_WAITS:

```
mysql> SELECT * FROM innodb_lock_waits\G
*************************** 1. row ***************************
requesting_trx_id: 3B86
requested_lock_id: 3B86:1120:3:6
  blocking_trx_id: 3B85
  blocking_lock_id: 3B85:1120:3:6
1 row in set (0.09 sec)
```

The column requesting_trx_id is the ID of our "hanging" transaction, and blocking_trx_id is the ID of the transaction that holds the lock. requested_lock_id and blocking_lock_id show information about the requested and blocked locks, respectively.

All we need to know now is the MySQL process ID of the blocking transaction, so we can do something with it. The content of the INNODB_TRX table will help us find it:

```
mysql> SELECT * FROM innodb_trx\G
*************************** 1. row ***************************
                    trx_id: 3B86
                 trx_state: LOCK WAIT
               trx_started: 2011-08-02 14:48:51
       trx_requested_lock_id: 3B86:1120:3:6
          trx_wait_started: 2011-08-02 14:49:59
                trx_weight: 2
         trx_mysql_thread_id: 28546
                 trx_query: UPDATE t SET a=36  WHERE a=6
       trx_operation_state: starting index read
          trx_tables_in_use: 1
         trx_tables_locked: 1
          trx_lock_structs: 2
     trx_lock_memory_bytes: 320
            trx_rows_locked: 1
          trx_rows_modified: 0
    trx_concurrency_tickets: 0
         trx_isolation_level: REPEATABLE READ
          trx_unique_checks: 1
      trx_foreign_key_checks: 1
    trx_last_foreign_key_error: NULL
   trx_adaptive_hash_latched: 0
   trx_adaptive_hash_timeout: 10000
*************************** 2. row ***************************
                    trx_id: 3B85
                 trx_state: RUNNING
               trx_started: 2011-08-02 14:48:41
       trx_requested_lock_id: NULL
          trx_wait_started: NULL
                trx_weight: 4
         trx_mysql_thread_id: 28544
                 trx_query: NULL
```

```
            trx_operation_state: NULL
             trx_tables_in_use: 0
             trx_tables_locked: 0
              trx_lock_structs: 2
        trx_lock_memory_bytes: 320
               trx_rows_locked: 1
             trx_rows_modified: 2
       trx_concurrency_tickets: 0
          trx_isolation_level: REPEATABLE READ
             trx_unique_checks: 1
        trx_foreign_key_checks: 1
      trx_last_foreign_key_error: NULL
      trx_adaptive_hash_latched: 0
      trx_adaptive_hash_timeout: 10000
2 rows in set (0.11 sec)
```

The `Id` of our blocking transaction is 3B85. So this is the second row in the output, with a `trx_mysql_thread_id` of 28544. We can confirm this using `SHOW PROCESSLIST`:

```
mysql> SHOW PROCESSLIST\G
*************************** 1. row ***************************
      Id: 28542
    User: root
    Host: localhost
      db: information_schema
 Command: Sleep
    Time: 46
   State:
    Info: NULL
*************************** 2. row ***************************
      Id: 28544
    User: root
    Host: localhost
      db: test
 Command: Sleep
    Time: 79
   State:
    Info: NULL
*************************** 3. row ***************************
      Id: 28546
    User: root
    Host: localhost
      db: test
 Command: Query
    Time: 1
   State: Updating
    Info: UPDATE t SET a=36 WHERE a=6
*************************** 4. row ***************************
      Id: 28547
    User: root
    Host: localhost
      db: test
 Command: Query
    Time: 0
   State: NULL
```

```
       Info: SHOW PROCESSLIST
    4 rows in set (0.01 sec)
```

Now that we know the MySQL thread ID, we can do whatever we want with the blocking transaction: either wait until it finishes or kill it. If we ran the offending command from an application, we can also analyze what led to such a locking issue and can fix it to prevent future problems.

Actually, the INNODB_TRX table contains a lot of useful information about transactions. If we go back to our example, we can see trx_state: LOCK WAIT for our waiting transaction and trx_state: RUNNING for the one that is running. I won't describe this additional information here, but I will touch on it in Chapter 6.

- We have just learned that an uncommitted transaction can hold locks, even if the query using the affected rows finished hours ago.

You should remember this while coding. I saw environments where users set autocommit=0 and left transactions running for hours. This leads to issues that are hard to uncover and understand, especially when the user was not prepared for it. Such environments are often used in popular Java frameworks that add autocommit=0 to a URL by default.

- To summarize, when you work with multistatement transactions, commit them as soon as you can. Don't leave an uncommitted transaction around after its last update has finished, even if it does not modify any further rows.

Deadlocks

Deadlock is a situation when two or more competing transactions are waiting for each other to free locks, and thus neither ever finishes. With row-level locking, deadlocks are not 100% avoidable.

InnoDB has an internal deadlock detector. When it finds one, it just rolls back one of the transactions, reporting an error that we'll see momentarily. When designing an application, you need to be prepared for such a situation and handle the rollback appropriately.

Information about deadlocks can be found in SHOW ENGINE INNODB STATUS. To demonstrate this, we will examine a trivial example of a deadlock.

The initial data is:

```
mysql> CREATE TABLE `t` (
`a` int(10) unsigned NOT NULL AUTO_INCREMENT,
PRIMARY KEY (`a`) ) ENGINE=InnoDB DEFAULT CHARSET=utf8;
Query OK, 0 rows affected (0.27 sec)

mysql> INSERT INTO t VALUES();
Query OK, 1 row affected (0.16 sec)

mysql> INSERT INTO t SELECT NULL FROM t;
```

```
Query OK, 1 row affected (0.11 sec)
Records: 1  Duplicates: 0   Warnings: 0

mysql> INSERT INTO t SELECT NULL FROM t;
Query OK, 2 rows affected (0.09 sec)
Records: 2  Duplicates: 0   Warnings: 0

mysql> SELECT * FROM t;
+---+
| a |
+---+
| 1 |
| 2 |
| 3 |
| 4 |
+---+
4 rows in set (0.00 sec)
```

Now let's start two transactions and insert one row in each of them:

```
mysql1> BEGIN;
Query OK, 0 rows affected (0.00 sec)

mysql1> INSERT INTO t VALUES();
Query OK, 1 row affected (0.00 sec)

mysql1> SELECT * FROM t;
+---+
| a |
+---+
| 1 |
| 2 |
| 3 |
| 4 |
| 8 |
+---+
5 rows in set (0.00 sec)

mysql2> BEGIN;
Query OK, 0 rows affected (0.00 sec)

mysql2> INSERT INTO t VALUES();
Query OK, 1 row affected (0.00 sec)

mysql2> SELECT * FROM t;
+---+
| a |
+---+
| 1 |
| 2 |
| 3 |
| 4 |
| 9 |
+---+
5 rows in set (0.00 sec)
```

Everything's OK so far. Both tables inserted one value into an auto-incremented field. Now let's try to modify a row in the first transaction:

```
mysql1> UPDATE t SET a=9 WHERE a=8;
```

While it waits, let's go to the second one and modify its row:

```
mysql2> UPDATE t SET a=8 WHERE a=9;
ERROR 1213 (40001): Deadlock found when trying to get lock; try restarting transaction
```

The query fails immediately, returning information about the deadlock that has occurred. Meanwhile, the second query completed with no problems:

```
Query OK, 1 row affected (9.56 sec)
Rows matched: 1  Changed: 1  Warnings: 0
```

You just saw how InnoDB's deadlock detector worked. To find out what happened, we can again examine SHOW ENGINE INNODB STATUS:

```
------------------------
LATEST DETECTED DEADLOCK
------------------------
110803  3:04:34
*** (1) TRANSACTION:
TRANSACTION 3B96, ACTIVE 29 sec, OS thread id 35542016 updating or deleting
mysql tables in use 1, locked 1
LOCK WAIT 3 lock struct(s), heap size 320, 2 row lock(s), undo log entries 2
MySQL thread id 30446, query id 772 localhost root Updating
update t set a=9 where a=8
*** (1) WAITING FOR THIS LOCK TO BE GRANTED:
RECORD LOCKS space id 1121 page no 3 n bits 80 index `PRIMARY` of table `test`.`t`
trx id 3B96 lock mode S locks rec but not gap waiting
Record lock, heap no 8 PHYSICAL RECORD: n_fields 3; compact format; info bits 32
 0: len 4; hex 00000009; asc     ;;
 1: len 6; hex 000000003b97; asc      ; ;;
 2: len 7; hex 510000022328d5; asc Q   #( ;;

*** (2) TRANSACTION:
TRANSACTION 3B97, ACTIVE 21 sec, OS thread id 35552256 updating or deleting
mysql tables in use 1, locked 1
3 lock struct(s), heap size 320, 2 row lock(s), undo log entries 2
MySQL thread id 30447, query id 773 localhost root Updating
update t set a=8 where a=9
*** (2) HOLDS THE LOCK(S):
RECORD LOCKS space id 1121 page no 3 n bits 80 index `PRIMARY` of table `test`.`t`
trx id 3B97 lock_mode X locks rec but not gap
Record lock, heap no 8 PHYSICAL RECORD: n_fields 3; compact format; info bits 32
 0: len 4; hex 00000009; asc     ;;
 1: len 6; hex 000000003b97; asc      ; ;;
 2: len 7; hex 510000022328d5; asc Q   #( ;;

*** (2) WAITING FOR THIS LOCK TO BE GRANTED:
RECORD LOCKS space id 1121 page no 3 n bits 80 index `PRIMARY` of table `test`.`t`
trx id 3B97 lock mode S locks rec but not gap waiting
Record lock, heap no 6 PHYSICAL RECORD: n_fields 3; compact format; info bits 32
 0: len 4; hex 00000008; asc     ;;
```

```
1: len 6; hex 000000003b96; asc    ; ;;
2: len 7; hex 50000002221b83; asc P   "  ;;
```

```
*** WE ROLL BACK TRANSACTION (2)
```

The output contains a lot of information about the latest deadlock and why it happened. You need to pay attention to the parts named `WAITING FOR THIS LOCK TO BE GRANTED` (which shows which lock the transaction is waiting for) and `HOLDS THE LOCK(S)` (which shows the locks that are holding up this transaction). This knowledge is especially important in applications where you cannot predict which queries are executed at particular times, such as queries invoked by interactions with users of a web application.

To cope with potential deadlocks, you need to add error-handling functionality into your application, as was described in Chapter 1. If you get an error indicating a deadlock and rollback has occurred, restart the transaction.

Implicit Commits

Some statements commit transactions even when you don't call `COMMIT` explicitly. This situation is called an `implicit commit`, and if you aren't aware you're doing a commit, you can end up with an inconsistent state.

A lot of statements cause implicit commits. I won't list them here, because they can vary from version to version. The general rule is that DDL, transaction-related, and administrative statements cause implicit commits, whereas those that work with data do not.

One symptom of an unanticipated implicit commit is when you see unwanted data in tables even though the statements inserting that data were supposed to be rolled back. Here's an example:

```
mysql> CREATE TABLE t1(f1 INT) ENGINE=InnoDB;
Query OK, 0 rows affected (0.14 sec)

mysql> SELECT * FROM t1;
Empty set (0.00 sec)

mysql> BEGIN;
Query OK, 0 rows affected (0.00 sec)

mysql> INSERT INTO t1 VALUES(100);
Query OK, 1 row affected (0.03 sec)

mysql> CREATE TABLE t2 LIKE t1;
Query OK, 0 rows affected (0.19 sec)

mysql> INSERT INTO t1 VALUES(200);
Query OK, 1 row affected (0.02 sec)

mysql> ROLLBACK;
Query OK, 0 rows affected (0.00 sec)
```

CREATE TABLE causes an implicit commit. So even though you may think you rolled back both inserts, t1 will contain one row with the value 100. The second insert with value 200 will be rolled back as desired.

This example assumes that you have set autocommit=0 so that multistatement transactions are used by default. While we're on the subject of commits, it's worth noting again that the default value of autocommit is 1, preventing the use of multistatement transactions when a BEGIN or START TRANSACTION is not called explicitly. When the value is 1, each statement will be committed right away, and in the previous situation you would actually end up with both rows in the table:

```
mysql> SELECT * FROM t1;
+------+
| f1   |
+------+
|  100 |
|  200 |
+------+
2 rows in set (0.00 sec)

mysql> SELECT @@autocommit;
+--------------+
| @@autocommit |
+--------------+
|            1 |
+--------------+
1 row in set (0.00 sec)
```

- Generally, to prevent such issues, keep transactions small, so that even if you interrupt a transaction by mistake with a statement causing an implicit commit, the side effect will be minimal.

Metadata Locking

To ensure data consistency, DDL operations on a table should be blocked if another transaction is using the table. Starting with version 5.5.3, this is achieved by using metadata locks.

When a transaction starts, it acquires metadata locks on all the tables it uses and releases the locks when it finishes. All other threads that try to modify the tables' definitions wait until the transaction ends.

DDL operations in MySQL servers prior to 5.5.3 knew nothing about parallel transactions. This would lead to collisions similar to the following:

```
mysql1> BEGIN;
Query OK, 0 rows affected (0.08 sec)

mysql1> SELECT * FROM t1;
+------+
| f1   |
```

```
+------+
| 100  |
| 200  |
+------+
2 rows in set (0.10 sec)
```

In one transaction, we are selecting data from a table, planning to use this result set during the current transaction. At the very same time, another thread drops the table:

```
mysql2> DROP TABLE t1;
Query OK, 0 rows affected (0.17 sec)
```

DROP is not an operation that can be rolled back, so the first thread is the one affected by the conflict:

```
mysql> SELECT * FROM t1;
ERROR 1146 (42S02): Table 'test.t1' doesn't exist
```

Our transaction obviously cannot complete. A metadata lock would allow our transaction to complete before the other connection's DROP statement could execute. To illustrate this, we will execute the same example on version 5.5.3 or later:

```
mysql1> BEGIN;
Query OK, 0 rows affected (0.00 sec)

mysql1> SELECT * FROM t1;
+------+
| f1   |
+------+
| 100  |
| 200  |
+------+
2 rows in set (0.00 sec)
```

Now the DROP attempt just blocks:

```
mysql2> DROP TABLE t1;
```

After issuing that command, I waited a few seconds, so you will see how long the drop was executing, and then rolled back the first transaction:

```
mysql1> ROLLBACK;
Query OK, 0 rows affected (0.00 sec)
```

Now we can look at the query execution time to be sure the DROP waited until the first transaction finished:

```
mysql2> DROP TABLE t1;
Query OK, 0 rows affected (1 min 0.39 sec)
```

The new model is much safer, and as such does not require any new troubleshooting techniques. But MySQL has been around for a long time before metadata locks were introduced, and users became used to the old behavior, even creating workarounds for it. So I want to add a few notes about the differences in server behavior created by metadata locking.

Metadata Locking Versus the Old Model

Metadata locks are acquired independently of the storage engine you use. So if you use a MyISAM table with `autocommit=0` or if you start an explicit transaction with `BEGIN` or `START TRANSACTION`, your connection will acquire the metadata lock. You can clearly see this in the output of `SHOW PROCESSLIST`, which will show the statement with the state "Waiting for table metadata lock."

A small example demonstrates the use of the lock. The first thread opens a transaction that accesses a MyISAM table. I used `BEGIN` here, but the same behavior can be seen if you use `autocommit=0`:

```
mysql1> SHOW CREATE TABLE tm\G
*************************** 1. row ***************************
       Table: tm
Create Table: CREATE TABLE `tm` (
  `a` int(10) unsigned NOT NULL AUTO_INCREMENT,
  PRIMARY KEY (`a`)
) ENGINE=MyISAM AUTO_INCREMENT=5 DEFAULT CHARSET=utf8
1 row in set (0.00 sec)

mysql1> BEGIN;
Query OK, 0 rows affected (0.00 sec)

mysql1> SELECT * FROM tm;
+---+
| a |
+---+
| 1 |
| 2 |
| 3 |
| 4 |
+---+
4 rows in set (0.00 sec)
```

At the same time, another thread calls `TRUNCATE`, which affects table metadata:

```
mysql2> TRUNCATE TABLE tm;
```

You can see the states of both threads if you run `SHOW PROCESSLIST` using a third connection:

```
mysql> SHOW PROCESSLIST\G
*************************** 1. row ***************************
     Id: 30970
   User: root
   Host: localhost
     db: test
Command: Sleep
   Time: 26
  State:
   Info: NULL
*************************** 2. row ***************************
     Id: 30972
   User: root
```

```
      Host: localhost
        db: test
   Command: Query
      Time: 9
     State: Waiting for table metadata lock
      Info: TRUNCATE TABLE tm
*************************** 3. row ***************************
        Id: 31005
      User: root
      Host: localhost
        db: NULL
   Command: Query
      Time: 0
     State: NULL
      Info: SHOW PROCESSLIST
3 rows in set (0.00 sec)
```

When a query blocks while waiting for the metadata lock, `SHOW PROCESSLIST` is your assistant again. After you move to a version of MySQL with support for the metadata lock, you may find that DDL queries start to run slowly. This is because they have to wait when another transaction has the lock.

In theory, the metadata lock can time out. The timeout is specified by a variable named `lock_wait_timeout`. By default, it is set to 31,536,000 seconds (one year), so effectively a locked query can never die:

```
mysql> truncate table tm;
Query OK, 0 rows affected (5 hours 12 min 52.51 sec)
```

To provide an effective timeout, you can set `lock_wait_timeout` to a smaller value, such as one second:

```
mysql> set lock_wait_timeout=1;
Query OK, 0 rows affected (0.00 sec)

mysql> truncate table tm;
ERROR 1205 (HY000): Lock wait timeout exceeded; try restarting transaction
```

How Concurrency Affects Performance

We just discussed cases when conflicts between parallel threads or transactions created performance issues or even aborted queries. You saw how locks set by SQL statements or the storage engines affect parallel threads. Such locks are visible to users and easy to track, although they are not always easy to debug. You need to account for the possibility of parallel, competing threads when an application is capable of creating multiple MySQL connections. This can be as common as a web server that opens parallel connections to a MySQL server because multiple users have opened a web page provided by that web server.

We also discussed wrong results or dramatic slowdowns that are hard to miss if your application handles errors. When I collected examples for this book, I put all such issues in "Wrong Results from a SELECT" on page 5. I distinguish those from performance problems because you can see their results immediately, whereas performance problems are generally hidden at first, and you notice them only after examining the slow query log or getting complaints from users about slow applications.

So let's tackle the subtler performance problems. If a query suddenly starts to run slowly, your first step is to make sure it is properly optimized. The easiest way to do this is to run the query in an isolated, single-threaded environment. If the query still runs slowly, either it requires optimization or the recent execution of a large number of updates caused the index statistic to become out of date. (Chapter 1 contains basic optimization techniques.)

If a query completes quickly in single-threaded environment but slowly in a multi-threaded one, this almost certainly means you are experiencing a concurrency issue. All the techniques that I illustrated for dealing with wrong results are suitable for this case as well. Slow queries are just a slightly more complex problem because in order to debug them, you have to reproduce the conditions under which they occur, and it can be hard to make the problem strike when you want it to.

 I always insist on reproducing problems, not just removing a problematic query. For concurrency problems, this is important because the problem query may be just a symptom of a deeper problem. If you stop executing it without solving the real problem, you may suffer from the same issue in another part of the application.

Monitoring InnoDB Transactions for Concurrency Problems

If you are debugging locks caused by an InnoDB transaction, InnoDB Monitors will make your life easier. Just turn a monitor on, and it will periodically dump messages into the error logfile, similar to the output you have already seen with the use of SHOW ENGINE INNODB STATUS.

To turn on InnoDB Monitors, create a table named innodb_monitor in any database:

```
$mysql test -A
Welcome to the MySQL monitor.  Commands end with ; or \g.
Your MySQL connection id is 2624
Server version: 5.1.59-debug Source distribution

Copyright (c) 2000, 2011, Oracle and/or its affiliates. All rights reserved.

Oracle is a registered trademark of Oracle Corporation and/or its
affiliates. Other names may be trademarks of their respective
owners.

Type 'help;' or '\h' for help. Type '\c' to clear the current input statement.

mysql> CREATE TABLE innodb_monitor(f1 INT) ENGINE=InnoDB;
Query OK, 0 rows affected (0.48 sec)
```

The -A option on the MySQL client command is useful when you're trying to debug problems related to concurrency. Normally, the client asks for a list of available tables. The client could then be held up by locks held by other connections, which defeats the purpose of running the client to debug them. The -A option suppresses the request for the table list.

Once you do this, InnoDB recognizes the table and starts printing information to the error logfile. So if you check for the time when the slow query was running against the transactions information recorded at that time, you can find out what was holding a lock that held up the query. More information about InnoDB Monitors appears in "SHOW ENGINE INNODB STATUS and InnoDB Monitors" on page 96 and also in Chapter 6.

Monitoring Other Resources for Concurrency Problems

If you debug a query that doesn't use the InnoDB storage engine or that you suspect is affected by a different kind of lock, there are still a couple of options. You can issue SHOW PROCESSLIST, but an even better choice is to schedule SELECT … FROM INFORMATION_SCHEMA.PROCESSLIST to run repeatedly and save its output into a file or a table together with information about when it was taken. This output is easier to control and read than SHOW PROCESSLIST. Check the process list information from the same time as when the slow query was running to get some clue about what was holding up the query.

The effects of concurrency on performance do not always lie at the level of SQL or the storage engine. Multiple threads of the MySQL server also share hardware resources, such as RAM and CPU. Some of these resources are dedicated to each thread, whereas others, such as temporary tables, are dedicated for particular kinds of operations and allocated only when necessary. Some resources are shared by all threads. You should also consider operating system limits when planning an application. In this section, I will describe the concepts that affect the performance of these resources, and Chapter 3 will discuss in detail the options that control resource usage.

Let's start with the memory allocated to each thread. The MySQL server has a group of options that allows you to set the size of thread-specific buffers. Roughly, the more memory you allocate, the faster the thread runs. But these buffers are allocated for every single thread you run, so the more resources you allocate to each thread, the fewer threads can run simultaneously. Always seek a balance between values that improve performance and the real amount of physical memory.

Resources allocated for certain kinds of operations are limited too. Don't set them very high until it is necessary, but don't set them too low either. A good compromise is to set high values for only a few sessions (connections) that need large buffers and leave the default value for others. This level of control can be set on a session-by-session basis dynamically:

```
SET SESSION join_buffer_size=1024*1024*1024;
```

The third kind of resources are those shared by all threads, usually internal caches. With such options, you generally don't need to worry that adding more connections will increase memory usage. One potential issue with them, though, is that changing the data can invalidate the cache and cause subsequent statements to take longer. Usually this is a very quick operation, but if a cache is very large, invalidation can take a long time, so this can affect the user while a thread waits for the cache to become accessible again.

Finally, performance can run up against limits on operating resources such as file descriptors and CPU. The number of file descriptors available on the system limits the number of connections the server can make, the number of tables that can be opened simultaneously, and even the number of partitions in a single table. You may find it impossible even to open a table if it has more partitions than available file descriptors. We will discuss how the operating system can affect MySQL in Chapter 4.

Other Locking Issues

Other resources that can affect your application are internal locks and mutexes acquired when the server executes particular operations. Most of them protect data integrity. With a few exceptions, such as InnoDB mutexes and spin locks, you cannot and should not try to control them, but because a few of them can become visible to user applications, I'll describe them here.

Transactions can create race conditions and therefore deadlocks, but so can other activities. When the MySQL server starts using a resource such as a file or modifies a variable that is shared between threads, it locks access to the resource to prevent concurrent access to the same resource by other threads. This is done for data consistency. But at the same time, such protection can lead to deadlocks.

These deadlocks are hard to diagnose and theoretically should never happen, but because they have turned up in the past, I'll describe what to do when you suspect it. As an example, I will create a deadlock of this kind using a test case from a bug report. This bug is not related to troubleshooting a metadata lock (MDL), so I will concentrate on just the debugging aspect, not on the actions that led to the deadlock.

 It might seem artificial to illustrate a problem caused by a MySQL bug instead of a user error, but the message is useful. Nobody is insured against hitting a bug, and it is good to be prepared. Forewarned is forearmed.

The symptoms of a "resource" deadlock are the same as for deadlocks caused by row locking: queries just hang. No internal mechanism can find such a deadlock and kill it, so don't expect that the thread will time out (as with an InnoDB lock) or immediately be rolled back (as with an InnoDB deadlock). SHOW PROCESSLIST will show something like this:

```
mysql> SHOW PROCESSLIST\G
*************************** 1. row ***************************
     Id: 2
   User: root
   Host: localhost
     db: performance_schema
Command: Query
   Time: 0
  State: NULL
   Info: SHOW PROCESSLIST
*************************** 2. row ***************************
     Id: 6
   User: root
   Host: localhost
     db: test
Command: Query
   Time: 9764
  State: Waiting for table metadata lock
   Info: SELECT * FROM t1, t2
*************************** 3. row ***************************
     Id: 7
   User: root
   Host: localhost
     db: test
Command: Query
   Time: 9765
  State: Waiting for table metadata lock
   Info: RENAME TABLE t2 TO t0, t4 TO t2, t0 TO t4
*************************** 4. row ***************************
     Id: 8
   User: root
   Host: localhost
     db: test
Command: Query
   Time: 9766
  State: Waiting for table level lock
   Info: INSERT INTO t3 VALUES ((SELECT count(*) FROM t4))
*************************** 5. row ***************************
     Id: 10
   User: root
   Host: localhost
     db: test
Command: Sleep
   Time: 9768
  State:
   Info: NULL
*************************** 6. row ***************************
     Id: 502
   User: root
   Host: localhost
     db: test
Command: Sleep
```

```
    Time: 2
    State:
     Info: NULL
6 rows in set (0.00 sec)
```

This output shows several queries waiting for different kinds of locks for more than 9,000 seconds.

The TRANSACTIONS part of the SHOW ENGINE INNODB STATUS output does not show any new information:

```
------------
TRANSACTIONS
------------
Trx id counter 4211
Purge done for trx's n:o < 4211 undo n:o < 0
History list length 127
LIST OF TRANSACTIONS FOR EACH SESSION:
---TRANSACTION 0, not started, OS thread id 35934208
MySQL thread id 502, query id 124 localhost root
show engine innodb status
---TRANSACTION 0, not started, OS thread id 33726976
MySQL thread id 6, query id 71 localhost root Waiting for table metadata lock
select * from t1, t2
---TRANSACTION 0, not started, OS thread id 35786240
mysql tables in use 2, locked 2
MySQL thread id 8, query id 69 localhost root Waiting for table level lock
insert into t3 values ((select count(*) from t4))
---TRANSACTION 4201, not started, OS thread id 35354624
mysql tables in use 2, locked 4
MySQL thread id 10, query id 68 localhost root
---TRANSACTION 0, not started, OS thread id 35633152
MySQL thread id 7, query id 70 localhost root Waiting for table metadata lock
rename table t2 to t0, t4 to t2, t0 to t4
```

Starting with version 5.5, additional information can be received from the performance_schema, which I'll describe in "PERFORMANCE_SCHEMA Tables" on page 100. Here I want to show what to do when the problem I just highlighted arises.

The first table to check is MUTEX_INSTANCES, which lists all mutexes created since the server started. Some of them are currently unused, so you should skip them in your SELECT and retrieve only the ones where LOCKED_BY_THREAD_ID is not null:

```
mysql> SELECT * FROM MUTEX_INSTANCES WHERE LOCKED_BY_THREAD_ID is
not null\G
*************************** 1. row ***************************
             NAME: wait/synch/mutex/sql/MDL_wait::LOCK_wait_status
OBJECT_INSTANCE_BEGIN: 35623528
  LOCKED_BY_THREAD_ID: 23
*************************** 2. row ***************************
             NAME: wait/synch/mutex/sql/MDL_wait::LOCK_wait_status
OBJECT_INSTANCE_BEGIN: 35036264
  LOCKED_BY_THREAD_ID: 22
*************************** 3. row ***************************
```

```
             NAME: wait/synch/mutex/mysys/THR_LOCK::mutex
OBJECT_INSTANCE_BEGIN: 508708108
  LOCKED_BY_THREAD_ID: 24
3 rows in set (0.26 sec)
```

To find out who waits on these mutexes, query the EVENTS_WAITS_CURRENT table:

```
mysql> SELECT THREAD_ID, EVENT_ID, EVENT_NAME, SOURCE,
TIMER_START,  OBJECT_INSTANCE_BEGIN, OPERATION FROM EVENTS_WAITS_CURRENT WHERE
THREAD_ID IN(SELECT LOCKED_BY_THREAD_ID FROM MUTEX_INSTANCES WHERE
LOCKED_BY_THREAD_ID IS NOT NULL)\G
*************************** 1. row ***************************
            THREAD_ID: 24
             EVENT_ID: 268
           EVENT_NAME: wait/synch/cond/mysys/my_thread_var::suspend
               SOURCE: thr_lock.c:461
          TIMER_START: 128382107931720
OBJECT_INSTANCE_BEGIN: 508721156
            OPERATION: timed_wait
*************************** 2. row ***************************
            THREAD_ID: 22
             EVENT_ID: 44
           EVENT_NAME: wait/synch/cond/sql/MDL_context::COND_wait_status
               SOURCE: mdl.cc:995
          TIMER_START: 130306657228800
OBJECT_INSTANCE_BEGIN: 35036372
            OPERATION: timed_wait
*************************** 3. row ***************************
            THREAD_ID: 23
             EVENT_ID: 42430
           EVENT_NAME: wait/synch/cond/sql/MDL_context::COND_wait_status
               SOURCE: mdl.cc:995
          TIMER_START: 7865906646714888
OBJECT_INSTANCE_BEGIN: 35623636
            OPERATION: timed_wait
3 rows in set (2.23 sec)
```

The THREAD_ID in the output is the actual number assigned internally to a thread by *mysqld*, not the number of the connection thread that can help us find the statement causing the deadlock. To find the number of the connection thread, query the THREADS table. I have not filtered the output here, because I want to show you all the threads that run inside the *mysqld* process while it serves the six connections from our example.

```
mysql> SELECT * FROM THREADS\G
*************************** 1. row ***************************
THREAD_ID: 0
       ID: 0
     NAME: thread/sql/main
*************************** 2. row ***************************
THREAD_ID: 24
       ID: 8
     NAME: thread/sql/one_connection
*************************** 3. row ***************************
THREAD_ID: 2
```

```
         ID: 0
       NAME: thread/innodb/io_handler_thread
*************************** 4. row ***************************
THREAD_ID: 14
       ID: 0
     NAME: thread/innodb/srv_monitor_thread
*************************** 5. row ***************************
THREAD_ID: 6
       ID: 0
     NAME: thread/innodb/io_handler_thread
*************************** 6. row ***************************
THREAD_ID: 518
       ID: 502
     NAME: thread/sql/one_connection
*************************** 7. row ***************************
THREAD_ID: 12
       ID: 0
     NAME: thread/innodb/srv_lock_timeout_thread
*************************** 8. row ***************************
THREAD_ID: 22
       ID: 6
     NAME: thread/sql/one_connection
*************************** 9. row ***************************
THREAD_ID: 7
       ID: 0
     NAME: thread/innodb/io_handler_thread
*************************** 10. row ***************************
THREAD_ID: 3
       ID: 0
     NAME: thread/innodb/io_handler_thread
*************************** 11. row ***************************
THREAD_ID: 26
       ID: 10
     NAME: thread/sql/one_connection
*************************** 12. row ***************************
THREAD_ID: 9
       ID: 0
     NAME: thread/innodb/io_handler_thread
*************************** 13. row ***************************
THREAD_ID: 16
       ID: 0
     NAME: thread/sql/signal_handler
*************************** 14. row ***************************
THREAD_ID: 23
       ID: 7
     NAME: thread/sql/one_connection
*************************** 15. row ***************************
THREAD_ID: 1
       ID: 0
     NAME: thread/innodb/io_handler_thread
*************************** 16. row ***************************
THREAD_ID: 4
       ID: 0
     NAME: thread/innodb/io_handler_thread
*************************** 17. row ***************************
```

```
     THREAD_ID: 5
           ID: 0
         NAME: thread/innodb/io_handler_thread
*************************** 18. row ***************************
     THREAD_ID: 8
           ID: 0
         NAME: thread/innodb/io_handler_thread
*************************** 19. row ***************************
     THREAD_ID: 15
           ID: 0
         NAME: thread/innodb/srv_master_thread
*************************** 20. row ***************************
     THREAD_ID: 18
           ID: 2
         NAME: thread/sql/one_connection
*************************** 21. row ***************************
     THREAD_ID: 13
           ID: 0
         NAME: thread/innodb/srv_error_monitor_thread
*************************** 22. row ***************************
     THREAD_ID: 10
           ID: 0
         NAME: thread/innodb/io_handler_thread
22 rows in set (0.03 sec)
```

Now we have all the information we can get about what is going on inside the server without engaging in special manipulations, such as attaching a debugger to the running *mysqld* process. In this case, we actually had all the information we needed after the first SHOW PROCESSLIST call. But I wanted to show what's available from performance_schema to help debug internal problems, such as deadlocks, when the state is not as clear as it was in this example.

What should be done to solve a deadlock? You need to pick a connection to serve as the victim and kill it. In this case, fortunately we can find a relatively unimportant connection in the SHOW ENGINE INNODB STATUS we saw earlier. Here is what it says about MySQL server's thread 10:

```
---TRANSACTION 4201, not started, OS thread id 35354624
mysql tables in use 2, locked 4
MySQL thread id 10, query id 68 localhost root
```

This is not waiting for any action, but it is locking two tables. Let's kill it:

```
mysql> KILL 10;
Query OK, 0 rows affected (0.09 sec)
```

We were lucky, and killing this single connection solved the problem:

```
mysql> SHOW PROCESSLIST\G
*************************** 1. row ***************************
      Id: 2
    User: root
    Host: localhost
      db: performance_schema
 Command: Query
```

```
    Time: 0
   State: NULL
    Info: SHOW PROCESSLIST
*************************** 2. row ***************************
      Id: 6
    User: root
    Host: localhost
      db: test
 Command: Sleep
    Time: 10361
   State:
    Info: NULL
*************************** 3. row ***************************
      Id: 7
    User: root
    Host: localhost
      db: test
 Command: Sleep
    Time: 10362
   State:
    Info: NULL
*************************** 4. row ***************************
      Id: 8
    User: root
    Host: localhost
      db: test
 Command: Sleep
    Time: 10363
   State:
    Info: NULL
*************************** 5. row ***************************
      Id: 502
    User: root
    Host: localhost
      db: test
 Command: Sleep
    Time: 152
   State:
    Info: NULL
5 rows in set (0.00 sec)

mysql> SELECT * FROM MUTEX_INSTANCES WHERE LOCKED_BY_THREAD_ID IS
NOT NULL\G
Empty set (0.11 sec)

mysql> SELECT THREAD_ID, EVENT_ID, EVENT_NAME, SOURCE,
TIMER_START,  OBJECT_INSTANCE_BEGIN, OPERATION FROM EVENTS_WAITS_CURRENT WHERE
THREAD_ID IN(SELECT LOCKED_BY_THREAD_ID FROM MUTEX_INSTANCES WHERE
LOCKED_BY_THREAD_ID IS NOT NULL)\G
Empty set (1.23 sec)
```

This was a short overview about system deadlocks and what to do if you meet them. The basic procedure is to make sure there are threads waiting essentially forever, find a thread you can live without, and kill it. You should not be afraid of killing stalled threads, because it is better to kill them and then fix any resulting error manually than to wait indefinitely until *mysqld* stops for another reason.

You may encounter other examples of the influence internal server locks have on applications. Some even cause server crashes. For instance, InnoDB uses semaphores for various locking purposes, such as to protect CHECK TABLE and OPTIMIZE TABLE, but if an InnoDB semaphore waits for more than 600 seconds, InnoDB intentionally crashes the server.

 Don't mix semaphores' long waiting times with user sessions that last more than 600 seconds. InnoDB semaphores do protect certain operations. A single session can issue none or dozens of them.

You can monitor the state of an application and prevent such situations. Thus, pertaining to InnoDB semaphores, the storage engine prints information about wait times in its monitor:

```
----------
SEMAPHORES
----------
OS WAIT ARRAY INFO: reservation count 179, signal count 177
--Thread 35471872 has waited at trx/trx0rec.c line 1253 for 0.00 seconds the semaphore:
X-lock (wait_ex) on RW-latch at 0x149b124c created in file buf/buf0buf.c line 898
a writer (thread id 35471872) has reserved it in mode  wait exclusive
number of readers 1, waiters flag 0, lock_word: ffffffff
Last time read locked in file buf/buf0flu.c line 1186
Last time write locked in file trx/trx0rec.c line 1253
Mutex spin waits 209, rounds 3599, OS waits 38
RW-shared spins 70, rounds 2431, OS waits 67
RW-excl spins 0, rounds 2190, OS waits 71
Spin rounds per wait: 17.22 mutex, 34.73 RW-shared, 2190.00 RW-excl
```

 Don't worry if InnoDB prints information about semaphore waits for operations that need to take a long time, such as CHECK TABLE on a huge table. What you need to take action on is a large waiting time during a normal operation.

Replication and Concurrency

Another important aspect of concurrency troubleshooting concerns replicated environments.

When troubleshooting replication, you need to remember that a master server is always multithreaded, whereas the slave runs all updates in a single thread.[2] This affects

---

2. This will change, as discussed in "Multithreaded Slave" on page 88.

performance and consistency during replication, regardless of the binary log formats or options you use.

The majority of replication issues involve data inconsistency, meaning that the data on the slave is different from that on the master. In most cases, MySQL replication takes care of data consistency, but sometimes you can still experience issues, especially if you use statement-based replication. This section focuses on consistency, with a few words at the end about how performance can be affected by replication.

Statement-Based Replication Issues

Starting with version 5.1, MySQL supports three binary logging formats: statement, row, and mixed. The majority of issues with data inconsistency happen with statement-basement replication (SBR), which uses the statement binary log format. This format has several advantages over row-based logging, and historically it was the only way to log changes, so its user base is still huge and it is still the default. But it is more risky than row-based logging.

Row-based logging records raw data about rows in the log. The slave does not execute the same queries as the master, but instead updates table rows directly. This is the safest binary logging format because it can't insert into the slave table any values that do not exist on the master. This format can be used safely even when you call nondeterministic functions such as NOW().

Statement-based logging just puts queries in the original SQL format into the log, so the slave executes the same commands as the master. If you use this format, network traffic usually—although not always—is much lower than if a row-based format is used because a query can take up less data than the actual changes it makes to rows. This is especially noticeable when you update several rows in a table with BLOB columns. The disadvantage of this format is that it forces you to ensure data consistency. For example, if you insert the output of the function NOW() into a column, you will most likely have different data on the master and slave.

The mixed binary logging format contains the advantages of both row and statement logging: it saves the majority of queries in statement format but switches to row format when a query is not safe, i.e., when it uses a nondeterministic function such as NOW().

When you plan an application under conditions where MySQL is using replication, be aware of how different statements affect consistency. Even when the master provides a lot of additional information to the slave, the latter cannot handle all issues.

The MySQL Reference Manual contains a list of statements that are not safe when statement-based replication is used, meaning that using such a statement can leave different results on the slave and master. *MySQL High Availability* by Charles Bell et al. (O'Reilly) covers consistency issues during replication in detail. Here I'll focus on concurrency-related problems, which can lead to different results if statements are run in many threads on the master and were put in a particular order on the slave.

Because a master server is multithreaded, it can run multiple connections in a nondeterministic order. But the slave, which is currently single-threaded, reissues the statements in the order in which they were logged, which may be different from the order in which they were issued on the server. This can lead to differences between the master and slave.

Multithreaded Slave

The Replication Team is working on a multithreaded slave. The current status of this enhancement is feature preview. A multithreaded slave can distribute transactions into different threads. You can tune the number of threads using the `slave_parallel_workers` variable.

This feature affects replication scalability, i.e., the speed of data updates, so it can prevent slaves from falling so far behind that consistency is threatened. But don't expect it to prevent data consistency issues.

You can learn more about multithreaded slaves in a blog post by Luís Soares (*http://d2 -systems.blogspot.com/2011/04/mysql-56x-feature-preview-multi.html*).

To illustrate ordering problems, I will use a simple table with a single field and no unique index. In real life, a similar pattern applies whenever queries search for rows without using a unique index.

Example 2-1. Example of replication issue happened due to wrong order of transactions

```
CREATE TABLE t1(f1 CHAR(2)) ENGINE=InnoDB;
```

Now I'll imitate the effect of concurrent transactions inserting rows in batch mode:

```
master1> BEGIN;
master1> INSERT INTO t1 VALUES(1);
master1> INSERT INTO t1 VALUES(2);
master1> INSERT INTO t1 VALUES(3);
master1> INSERT INTO t1 VALUES(4);
master1> INSERT INTO t1 VALUES(5);
```

Note that this transaction is not yet committed. Next, I open a new transaction in another connection and insert yet another bunch of rows:

```
master2> BEGIN;
master2> INSERT INTO t1 VALUES('a');
master2> INSERT INTO t1 VALUES('b');
master2> INSERT INTO t1 VALUES('c');
master2> INSERT INTO t1 VALUES('d');
```

```
master2> INSERT INTO t1 VALUES('e');
master2> COMMIT;
```

This second transaction is committed. Now I'll commit the first one:

```
master1> COMMIT;
```

You probably expect that the table will have 1, 2, 3, 4, 5 as the first rows and a, b, c, d, e as the following rows. This is absolutely correct, because the first transaction started earlier than the second one:

```
master1> SELECT * FROM t1;
+------+
| f1   |
+------+
| 1    |
| 2    |
| 3    |
| 4    |
| 5    |
| a    |
| b    |
| c    |
| d    |
| e    |
+------+
10 rows in set (0.04 sec)
```

But the master doesn't write anything to the binary log until the transaction is committed. Therefore, the slave will have a, b, c, d, e as the first rows and 1, 2, 3, 4, 5 as the second set:

```
slave> SELECT * FROM t1;
+------+
| f1   |
+------+
| a    |
| b    |
| c    |
| d    |
| e    |
| 1    |
| 2    |
| 3    |
| 4    |
| 5    |
+------+
10 rows in set (0.04 sec)
```

This is fine so far: the master and slave contain same the data, although in a different order. Things break when one runs an unsafe UPDATE:

```
master1> UPDATE t1 SET f1='A' LIMIT 5;
Query OK, 5 rows affected, 1 warning (0.14 sec)
Rows matched: 5  Changed: 5  Warnings: 1
```

```
mysql> SHOW WARNINGS\G
*************************** 1. row ***************************
  Level: Note
   Code: 1592
Message: Unsafe statement written to the binary log using statement format since
BINLOG_FORMAT = STATEMENT. The statement is unsafe because it uses a LIMIT
clause. This is unsafe because the set of rows included cannot be predicted.
1 row in set (0.00 sec)
```

As you see, the server warns us that this query is not safe. Let's see why. On the master we end up with:

```
master1> SELECT * FROM t1;
+------+
| f1   |
+------+
| A    |
| A    |
| A    |
| A    |
| A    |
| a    |
| b    |
| c    |
| d    |
| e    |
+------+
```

whereas the slave has a completely different data set:

```
slave> SELECT * FROM t1;
+------+
| f1   |
+------+
| A    |
| A    |
| A    |
| A    |
| A    |
| 1    |
| 2    |
| 3    |
| 4    |
| 5    |
+------+
```

This example is quite simple. In real life, mix-ups are usually much worse. In this example, I used a transactional storage engine and multistatement transactions just to reproduce an erroneous result easily. With a nontransactional storage engine, you can see similar issues when using MySQL extensions that delay actual data changes, such as INSERT DELAYED.

The best way to prevent such a situation is to use row-based or mixed replication. If you stick to statement-based replication, it is absolutely necessary to design the application to prevent such situations. Keep in mind that every transaction is written to the binary log when and only when it is committed. You also need to use the techniques to check warnings described in Chapter 1. If this sounds too hard to do for every single query in production (e.g., due to performance considerations), do it at least during the development stage.

Mixing Transactional and Nontransactional Tables

It is important not to mix transactional and nontransactional tables in the same transaction.[3] Once you make changes to a nontransactional table, you cannot roll them back, so if the transaction is aborted or rolled back, your data can become inconsistent.

> The same issue occurs when mixing transactional tables using different engines in the same transaction. If engines have different transaction isolation levels or different rules for statements that cause implicit commits, you can end up with problems similar to those described for mixing transactional and nontransactional tables.

This can happen even when using a single MySQL server, but in replicated environments things sometimes get even worse. So I'm including this section in the part about replication, even though it contains lessons for nonreplicated environments as well.

For our example, we will show a stored procedure using the same concept as the example from "Tracing Back Errors in Data" on page 19. I'm changing the temporary table here to a persistent one and adding another procedure that will fill rows in table t2. Table t2 will also use the MyISAM storage engine. MyISAM was the default engine before 5.5, so such a temporary table can be created easily if the user forgets to add the ENGINE option to the CREATE TABLE statement. The user may also use MyISAM in the mistaken hope of improving performance:

```
CREATE TABLE t1(f1 INT) ENGINE=InnoDB;
CREATE TABLE t2(f1 INT) ENGINE=MyISAM;
CREATE TABLE t3(f1 INT) ENGINE=InnoDB;

INSERT INTO t3 VALUES(1),(2),(3);

CREATE PROCEDURE p1()
BEGIN
DECLARE m INT UNSIGNED DEFAULT NULL;
SELECT max(f1) INTO m FROM t2;
IF m IS NOT NULL
THEN
  INSERT INTO t1(f1) SELECT f1 FROM t2;
END IF;
```

---

3. There are exceptions to this rule that I would call "semi-safe," like when a nontransactional table is read-only or write-only (a log table, for instance, is write-only in this context). When you use such tables together with transactional tables, plan carefully.

```
END
|
```

Now I will add values into t2 in a transaction:

```
master>  BEGIN;
Query OK, 0 rows affected (0.00 sec)

master>  INSERT INTO t1 VALUES(5);
Query OK, 1 row affected (0.00 sec)

master>  INSERT INTO t2 SELECT f1 FROM t3;
Query OK, 3 rows affected, 1 warning (0.00 sec)
Records: 3  Duplicates: 0  Warnings: 1
```

And I'll call p1() without committing the transaction in the parallel master connection:

```
master>  BEGIN;
Query OK, 0 rows affected (0.00 sec)

master>  CALL p1();
Query OK, 3 rows affected (0.00 sec)

master>  COMMIT;
Query OK, 0 rows affected (0.00 sec)

master>  SELECT * FROM t1;
+------+
| f1   |
+------+
|    1 |
|    2 |
|    3 |
+------+
3 rows in set (0.00 sec)
```

As you see, there are three rows on the master. Let's see how many we have on the slave:

```
slave>  SELECT * FROM t1;
Empty set (0.00 sec)
```

The slave actually has no rows. This happened because the master wrote updates to nontransactional tables into the transaction cache. But as we saw earlier, cache content is written to the binary log only after a transaction actually ends. In this case, perhaps the slave actually corresponds more closely to the user's intent than the master (because the master has "ghost" entries in t1 corresponding to a transaction that never completed), but the point is that we end up with data inconsistency thanks to the nontransactional table.

 The section "Replication options" on page 124 discusses the binlog_direct_non_transactional_updates option, which controls when updates on nontransactional tables are written to the binary log.

- So, don't mix transactional and nontransactional tables in a transaction. If it is absolutely necessary, use other locking methods, such as `LOCK TABLE`, to ensure consistency in case of a rollback or crash.

You can solve most replication-related issues using the row-based or mixed binary log format, but that won't help if the data on the master is not what you expect.

Issues on the Slave

We just discussed concurrency problems that arise because the master is multithreaded while the slave is single-threaded. If the slave SQL thread was the only one running, we wouldn't have any additional concurrency issues on the slave. But in real life, a slave also does other jobs besides replicating from the master, and therefore the slave's SQL thread can be affected by concurrency issues just like any other connection thread.

When the slave SQL thread writes to tables that are currently used by user threads, it acquires all locks for such tables, just like any other multithreaded case. You can see this by running `SHOW PROCESSLIST`:

```
slave> SHOW PROCESSLIST\G
*************************** 1. row ***************************
     Id: 1
   User: system user
   Host:
     db: NULL
Command: Connect
   Time: 115
  State: Waiting for master to send event
   Info: NULL
*************************** 2. row ***************************
     Id: 2
   User: system user
   Host:
     db: test
Command: Connect
   Time: 16
  State: update
   Info: INSERT INTO t1 VALUES(3)
*************************** 3. row ***************************
     Id: 3
   User: msandbox
   Host: localhost
     db: test
Command: Sleep
   Time: 28
  State:
   Info: NULL
*************************** 4. row ***************************
     Id: 4
   User: msandbox
   Host: localhost
     db: test
```

```
   Command: Query
      Time: 0
     State: NULL
      Info: SHOW PROCESSLIST
4 rows in set (0.00 sec)
```

The slave SQL thread is listed in row 2 and is run by `system user`, a special user that executes slave queries. I now run the following query in a parallel connection, before starting the slave, to demonstrate how the SQL thread waits for other threads to finish before it can execute the update:

```
SELECT * FROM t1 FOR UPDATE;
```

After taking this `SHOW PROCESSLIST` output, I rolled back the parallel query, so the SQL thread could successfully finish the query:

```
slave> SHOW PROCESSLIST\G
*************************** 1. row ***************************
      Id: 1
    User: system user
    Host:
      db: NULL
 Command: Connect
    Time: 267
   State: Waiting for master to send event
    Info: NULL
*************************** 2. row ***************************
      Id: 2
    User: system user
    Host:
      db: NULL
 Command: Connect
    Time: 168
   State: Slave has read all relay log; waiting for the slave I/O thread to update it
    Info: NULL
...
```

You can also encounter a situation where the slave SQL thread is holding locks on rows that your application is trying to access. To see when this happens, examine the output of `SHOW PROCESSLIST` and `SHOW ENGINE INNODB STATUS`.

The solution to both of these situations is either to wait until the active thread finishes or to roll back a user transaction if it waits for a lock for a long time.

Effectively Using MySQL Troubleshooting Tools

To end this chapter, I want to repeat the descriptions of tools we used and describe some of their useful features that I bypassed before.

SHOW PROCESSLIST and the INFORMATION_SCHEMA.PROCESSLIST Table

SHOW PROCESSLIST is the first tool to use when you suspect a concurrency issue. It will not show the relationships among statements in multistatement transactions, but will expose the symptoms of the problem to confirm that more investigation of concurrency is needed. The main symptom is a thread that's in the "Sleep" state for a long time.

The examples in this chapter used the short version of SHOW PROCESSLIST, which crops long queries. SHOW FULL PROCESSLIST shows the full query, which can be convenient if you have long queries and it's not easy to guess the full version from just the beginning of the query.

Starting with version 5.1, MySQL also offers the INFORMATION_SCHEMA.PROCESSLIST table, with the same data as SHOW FULL PROCESSLIST. On busy servers, the table greatly facilitates troubleshooting because you can use SQL to narrow down what you see:

```
slave2> SELECT * FROM INFORMATION_SCHEMA.PROCESSLIST\G
*************************** 1. row ***************************
     ID: 5
   USER: msandbox
   HOST: localhost
     DB: information_schema
COMMAND: Query
   TIME: 0
  STATE: executing
   INFO: SELECT * FROM INFORMATION_SCHEMA.PROCESSLIST
*************************** 2. row ***************************
     ID: 4
   USER: msandbox
   HOST: localhost
     DB: test
COMMAND: Sleep
   TIME: 583
  STATE:
   INFO: NULL
*************************** 3. row ***************************
     ID: 2
   USER: system user
   HOST:
     DB: NULL
COMMAND: Connect
   TIME: 940
  STATE: Slave has read all relay log; waiting for the slave I/O thread t
   INFO: NULL
*************************** 4. row ***************************
     ID: 1
   USER: system user
   HOST:
     DB: NULL
COMMAND: Connect
   TIME: 1936
  STATE: Waiting for master to send event
```

```
        INFO: NULL
    4 rows in set (0.00 sec)
```

So why did I use SHOW PROCESSLIST instead of the PROCESSLIST table in the majority of my examples? First, SHOW PROCESSLIST is supported in all MySQL versions. When doing my support job, I can request this information from customers without checking in advance what version of MySQL they use. Another explanation comes from my support job as well: when working with customers, we don't know all the details about their environment, so looking at the nonfiltered process list can provide some insights about it.

Considerations are different when you debug your own application. Because you already have information about which processes are important, you can limit output using queries with a WHERE condition, such as:

```
mysql> SELECT * FROM INFORMATION_SCHEMA.PROCESSLIST WHERE TIME > 50
mysql> SELECT * FROM INFORMATION_SCHEMA.PROCESSLIST WHERE INFO LIKE 'my query%'
```

This can save time when analyzing the results.

SHOW ENGINE INNODB STATUS and InnoDB Monitors

These tools display the most important information you need when using InnoDB tables. You can get the same information through a SHOW ENGINE INNODB STATUS command or by creating InnoDB monitor tables. These are not tables intended for users, but a way to tell InnoDB to write information about InnoDB's status in the error log every few seconds.

We will discuss standard and lock monitors here. InnoDB also offers Tablespace and Table monitors, which print information from the shared tablespace and the InnoDB internal dictionary, respectively. Tablespace and Table monitors are not directly related to the topic of concurrency, so I'm skipping them here.

The standard InnoDB monitor is what you get when you call SHOW ENGINE INNODB STATUS. In regards to concurrency, we are interesting in SEMAPHORES, LATEST DETECTED DEADLOCK, and TRANSACTIONS.

The SEMAPHORES section contains information about threads waiting for a mutex or a rw-lock semaphore. Pay attention to the number of waiting threads or to threads that wait for a long time. Long waits are not necessarily symptoms of a problem, however. For example, CHECK TABLE running on a huge table will hold a semaphore for a long time. But if you see a long wait during normal operations, you should check whether your installation can handle the number of InnoDB threads you have. Lowering the value of innodb_thread_concurrency can help.

The LATEST DETECTED DEADLOCK section contains information about the most recently detected deadlock. It is empty if no deadlock has been detected since server startup. You can monitor this section to see whether there are deadlocks in your application.

Knowing there are deadlocks, you can either move queries apart in your application so there is no conflict leading to deadlock or add code that will handle it gracefully.

The `TRANSACTIONS` section contains information about all currently running transactions. For the discussion in this chapter, it is especially important to note that this section lists information about all locks for which all active transactions are waiting. If InnoDB Lock Monitor is turned on, this section will also contain information about which locks it holds. This is very useful information for debugging lock waits.

To demonstrate how the InnoDB Lock Monitor can help you debug locks, let's go back to the example in "Hidden Queries" on page 63. If we turn on the InnoDB Lock Monitor and run same queries, we will see a bit more in the `SHOW ENGINE INNODB STATUS` output:

```
mysql> SHOW ENGINE INNODB STATUS \G
*************************** 1. row ***************************
  Type: InnoDB
  Name:
Status:
=====================================
110809 14:03:45 INNODB MONITOR OUTPUT
=====================================
Per second averages calculated from the last 6 seconds
----------
SEMAPHORES
----------
OS WAIT ARRAY INFO: reservation count 12, signal count 12
Mutex spin waits 0, rounds 209, OS waits 7
RW-shared spins 10, OS waits 5; RW-excl spins 0, OS waits 0
------------
TRANSACTIONS
------------
Trx id counter 0 26244358
Purge done for trx's n:o < 0 26244356 undo n:o < 0 0
History list length 4
LIST OF TRANSACTIONS FOR EACH SESSION:
---TRANSACTION 0 0, not started, OS thread id 101493760
MySQL thread id 219, query id 96 localhost root
show engine innodb status
---TRANSACTION 0 26244357, ACTIVE 1 sec, OS thread id 101357568 starting index read
mysql tables in use 1, locked 1
LOCK WAIT 2 lock struct(s), heap size 320, 1 row lock(s)
MySQL thread id 217, query id 95 localhost root Updating
update t set a=36 where a=6
------- TRX HAS BEEN WAITING 1 SEC FOR THIS LOCK TO BE GRANTED:
RECORD LOCKS space id 349 page no 3 n bits 88 index `PRIMARY` of table `test`.`t`
trx id 0 26244357 lock_mode X locks rec but not gap waiting
Record lock, heap no 6 PHYSICAL RECORD: n_fields 3; compact format; info bits 32
 0: len 4; hex 00000006; asc      ;; 1: len 6; hex 000001907504; asc      u ;; 2:
 len 7; hex 0000000032081c; asc     2 ;;

------------------
TABLE LOCK table `test`.`t` trx id 0 26244357 lock mode IX
RECORD LOCKS space id 349 page no 3 n bits 88 index `PRIMARY` of table `test`.`t`
trx id 0 26244357 lock_mode X locks rec but not gap waiting
```

```
Record lock, heap no 6 PHYSICAL RECORD: n_fields 3; compact format; info bits 32
 0: len 4; hex 00000006; asc      ;; 1: len 6; hex 000001907504; asc     u ;; 2:
 len 7; hex 0000000032081c; asc        2 ;;

---TRANSACTION 0 26244356, ACTIVE 6 sec, OS thread id 101099008
2 lock struct(s), heap size 320, 1 row lock(s), undo log entries 2
MySQL thread id 184, query id 93 localhost root
TABLE LOCK table `test`.`t` trx id 0 26244356 lock mode IX
RECORD LOCKS space id 349 page no 3 n bits 88 index `PRIMARY` of table `test`.`t`
trx id 0 26244356 lock_mode X locks rec but not gap
Record lock, heap no 6 PHYSICAL RECORD: n_fields 3; compact format; info bits 32
 0: len 4; hex 00000006; asc      ;; 1: len 6; hex 000001907504; asc     u ;; 2:
 len 7; hex 0000000032081c; asc        2 ;;
```

Compare this output with the output without locks you saw earlier. The important difference is that now you have information about the transaction that holds the lock:

```
---TRANSACTION 0 26244356, ACTIVE 6 sec, OS thread id 101099008
2 lock struct(s), heap size 320, 1 row lock(s), undo log entries 2
MySQL thread id 184, query id 93 localhost root
TABLE LOCK table `test`.`t` trx id 0 26244356 lock mode IX
RECORD LOCKS space id 349 page no 3 n bits 88 index `PRIMARY` of table `test`.`t`
trx id 0 26244356 lock_mode X locks rec but not gap
Record lock, heap no 6 PHYSICAL RECORD: n_fields 3; compact format; info bits 32
 0: len 4; hex 00000006; asc      ;; 1: len 6; hex 000001907504; asc     u ;; 2:
 len 7; hex 0000000032081c; asc        2 ;;
```

I put in the whole transaction information to show the identification information for the lock "Record lock, heap no 6." We are interested in the following:

```
Record lock, heap no 6 PHYSICAL RECORD: n_fields 3; compact format; info bits 32
 0: len 4; hex 00000006; asc      ;; 1: len 6; hex 000001907504; asc     u ;; 2:
 len 7; hex 0000000032081c; asc        2 ;;
```

This is the physical content of the locked record. And when you check the waiting transaction, you can see that it waits for exactly the same lock (pay attention to PHYSICAL RECORD):

```
update t set a=36 where a=6
------- TRX HAS BEEN WAITING 1 SEC FOR THIS LOCK TO BE GRANTED:
RECORD LOCKS space id 349 page no 3 n bits 88 index `PRIMARY` of table `test`.`t`
trx id 0 26244357 lock_mode X locks rec but not gap waiting
Record lock, heap no 6 PHYSICAL RECORD: n_fields 3; compact format; info bits 32
 0: len 4; hex 00000006; asc      ;; 1: len 6; hex 000001907504; asc     u ;; 2:
 len 7; hex 0000000032081c; asc        2 ;;
```

This is very useful information because you can clearly correlate the transactions waiting for locks with those holding locks.

Earlier we discussed InnoDB INFORMATION_SCHEMA tables. Why would one use InnoDB Monitors when you could just look at these tables? The reason is that INFORMATION_SCHEMA contains only current information, whereas InnoDB monitors can dump information into the error logfile so that you can analyze it later. This information is very useful when you want to find out what is going on while your application is running.

There are other useful parts to the InnoDB Monitor output. It makes sense to look at FILE I/O, INSERT BUFFER AND ADAPTIVE HASH INDEX, BUFFER POOL AND MEMORY, and ROW OPERATIONS when you suspect an undiagnosed deadlock or just a very long lock. Whenever read/write operations are stopped and threads are waiting for each other, this is probably a locking issue, even if the locked thread is in the "Updating" State.

INFORMATION_SCHEMA Tables

Starting with the InnoDB Plugin for version 5.1, MySQL supports new InnoDB INFORMATION_SCHEMA tables. Those related to concurrency issues are:

INNODB_TRX
> Contains a list of all transactions that are currently running

INNODB_LOCKS
> Contains information about the current locks held by transactions and which locks each transaction is waiting for

INNODB_LOCK_WAITS
> Contains information about the locks transactions are waiting for

These tables are easy to use and can quickly provide information about transaction states and locks. You saw examples earlier in this chapter that illustrate everything I need to say on the subject.

Typical INFORMATION_SCHEMA Queries That Are Useful When Debugging Concurrency Issues

Information about all locks transactions are waiting for:

```
SELECT * FROM INNODB_LOCK_WAITS
```

A list of blocking transactions:

```
SELECT * FROM INNODB_LOCKS WHERE LOCK_TRX_ID IN
  (SELECT BLOCKING_TRX_ID FROM INNODB_LOCK_WAITS)
```

or:

```
SELECT INNODB_LOCKS.* FROM INNODB_LOCKS JOIN INNODB_LOCK_WAITS
  ON (INNODB_LOCKS.LOCK_TRX_ID = INNODB_LOCK_WAITS.BLOCKING_TRX_ID)
```

A list of locks on particular table:

```
SELECT * FROM INNODB_LOCKS WHERE LOCK_TABLE = 'db_name.table_name'
```

A list of transactions waiting for locks:

```
SELECT TRX_ID, TRX_REQUESTED_LOCK_ID, TRX_MYSQL_THREAD_ID, TRX_QUERY
FROM INNODB_TRX WHERE TRX_STATE = 'LOCK WAIT'
```

PERFORMANCE_SCHEMA Tables

The performance schema lets you monitor MySQL server execution at a low level. It is implemented as a database containing tables based on the PERFORMANCE_SCHEMA storage engine. This storage engine collects event data using "instrumentation points" defined in the server source code. Tables in PERFORMANCE_SCHEMA do not use persistent disk storage.

To debug concurrency issues, you can use the COND_INSTANCES, FILE_INSTANCES, MUTEX_INSTANCES, and RWLOCK_INSTANCES tables along with various EVENTS_WAITS_* tables. The THREADS table can help you correlate internal threads with MySQL's user threads.

All *INSTANCES tables contain NAME and OBJECT_INSTANCE_BEGIN fields, which are the name of the instance and the memory address of the object being instrumented, respectively.

The COND_INSTANCES table contains a list of wait conditions that were created after the server started. Conditions (a term that will be familiar to programmers who have studied concurrency) are a way to make one thread wait for another.

The FILE_INSTANCES table contains a list of files seen by the performance schema. A filename is inserted into this table the first time a server opens it and stays there until it is deleted from the disk. Currently open files have a positive OPEN_COUNT. The Number field contains the number of file handles that currently use the file.

The MUTEX_INSTANCES table contains a list of mutexes seen by the performance schema. Mutexes where LOCKED_BY_THREAD_ID is NOT NULL are those that are currently locked.

The RWLOCK_INSTANCES table is a list of all read/write lock instances. WRITE_LOCKED_BY_THREAD_ID shows the ID of the thread that holds the lock. READ_LOCKED_BY_COUNT shows how many read locks are currently acquired on the instance.

EVENTS_WAITS_* tables contain information about wait events for each thread.

For example, to find out which kind of lock a transaction is waiting for, you can use following query:

```
mysql> SELECT THREAD_ID, EVENT_NAME, SOURCE, OPERATION, PROCESSLIST_ID \
FROM events_waits_current JOIN threads USING (THREAD_ID) WHERE PROCESSLIST_ID > 0\G
*************************** 1. row ***************************
    THREAD_ID: 36
   EVENT_NAME: wait/synch/mutex/mysys/THR_LOCK::mutex
       SOURCE: thr_lock.c:550
    OPERATION: lock
PROCESSLIST_ID: 20
*************************** 2. row ***************************
    THREAD_ID: 41
   EVENT_NAME: wait/synch/mutex/sql/THD::LOCK_thd_data
       SOURCE: sql_class.cc:3754
    OPERATION: lock
```

```
PROCESSLIST_ID: 25
*************************** 3. row ***************************
      THREAD_ID: 40
     EVENT_NAME: wait/synch/mutex/innodb/kernel_mutex
         SOURCE: srv0srv.c:1573
      OPERATION: lock
PROCESSLIST_ID: 24
3 rows in set (0.00 sec)
```

This shows that thread 24 is waiting on InnoDB `kernel_mutex`, while in `SHOW PROCESS LIST`, the same query is in the `Updating` state:

```
mysql> SHOW PROCESSLIST \G
*************************** 1. row ***************************
     Id: 20
   User: root
   Host: localhost
     db: performance_schema
Command: Query
   Time: 0
  State: NULL
   Info: show processlist
*************************** 2. row ***************************
     Id: 24
   User: root
   Host: localhost
     db: sbtest
Command: Query
   Time: 3
  State: Updating
   Info: update example set f2=f2*2
*************************** 3. row ***************************
     Id: 25
   User: root
   Host: localhost
     db: sbtest
Command: Sleep
   Time: 228
  State:
   Info: NULL
3 rows in set (0.00 sec)
```

The `THREADS` table contains a list of all currently running threads. The IDs are internally assigned and are totally different from the IDs of the connection threads. Furthermore, the server runs a lot of internal threads that are not related to connection threads. (For instance, slaves run an SQL thread and I/O thread.) This table contains a `PROCESS LIST_ID` field that shows which connection thread ID, if any, is associated with each particular thread.

`*_SUMMARY_*` tables contain aggregate information for terminated events.

As an example, to find out which tables are used most, you can try the following query. It will work for storage engines that store table data in separate files, such as MyISAM or InnoDB, when the option `innodb_file_per_table` is in use.

```
mysql> SELECT * FROM file_summary_by_instance WHERE file_name \
LIKE CONCAT(@@datadir,'sbtest/%') ORDER BY SUM_NUMBER_OF_BYTES_WRITE DESC, \
SUM_NUMBER_OF_BYTES_READ DESC \G
*************************** 1. row ***************************
                FILE_NAME: /home/ssmirnov/mysql-5.5/data/sbtest/example.ibd
               EVENT_NAME: wait/io/file/innodb/innodb_data_file
               COUNT_READ: 0
              COUNT_WRITE: 8
    SUM_NUMBER_OF_BYTES_READ: 0
   SUM_NUMBER_OF_BYTES_WRITE: 196608
*************************** 2. row ***************************
                FILE_NAME: /home/ssmirnov/mysql-5.5/data/sbtest/example.frm
               EVENT_NAME: wait/io/file/sql/FRM
               COUNT_READ: 14
              COUNT_WRITE: 17
    SUM_NUMBER_OF_BYTES_READ: 948
   SUM_NUMBER_OF_BYTES_WRITE: 4570
*************************** 3. row ***************************
                FILE_NAME: /home/ssmirnov/mysql-5.5/data/sbtest/sbtest.ibd
               EVENT_NAME: wait/io/file/innodb/innodb_data_file
               COUNT_READ: 5236
              COUNT_WRITE: 0
    SUM_NUMBER_OF_BYTES_READ: 85786624
   SUM_NUMBER_OF_BYTES_WRITE: 0
*************************** 4. row ***************************
                FILE_NAME: /home/ssmirnov/mysql-5.5/data/sbtest/sbtest.frm
               EVENT_NAME: wait/io/file/sql/FRM
               COUNT_READ: 7
              COUNT_WRITE: 0
    SUM_NUMBER_OF_BYTES_READ: 1141
   SUM_NUMBER_OF_BYTES_WRITE: 0
*************************** 5. row ***************************
                FILE_NAME: /home/ssmirnov/mysql-5.5/data/sbtest/db.opt
               EVENT_NAME: wait/io/file/sql/dbopt
               COUNT_READ: 0
              COUNT_WRITE: 0
    SUM_NUMBER_OF_BYTES_READ: 0
   SUM_NUMBER_OF_BYTES_WRITE: 0
5 rows in set (0.00 sec)
```

Log Files

There are two MySQL server logfiles that can help you with concurrency problems: the error logfile and the general query logfile.

The error logfile contains information about what is going wrong. It will contain information about unsafe replication statements, intentional crashes due to long semaphore waits, and so on. I have already advised in Chapter 1 that the error logfile is the first place to look when you encounter a problem. The same tip applies to concurrency as well. When you don't know the source of a problem, look at the error log first.

The general query log can help you to find a query that cannot be found by other means. One example is a multistatement transaction that blocks others. If this is called from an application, it is sometimes hard to determine which exact query caused the problem. In such cases, turn on the general query log, wait until the problem reoccurs, and then search the general log for queries by a particular thread. A typical troubleshooting pattern is to look in the InnoDB Monitor output, find the ID of the MySQL thread of the transaction that probably blocking another transaction, and then run the query:

```
SELECT argument, event_time FROM mysql.general_log WHERE thread_id =
THIS_THREAD_ID ORDER BY event_time
```

This will return a list of queries that were run by the locking thread. You should be able to find a `BEGIN` or `START TRANSACTION` statement that kicks off the whole multistatement transaction. Once you discover the offending transaction, you can research what to change in the application to prevent similar locking in the future.

To illustrate this, let's return to the example from "Hidden Queries" on page 63. In the output from `SHOW PROCESSLIST` we saw:

```
mysql> SHOW PROCESSLIST\G
*************************** 1. row ***************************
     Id: 184
   User: root
   Host: localhost
     db: test
Command: Sleep
   Time: 25
  State:
   Info: NULL
*************************** 2. row ***************************
     Id: 217
   User: root
   Host: localhost
     db: test
Command: Query
   Time: 5
  State: Updating
   Info: UPDATE t SET a=36 WHERE a=6
*************************** 3. row ***************************
     Id: 219
   User: root
   Host: localhost
     db: mysql
Command: Query
   Time: 0
  State: NULL
   Info: SHOW PROCESSLIST
3 rows in set (0.00 sec)
```

`SHOW ENGINE INNODB STATUS` shows:

```
mysql> SHOW ENGINE INNODB STATUS \G
*************************** 1. row ***************************
  Type: InnoDB
```

```
    Name:
Status:
=====================================
110809 13:57:21 INNODB MONITOR OUTPUT
=====================================
Per second averages calculated from the last 33 seconds
----------
SEMAPHORES
----------
OS WAIT ARRAY INFO: reservation count 5, signal count 5
Mutex spin waits 0, rounds 80, OS waits 2
RW-shared spins 6, OS waits 3; RW-excl spins 0, OS waits 0
------------
TRANSACTIONS
------------
Trx id counter 0 26244354
Purge done for trx's n:o < 0 26243867 undo n:o < 0 0
History list length 3
LIST OF TRANSACTIONS FOR EACH SESSION:
---TRANSACTION 0 0, not started, OS thread id 101493760
MySQL thread id 219, query id 86 localhost root
SHOW ENGINE INNODB STATUS
---TRANSACTION 0 26244353, ACTIVE 119 sec, OS thread id 101357568 starting index read
mysql tables in use 1, locked 1
LOCK WAIT 2 lock struct(s), heap size 320, 1 row lock(s)
MySQL thread id 217, query id 85 localhost root Updating
UPDATE t SET a=36 WHERE a=6
------- TRX HAS BEEN WAITING 1 SEC FOR THIS LOCK TO BE GRANTED:
RECORD LOCKS space id 349 page no 3 n bits 88 index `PRIMARY` of table `test`.`t`
trx id 0 26244353 lock_mode X locks rec but not gap waiting
Record lock, heap no 6 PHYSICAL RECORD: n_fields 3; compact format; info bits 32
 0: len 4; hex 00000006; asc     ;; 1: len 6; hex 000001907500; asc     u ;; 2:
 len 7; hex 00000000320762; asc     2 b;;


------------------
---TRANSACTION 0 26244352, ACTIVE 139 sec, OS thread id 101099008
2 lock struct(s), heap size 320, 1 row lock(s), undo log entries 2
MySQL thread id 184, query id 79 localhost root
 ...
```

Our blocked transaction is 26244353 of MySQL thread 217. The only transaction currently holding locks is 26244352 of MySQL thread 184. But it is not at all clear what thread 184 is doing until we look at the general query logfile:

```
mysql> SELECT argument, event_time FROM mysql.general_log WHERE
thread_id=184 ORDER BY event_time;
+-------------------------------+---------------------+
| argument                      | event_time          |
+-------------------------------+---------------------+
| begin                         | 2011-08-09 13:55:58 |
| update t set a=26 where a=6   | 2011-08-09 13:56:09 |
+-------------------------------+---------------------+
2 rows in set (0.15 sec)
```

From this output, we can easily see that our transaction is updating the same row in the same table as the blocked transaction. With this knowledge, we can recode our application.

CHAPTER 3

Effects of Server Options

The MySQL server provides an enormous number of options that you can set in various ways: in the *my.cnf* configuration file, on the command line that starts the server, or by setting variables at runtime. Most MySQL variables can be set dynamically, and there is generally one variable corresponding to each configuration option.

Some of the options are global, some apply to specific storage engines, some, called session, apply to connection, and some apply to particular activities, such as replication. This chapter is not a general guide to MySQL server options, but covers the problems that some can create or the ways in which changing an option can help you troubleshoot MySQL.

Before embarking on this chapter, we need to agree on certain terms.

I will use both *option* and *variable* to denote a server option. MySQL uses a separate syntax for options and variables: options are usually spelled with hyphens (*variable-name*), whereas the corresponding variables are spelled with underscores (*variable_name*). Usually the MySQL server supports both types of syntax for the command line and configuration file, but supports only the *variable_name* syntax for variables. Therefore, we will use the latter syntax in this book whenever it is supported.

Variables can be split into different groups depending on their purpose: to point the server to directories, to limit hardware resources, to change how *mysqld* treats one or another situation, and so on. They can also be split into different groups depending on when they are allocated: at server start, when a connection thread is created, or when the server starts a particular operation.

Service Options

I use the term *service options* because this single word explains all the varieties of their functionality: pointing the server to directories and files, telling it whether a particular log should be turned on, and so on. These options usually don't create problems. I found only two typical troubleshooting cases with them: when an option points to a wrong path and when a particular feature, when turned on, changes the behavior of the mysqld command. The latter case can be hard to diagnose because you simply cannot expect these changes.

When an option uses the wrong path, you'll usually notice the problem at server startup. For example, if you point to the wrong datadir, mysqld will refuse to start and will print a message such as:

```
$./bin/mysqld --datadir=/wrong/path &
[1] 966

$110815 14:08:50 [ERROR] Can't find messagefile
'/users/ssmirnova/blade12/build/mysql-trunk-bugfixing/share/errmsg.sys'
110815 14:08:50 [Warning] Can't create test file /wrong/path/blade12.lower-test
110815 14:08:50 [Warning] Can't create test file /wrong/path/blade12.lower-test
./bin/mysqld: Can't change dir to '/wrong/path/' (Errcode: 2)
110815 14:08:50 [ERROR] Aborting

110815 14:08:50 [Note] Binlog end
110815 14:08:50 [Note]

[1]+  Exit 1                    ./bin/mysqld --datadir=/wrong/path
```

But of course you don't see this message on the command line if *mysqld* is started in a system startup file as a daemon. In that case, users usually notice the problem when their first connection attempt fails with an error like the following:

```
$./bin/mysql -uroot -S /tmp/mysql_ssmirnova.sock
ERROR 2002 (HY000): Can't connect to local MySQL server through socket
'/tmp/mysql_ssmirnova.sock' (2)
```

The error simply indicates that no server is running. In such cases, you need to examine the error logfile or, if there is no error logfile, check the operating system log for messages concerning *mysqld*. The MySQL error logfile would contain the same message as we saw in the earlier listing. An operating system message can vary but usually says that some automatic script, such as *mysql.server* from the MySQL installation, failed to start *mysqld*. You can also check that no MySQL server is running by looking at a process listing. Here is an example for Linux, showing that *mysqld* doesn't appear anywhere in the system's processes:

```
$ps -ef | grep mysqld
10149    7076  6722  0 23:35 pts/0    00:00:00 grep mysqld
```

The *mysqladmin* utility has ping command that reports whether the MySQL server is alive or stopped:

```
$mysqladmin -h127.0.0.1 -P3306 ping
mysqladmin: connect to server at '127.0.0.1' failed
error: 'Can't connect to MySQL server on '127.0.0.1' (10061)'
Check that mysqld is running on 127.0.0.1 and that the port is 3306.
You can check this by doing 'telnet 127.0.0.1 3306'
```

A few options pointing to specific paths do not prevent the MySQL server from starting, but simply turn off a particular option. For example, let's see what a corrupt InnoDB startup sequence might look like:

```
110815 14:14:45 [Note] Plugin 'FEDERATED' is disabled.
110815 14:14:45 [Note] Plugin 'ndbcluster' is disabled.
110815 14:14:45 [ERROR] InnoDB: syntax error in innodb_data_file_path
110815 14:14:45 [ERROR] Plugin 'InnoDB' init function returned error.
110815 14:14:45 [ERROR] Plugin 'InnoDB' registration as a STORAGE ENGINE failed.
110815 14:14:45 [Note] Event Scheduler: Loaded 0 events
110815 14:14:45 [Note] ./libexec/mysqld: ready for connections.
Version: '5.1.60-debug'  socket: '/tmp/mysql_ssmirnova.sock'  port: 33051
Source distribution
```

The server was successfully started, but the InnoDB engine was not loaded:

```
mysql> SHOW ENGINES\G
*************************** 1. row ***************************
      Engine: ndbcluster
     Support: NO
     Comment: Clustered, fault-tolerant tables
Transactions: NULL
          XA: NULL
  Savepoints: NULL
*************************** 2. row ***************************
      Engine: MRG_MYISAM
     Support: YES
     Comment: Collection of identical MyISAM tables
Transactions: NO
          XA: NO
  Savepoints: NO
*************************** 3. row ***************************
      Engine: BLACKHOLE
     Support: YES
     Comment: /dev/null storage engine (anything you write to it disappears)
Transactions: NO
          XA: NO
  Savepoints: NO
*************************** 4. row ***************************
      Engine: CSV
     Support: YES
     Comment: CSV storage engine
Transactions: NO
          XA: NO
  Savepoints: NO
*************************** 5. row ***************************
      Engine: MEMORY
     Support: YES
     Comment: Hash based, stored in memory, useful for temporary tables
Transactions: NO
```

```
            XA: NO
    Savepoints: NO
*************************** 6. row ***************************
        Engine: FEDERATED
       Support: NO
       Comment: Federated MySQL storage engine
  Transactions: NULL
            XA: NULL
    Savepoints: NULL
*************************** 7. row ***************************
        Engine: ARCHIVE
       Support: YES
       Comment: Archive storage engine
  Transactions: NO
            XA: NO
    Savepoints: NO
*************************** 8. row ***************************
        Engine: MyISAM
       Support: DEFAULT
       Comment: Default engine as of MySQL 3.23 with great performance
  Transactions: NO
            XA: NO
    Savepoints: NO
8 rows in set (0.00 sec)
```

I turned the error logfile off so that we could see the error on the console, but in production, the error log would be the place to look for the error message. Therefore, if you find out that one of the features you need does not exist, check the error logfile first.

It is very important to understand how a desired feature affects the work a server does. For example, when InnoDB is not available, we still can create tables successfully if the SQL mode does not contain NO_ENGINE_SUBSTITUTION:

```
mysql> CREATE TABLE t1(f1 INT) ENGINE=InnoDB;
Query OK, 0 rows affected, 2 warnings (0.01 sec)
```

This example shows that it's always important to check warnings. In this case, the table was created using the wrong storage engine because we had an error trying to start InnoDB:

```
mysql> SHOW WARNINGS;
+---------+------+---------------------------------------------+
| Level   | Code | Message                                     |
+---------+------+---------------------------------------------+
| Warning | 1286 | Unknown table engine 'InnoDB'               |
| Warning | 1266 | Using storage engine MyISAM for table 't1'  |
+---------+------+---------------------------------------------+
2 rows in set (0.00 sec)
```

If you don't check the warnings, a user might start using this table and discover the problem only when your whole application is affected. As you know from the previous chapter, MyISAM and InnoDB use different locking methods, so an application written to use the advantages of InnoDB can run into huge issues if the tables are MyISAM instead. And I haven't even talked about the absence of transactions!

- Check whether a feature you rely on exists in the server instance if you experience problems with it.

The other major set of problems with service options concerns options that change the behavior of MySQL, although their main purpose is different. When setting a service option, you can expect it will provide one feature or another, but you may not expect it to affect your queries.

A trivial example is the effect of binary logging on creating stored functions. When enabled, you can expect it will store all events that modify data, but you might not be aware of its other side effects.

First, I will show how one can create a dummy stored function if the server does not use the binary log:

```
root> GRANT ALL ON test.* TO sveta@'%';
Query OK, 0 rows affected (0.01 sec)
```

Then, I connect as user *sveta* and run:

```
sveta> CREATE FUNCTION f1() RETURNS INT RETURN 1;
Query OK, 0 rows affected (0.02 sec)
```

Everything is fine. But things change when I start *mysqld* with the log_bin option:

```
$./libexec/mysqld --defaults-file=support-files/my-small.cnf \
--basedir=. --datadir=./data --socket=/tmp/mysql_ssmirnova.sock --port=33051 \
--log_error --log_bin &
[1] 3658
```

and try to recreate the same function:

```
sveta> DROP FUNCTION f1;
Query OK, 0 rows affected (0.00 sec)

sveta> CREATE FUNCTION f1() RETURNS INT RETURN 1;
ERROR 1418 (HY000): This function has none of DETERMINISTIC, NO SQL, or READS
SQL DATA in its declaration and binary logging is enabled (you *might* want to
use the less safe log_bin_trust_function_creators variable)
```

The error message clearly explains the issue. I wanted to show this example to demonstrate how an option can change server behavior, even if its main purpose is not to affect user queries. Usually when a user meets such a problem, the cause is not so clear and can be confusing.

Variables That Are Supposed to Change the Server Behavior

Another set of variables affects how the MySQL server handles user input.

I will show a trivial example that clearly shows the effect of setting such a variable. In this case, we will set SQL Mode to `STRICT_TRANS_TABLES` so that attempts to insert invalid data into transactional tables will be rejected instead of being smoothed over. However, we expect the server to fix the statements, if possible, for nontransactional tables instead of rejecting the statements:

```
mysql> SET @@sql_mode = 'strict_trans_tables';
Query OK, 0 rows affected (0.03 sec)

mysql> CREATE TABLE `myisam` (
    ->             `id` bigint(20) NOT NULL AUTO_INCREMENT,
    ->             `a` varchar(50) NOT NULL,
    ->             `b` varchar(50) NOT NULL,
    ->             PRIMARY KEY (`id`)
    ->          ) ENGINE=MyISAM DEFAULT CHARSET=latin1 ;
Query OK, 0 rows affected (0.05 sec)

mysql> INSERT INTO `myisam` (id,a) VALUES (1,'a');
ERROR 1364 (HY000): Field 'b' doesn't have a default value
```

I deliberately issued an erroneous `INSERT`, omitting a value for the `b` column. I expect the server to insert an empty string for `b`. But even though this table uses the MyISAM storage engine, the insert fails with an error message.

The MySQL Reference Manual explains the behavior (see *http://dev.mysql.com/doc/refman/5.1/en/server-sql-mode.html*):

> `STRICT_TRANS_TABLES`: If a value could not be inserted as given into a transactional table, abort the statement. For a nontransactional table, abort the statement if the value occurs in a single-row statement or the first row of a multirow statement.

My `INSERT` statement was a single-row statement, so the server refused to correct it. But this doesn't seem intuitive, does it?

- Carefully check what an option does if you see behavior you don't expect.

Options That Limit Hardware Resources

The options in this group set limits on various hardware resources. They can be used for two purposes: to tune performance and to limit use for certain operations. The latter options are useful when you want to limit traffic between clients and the server or prevent Denial of Service attacks. It's better for particular users to get graceful errors because of lack of resources than for *mysqld* to die because it can't handle all incoming requests.

Later in this chapter, I will describe the tactics one should follow when adjusting these options. Here I want to point to cases when such variables lead to different and perhaps unexpected behavior compared to setups where the variables were not set. As always, I will show by example.

In my day-to-day job, I see many users who are affected by ignoring the value of max_allowed_packet. This variable limits the number of bytes that can be set in a single packet between the server and the client. In this example, I lower the default 1MB value of max_allowed_packet just to demonstrate its effect:

```
mysql> SELECT repeat('a',1025);
+------------------+
| repeat('a',1025) |
+------------------+
| NULL             |
+------------------+
1 row in set, 1 warning (0.00 sec)

mysql> SHOW WARNINGS\G
*************************** 1. row ***************************
  Level: Warning
   Code: 1301
Message: Result of repeat() was larger than max_allowed_packet (1024) - truncated
1 row in set (0.00 sec)
```

This time, it is clear from the warning message why the error happened. But sometimes it is not so clear:

```
$ ./my sql test <phpconf2009_1.sql
ERROR 1064 (42000) at line 33: You have an error in your SQL syntax; check the
manual that corresponds to your MySQL server version for the right syntax to use
near
'00000000000000000000000000000000000000000000000000000000000000000000000000000000'
at line 2
```

The exact message you get depends on the particular statement you sent to the server, usually when selecting data from very large table or accessing a BLOB field.

- If you start getting syntax errors for valid queries, check whether their size exceeds max_allowed_packet.

Using the --no-defaults Option

It is hard to remember by heart what every variable does. Even I cannot do it, and I work with them every day. One solution is to go to the list of options and exclude each of them one by one. But that's not easy. Version 5.1 of MySQL has 291 variables, my outdated 5.5 installation has 321, and no one can guarantee that this value will not grow in the future. If you use a custom storage engine, it can have its own options as well.

It is much easier to check how the MySQL server should work with no options specified, i.e., if it uses the defaults for all values. If you have a rough guess about how mysqld should work with no custom options set, you can start the server with the --no-defaults option and compare the results to those you get when custom options are set.

Both the `--no-defaults` and `--defaults-file` options must be specified as the first options passed to *mysqld*. Otherwise, the server will not recognize them.

If the results are different, start adding options that you used before one by one, and test to see if the wrong behavior comes back. Once you find which variable causes the changes, you can refer to its documentation and adjust it accordingly.

Performance Options

These options generally don't cause errors, but can have a dramatic effect on performance. Usually you run the server under various real-life loads while tuning them until you have a combination that works well for your particular environment.

However, there is one situation when such an option can cause an error, and removing it from the configuration file or reducing its value can make sense. This is when your server hits an out-of-resources error. The most common cases involve a lack of memory or file descriptors. If you find yourself in such a situation, use the `--no-defaults` method from the previous section to find the option that's too big.

Haste Makes Waste

This popular English proverb has an equivalent in many other languages. Russians have one that can be translated literally as "sliding slowly, arriving further." I think this wisdom is good when you tune the MySQL server too, at least when you are not 100% sure what you are doing.

- Unless you are 100% sure what is wrong, add options one by one, and then test the configuration each time.

This means that if you think some set of options can make the MySQL server's behavior better for your application, change one option first, then test, and then, if you are happy with the result, add another option, and so on, until you have checked every relevant option. This can appear slow, but if something goes wrong, you can safely roll back the most recent change and quickly return your server to a working stage.

This method is especially important when you adjust buffers or other options that limit hardware resources, but can be used for options that change server behavior as well. Even with a good knowledge of what variables are doing, it is much easier to find and fix a single mistake than find out what is wrong in dozens of options.

When using this method, save the results of every test. For example, if you are working on improving performance, run benchmarks or measure query execution time before changing anything, and then repeat the same test after modifying each option.

The SET Statement

MySQL supports two kinds of variables: SESSION and GLOBAL. SESSION variables are set for the current connection only and do not affect others. GLOBAL variables apply to all connections created after you set such a variable. But setting a GLOBAL variable does not affect the current connection,[1] so you should either set both SESSION and GLOBAL variables or reconnect if you need to use a new value in the current connection.

You can set a session variable using the statement:

```
SET [SESSION] var_name=value
```

I put SESSION in square brackets because you can omit this keyword; the set command uses SESSION as the default.

To set a GLOBAL variable, use the statement:

```
SET GLOBAL var_name=value
```

When you test options, I suggest you try to use a SESSION variable whenever possible. After you are happy with the results, you can use a GLOBAL variable to change the running server's configuration, and then change the configuration file so that this value will be applied after a restart.

> Using SET SESSION is also very helpful when you want to check the effect of an option on a particular query. In this case, you can set the variable before the query, test, and then return back to the default value using the statement SET [SESSION] variable_name=DEFAULT.

If an option is shared among threads, you can start by setting a GLOBAL variable, and then examine how the server behaves. After you are happy with the result, change the configuration file to include the new variable and its setting.

This method allows you to test changes without interrupting the application, because it puts your desired change into effect while delaying the server restart until a scheduled time.

There are a few options that cannot be set dynamically. In these cases, you have to restart the MySQL server, even if you just want to test their effects.

How to Check Whether Changes Had an Effect

There are status variables that show the current server status. As opposed to configuration variables, these do not affect server behavior, but instead contain information

---

1. There are few exceptions, such as SET GLOBAL general_log=1. Usually such exceptions do not have a SESSION equivalent.

about what is happening in the *mysqld* process. Status variables are read-only, i.e., it is the MySQL server that changes them, not the user. They show such things as how many queries were executed and of what kind, network traffic, how indexes are used (you can find an example in "Queries That Modify Data" on page 36), buffer usage, how many tables are open, how many temporary tables were created, and a lot of other useful information. I won't describe each of them here, but will note which status variable to watch while covering the variables themselves later in this chapter, as I did in "Queries That Modify Data" on page 36.

In the context of altering variables, the status variables are useful mostly in "Performance-Related Options" on page 132. We will also discuss how to get information about what is going on in your MySQL configuration in Chapter 6.

Like other variables, status variables can apply to both individual sessions and all sessions (global). Session variables show the status for the current session, whereas global variables show the status since the server was started or since the last FLUSH STATUS command was executed.

> Some variables are not independent. For example, variables that control the query cache change nothing when query_cache_size is set to zero. When tuning such options, always think about the effect of the whole group, not just a single variable.

When you change a server option, it can affect changes to status variables. For example, if you change the table cache, you should look at the dynamics of the Open_tables and Opened_tables status variables. Opened_tables should not grow, whereas all Open_tables should be in the cache if the table cache is set properly.

> Sometimes a variable's value that was just set can be discarded because the specified value was either too big or too small. If you suspect that your change had no effect, check whether it was really made by using the query SHOW [SESSION|GLOBAL] VARIABLES LIKE 'variable_name' or the query SELECT VARIABLE_VALUE FROM INFORMATION_SCHEMA.[SESSION| GLOBAL]_VARIABLES WHERE VARIABLE_NAME='variable_name'.

Descriptions of Variables

Now that you are familiar with risk-free tuning methods for server variables, we are ready to discuss a few important ones. This is not a complete guide, but a starting point for further research.

You can read the rest of this section in any order: go through it from beginning to end, check the particular topics of most interest to you at the moment, or even skip it and use it as a reference when you encounter a problem. I don't describe every option, but concentrate on those that I've found are often used improperly or require an expanded understanding.

 At first, I doubted whether I should devote a section of this book to individual variables because each one is fully described in other sources. But the MySQL Reference Manual does not describe them specifically from a troubleshooting approach, so I decided to offer this short overview.

Options That Affect Server and Client Behavior

This section discusses general server options as well as options related to replication, connections, and storage engines. In the latter set, I'll cover only the MyISAM and InnoDB storage engines.

Server-related options

These affect all connections and statements.

Limits and max_* *variables*

You already saw how max_allowed_packet affects an application earlier in "Options That Limit Hardware Resources" on page 112. Other options restrict the size of result sets. Examples include group_concat_max_len, which limits the number of bytes that the GROUP_CONCAT function can return. Just compare:

```
mysql> SELECT @@group_concat_max_len;
+------------------------+
| @@group_concat_max_len |
+------------------------+
|                   1024 |
+------------------------+
1 row in set (0.00 sec)

mysql> SELECT group_concat(table_name) FROM tables WHERE
table_schema='mysql'\G
*************************** 1. row ***************************
group_concat(table_name):
columns_priv,db,event,func,general_log,help_category,help_keyword,help_relation,
help_topic,host,ndb_binlog_index,plugin,proc,procs_priv,servers,slow_log,
tables_priv,time_zone,time_zone_leap_second,time_zone_name,time_zone_transition,
time_zone_transition_type,user
1 row in set (0.15 sec)
```

and:

```
mysql> SET group_concat_max_len=100; ❶
Query OK, 0 rows affected (0.00 sec)

mysql> SELECT group_concat(table_name) FROM tables WHERE
table_schema='mysql'\G
*************************** 1. row ***************************
```

```
group_concat(table_name): columns_priv,db,event,func,general_log,help_category,
help_keyword,help_relation,help_topic,host,ndb_
1 row in set, 1 warning (0.06 sec)

mysql> SHOW WARNINGS\G
*************************** 1. row ***************************
  Level: Warning
   Code: 1260
Message: Row 11 was cut by GROUP_CONCAT()
1 row in set (0.00 sec)
```

❶ I decreased the value of group_concat_max_len to show an example that can fit
in this book. In real life, this problem usually happens when the user runs this
function on a large data set for which the default value is too small.

I won't describe each variable of the max_* group. Just check their values if you find
that *mysqld* is limiting either the size of the statement you're sending or the results
returned.

Permissions

Another possibility you should consider, if a statement fails, is whether your user
has the permissions to issue it, or rights to a particular database or table. For
example, the local_infile option can allow or disallow running the LOAD DATA
LOCAL INFILE query. The MySQL server usually gives a clear error message to
explain why one or another operation is not allowed.

SQL modes

The MySQL server defines SQL modes that can change how the server treats client
input. You already saw how NO_ENGINE_SUBSTITUTION and STRICT_TRANS_TABLES can
affect an application. Other modes can modify other behavior.

Here is another example that uses the ANSI_QUOTES mode. This mode tells the
MySQL server to use quotes defined in the ANSI SQL standard instead of MySQL's
default. The problem I describe here happens not when this mode is in use, but
when the user relies on the default empty mode in the hope that the server will
reject ANSI quotes set by mistake.

```
mysql> SELECT @@sql_mode;
+------------+
| @@sql_mode |
+------------+
|            |
+------------+
1 row in set (0.00 sec)

mysql> SELECT * FROM t1 WHERE "f1"=1;
Empty set, 1 warning (0.00 sec)

mysql> SET SQL_MODE='ansi_quotes';

Query OK, 0 rows affected (0.00 sec)

mysql> SELECT * FROM t1 WHERE "f1"=1;
```

```
+----+--------------------------------+
| f1 | f2                             |
+----+--------------------------------+
|  1 | f9f760a2dc91dfaf1cbc95046b249a3b |
+----+--------------------------------+
1 row in set (0.21 sec)
```

In the first case where the default is in effect, the MySQL treats "f1" as a string and converts it to DOUBLE. This is a valid value in the default SQL mode, but is treated differently from what the user expects.

```
mysql> SHOW WARNINGS;
+---------+------+----------------------------------------+
| Level   | Code | Message                                |
+---------+------+----------------------------------------+
| Warning | 1292 | Truncated incorrect DOUBLE value: 'f1' |
+---------+------+----------------------------------------+
1 row in set (0.09 sec)
```

When converted to a DOUBLE, the value "f1" is translated to 0, and "0" is not equal to "1". In the ANSI_QUOTES mode, "f1" is treated as a field name, so the query works. This is very common issue that can be easily missed in complicated queries with multiple conditions.

- When you meet "strange" query results, check the SQL mode and analyze whether it can be affecting your query.

I included several examples of SQL mode in this book to show how they can make different aspects of the server behave differently. I recommend that you study the list of SQL modes and what they do in the MySQL Reference Manual (*http://dev .mysql.com/doc/refman/5.5/en/server-sql-mode.html*).

One detail worth mentioning is that, starting with version 5.1.38, the InnoDB Plugin has an innodb_strict_mode option, which, if set, turns on strict checks of data inserted into InnoDB tables. This behaves similarly to, but slightly differently from, the strict SQL modes. So if you are using the InnoDB Plugin, you need to check the description of this variable. The option is turned off by default.

Character sets and collations

Understanding these variables is critical for those who use MySQL to store data in non-English languages, which applies when the latin1 character set doesn't suit your needs.

The character set is a map that matches a character or symbol to a byte sequence that represents it. Collation is a sorting rule. A character set can have multiple collations.

This topic is huge, so I will not try to cover it here exhaustively, but will give you a few starting points.

Character set and collation support in MySQL is really good, but a lot of its aspects can be tuned, and therefore people often get confused by them. When you suspect a character-set-related error, I recommend you study the chapter about character sets and collations in the MySQL Reference Manual carefully. Usually you will find answers to your questions there.

The following example shows how changing just the collation for a table can affect your data:

```
mysql> SET NAMES latin1;
Query OK, 0 rows affected (0.13 sec)

mysql> CREATE TEMPORARY TABLE t1(f1 VARCHAR(255)) DEFAULT
CHARSET=latin1 COLLATE=latin1_german2_ci;
Query OK, 0 rows affected (0.23 sec)

mysql> INSERT INTO t1 VALUES('Sveta'), ('Andy');
Query OK, 2 rows affected (0.29 sec)
Records: 2  Duplicates: 0  Warnings: 0

mysql> CREATE TEMPORARY TABLE t2 AS SELECT 'Sveta' AS
f1;
Query OK, 1 row affected (0.21 sec)
Records: 1  Duplicates: 0  Warnings: 0

mysql> SELECT * FROM t1 JOIN t2 USING(f1);
ERROR 1267 (HY000): Illegal mix of collations (latin1_german2_ci,IMPLICIT) and
(latin1_swedish_ci,IMPLICIT) for operation '='
```

Why did the query with a JOIN fail? We specified the latin1_german2_ci collation for the first table, whereas the second one used the default collation for the connection.

I'll return to this example in a moment, but first I'll show two queries that are extremely helpful for diagnosing such issues:

```
mysql> SHOW VARIABLES LIKE '%char%';
+--------------------------+------------------------------------------+
| Variable_name            | Value                                    |
+--------------------------+------------------------------------------+
| character_set_client     | latin1                                   |
| character_set_connection | latin1                                   |
| character_set_database   | utf8                                     |
| character_set_filesystem | binary                                   |
| character_set_results    | latin1                                   |
| character_set_server     | utf8                                     |
| character_set_system     | utf8                                     |
| character_sets_dir       | /Users/apple/mysql-5.1/share/mysql/charsets/ |
+--------------------------+------------------------------------------+
8 rows in set (0.09 sec)

mysql> SHOW VARIABLES LIKE '%coll%';
+---------------------+-------------------+
| Variable_name       | Value             |
```

```
+----------------------+--------------------+
| collation_connection | latin1_swedish_ci |
| collation_database   | utf8_general_ci   |
| collation_server     | utf8_general_ci   |
+----------------------+--------------------+
3 rows in set (0.01 sec)
```

Run these every time you suspect something is wrong with the character set or collation, then analyze the result and context of the query. The general safe rule is to have all character_set_* variables, collation_* variables, and create options the same for any tables and connections that work together. The easiest way to set client options is to use the SET NAMES statement. Of course, there can be cases when you need different character sets or collations, but you should understand their effects.

If we go back to our collation_connection example, the different collations lie behind why the JOIN query cannot be executed. We can confirm this if we change the value of the variable:

```
mysql> SET COLLATION_CONNECTION='latin1_german2_ci';
Query OK, 0 rows affected (0.00 sec)

mysql> DROP TABLE t2;
Query OK, 0 rows affected (0.04 sec)

mysql> CREATE TEMPORARY TABLE t2 AS SELECT 'Sveta' AS
f1;
Query OK, 1 row affected (0.01 sec)
Records: 1  Duplicates: 0  Warnings: 0

mysql> SELECT * FROM t1 JOIN t2 USING(f1);
+-------+
| f1    |
+-------+
| Sveta |
+-------+
1 row in set (0.00 sec)
```

- Check character set options and table definitions when you encounter issues while doing sorts or comparisons.

Operating system handling for lower_case* *options*

The lower_case_filesystem and lower_case_table_names options are similar to those that affect character sets. These variables determine how the operating system handles the case of database objects.

It is better not to touch these values, especially if your operating system is case-insensitive. Changing them can lead to unexpected behavior, as in the following example:

```
mysql> SELECT @@lower_case_table_names;
+--------------------------+
| @@lower_case_table_names |
+--------------------------+
```

```
|                        0 |
+--------------------------+
1 row in set (0.10 sec)

mysql> CREATE TABLE Table1(F1 INT NOT NULL AUTO_INCREMENT PRIMARY
KEY) ENGINE=InnoDB;
Query OK, 0 rows affected (0.27 sec)

mysql> CREATE TABLE Table2(F1 INT, CONSTRAINT F1 FOREIGN KEY(F1)
REFERENCES Table1(F1)) ENGINE=InnoDB;
Query OK, 0 rows affected (0.04 sec)

mysql> \q
Bye

$mysqldump --socket=/tmp/mysql50.sock -uroot test Table1
Table2
-- MySQL dump 10.11
<skipped>
--
-- Table structure for table `Table1`
--

DROP TABLE IF EXISTS `Table1`;
SET @saved_cs_client     = @@character_set_client;
SET character_set_client = utf8;
CREATE TABLE `Table1` (
  `F1` int(11) NOT NULL auto_increment,
  PRIMARY KEY  (`F1`)
) ENGINE=InnoDB DEFAULT CHARSET=utf8;
SET character_set_client = @saved_cs_client;


--
-- Dumping data for table `Table1`
--

LOCK TABLES `Table1` WRITE;
/*!40000 ALTER TABLE `Table1` DISABLE KEYS */;
/*!40000 ALTER TABLE `Table1` ENABLE KEYS */;
UNLOCK TABLES;


--
-- Table structure for table `Table2`
--

DROP TABLE IF EXISTS `Table2`;
SET @saved_cs_client     = @@character_set_client;
SET character_set_client = utf8;
CREATE TABLE `Table2` (
  `F1` int(11) default NULL,
  KEY `F1` (`F1`),

  CONSTRAINT `F1` FOREIGN KEY (`F1`) REFERENCES `table1` (`F1`)

) ENGINE=InnoDB DEFAULT CHARSET=utf8;
```

```
    SET character_set_client = @saved_cs_client;

%lt;skipped>
-- Dump completed on 2008-02-02 21:12:22
```

I have put the important part of the output in bold. A foreign key definition refers to a table named table1, but no table of that name exists. You could not restore this dump taken on a case-insensitive operating system (e.g., Windows) on a case-sensitive operating system (e.g., Linux).

It also is best to use consistent naming for tables in all statements and to not mix lowercase and uppercase in names on case-insensitive operating systems.

Init SQL

These options determine whether the server should execute some SQL statements automatically at various times:

init_file

Points to a file containing SQL statements that should be executed at server startup

init_connect

Contains an SQL string that should run when each client connects

init_slave

Contains an SQL string that should run when the server starts its SQL thread as a slave

There are two typical usage errors with these options.

The first problem is that it's easy to forget about what you put in the options. Usually the options are used to set some defaults for connections. So if you get results different from those that are returned when the default options are in use, check to see whether you have set one or more of these variables.

You can also issue SHOW [GLOBAL] VARIABLES to find out which defaults your connection uses. If you connect using a programming API, check the variable values using the same API because other environments, such as the MySQL command-line client, might use a different configuration file and thus have different default values.

The content of the init_connect option is executed only if the connecting user does not have the SUPER privilege. This was done to let a user with the SUPER privilege connect even if init_connect contains errors. This is another common usage mistake, when a user connects as a SUPER user and expects the content of init_con nect to be executed.

open_files_limit

This important option limits the number of file handles the MySQL server can open simultaneously. The higher this limit, the more table files and temporary tables you can have open, and therefore the greater the number of simultaneous connections you can handle. If this limit is too low for your environment, you will get errors when trying to connect, open a table, or execute a query that requires creating temporary tables.

Because the setting for this option reflects hardware limitations, we will discuss it further in the next chapter.

log_warnings

When turned on (nonzero), this option writes warnings into the server's error logfile. These are not warnings that happen during SQL execution, but rather debugging messages that show what is going on inside the server.

If set to 2, this option tells the server to log connection errors. This is very important when you are troubleshooting situations where clients cannot connect or are losing their connections. The log cannot always identify the problem, but its warning message can often shed some light on what is going on. It is very important to have this option enabled on the master server when using replication because you can identify when a slave I/O thread loses its connection. This in turn can be a symptom of a network failure, which can lead to worse problems in the future.

When set to 1 (the default) on a slave, it prints its own diagnostic messages, such as its positions in the binary and relay logs and its replication status. Starting with version 5.1.38, you need to enable this option enabled in order for the slave to print information about statements that are not safe in statement-based replication. (Before 5.1.38, the slave printed such messages in any case.) Starting with 5.1.38, you can turn off this option (set it to zero) to get rid of the log if you are sure you don't need the messages.

Replication options

These options determine the relationship between the master and slaves.

binlog-* *and* replicate-* *filters*

MySQL has the ability to filter objects subject to replication using the binlog-do-*, replicate-do-*, binlog-ignore-*, and replicate-ignore-* options. binlog-* options reduce the events that go into the binary logfile on the master, whereas replicate-* specify those that go into the relay logfile on the slave. Slaves also have replicate-wild-do-* and replicate-wild-ignore-*, which allow them to specify, through patterns, objects that should or should not be replicated.

The most common problems with these options are:

- People forget they specified the options.
- Filters specified in binlog-do-*, replicate-do-*, binlog-ignore-*, and replicate-ignore-* work if and only if USE *dbname* was called explicitly.

Symptoms of the problems are:

- A particular query was not replicated.
- An "unknown table *xxx* on query" error on the slave.

- When you use Statement-Based Replication (SBR) and find that some queries were either not replicated or replicated by mistake, check whether you have set these options and issued USE *dbname*.

It's always better to use the `replicate-wild-*` variants of these options, because these do not depend on calling USE.

Binary log formats

The `binlog_format` variable allows you to choose the format for replication: STATEMENT, ROW, or MIXED.

This is a dynamic variable that can be changed at the session level. If you don't want to use the mode currently set as the default for a particular query, you can temporarily switch formats using SET `binlog_format='row'` or SET `binlog_format='statement'`.

`binlog_direct_non_transactional_updates`

This option specifies when updates to nontransactional tables should be written into the binary log.

By default, when transactions are used, MySQL writes updates to nontransactional tables into the transaction cache and flushes this cache to the binary log only after a commit. This is done so that the slave is more likely to end up with the same data as the master, even if updates on nontransactional tables depend on data in transactional tables and the master is updating the same tables in many concurrent threads simultaneously.

But this solution causes problems when another transaction causes changes based on data that was modified by an uncommitted parallel transaction in a nontransactional table. We discussed a similar issue in the example in "Mixing Transactional and Nontransactional Tables" on page 91. If you experience such a problem, you can turn this option on. Before doing this, be sure that data in nontransactional tables cannot be modified by any statement that uses a transactional table.

This is a dynamic variable that can be changed at the session level, so you can use it for particular statements. It works, and makes sense, only if statement-based replication is used.

`log_bin_trust_function_creators`

This option tells *mysqld* not to fire a warning when a user without SUPER privileges tries to create a nondeterministic function on the master. See the example of default behavior in "Service Options" on page 111.

`binlog_cache_size` *and friends*

This item covers the following options:

- `binlog_cache_size`
- `binlog_stmt_cache_size`
- `max_binlog_cache_size`

- `max_binlog_stmt_cache_size`

These are caches that hold transactional and nontransactional statements issued during a transaction before writing to the binary log. If `max_binlog_cache_size` is reached, the statement aborts with the error `"Multi-statement transaction required more than 'max_binlog_cache_size' bytes of storage"`.

Check the `Binlog_cache_use`, `Binlog_stmt_cache_use`, `Binlog_cache_disk_use`, and `Binlog_stmt_cache_disk_use` status variables to find out how often the binlog cache was used and how often the size of the transaction exceeded `Binlog_cache_use` and `Binlog_stmt_cache_use`. When the size of the transaction exceeds the cache size, a temporary table is created to store the transaction cache.

`slave_skip_errors`

This option allows the slave SQL thread to run even when it encounters certain types of errors. For example, if the master is run with a forgiving SQL mode while the slave has a strict one, you can set `slave_skip_errors` to, say, `1366 (ERROR 1366 (HY000): Incorrect integer value)` so the slave does not fail due to a data format inconsistency when one inserts a string into an integer field.

Using this option can lead to data inconsistencies between master and slave that are hard to diagnose, so if you meet such an issue, check whether the option was not set.

`read_only`

This option makes the slave server read-only. This means that only the slave SQL thread can update its data, and other connections can only read data. This is valuable to preserve data consistency on the slave. However, the option does not restrict a user with the `SUPER` privilege from changing tables. Additionally, all users are still allowed to create temporary tables.

Engine options

This section describes options specific to particular storage engines. I will discuss a few InnoDB and MyISAM options here. Options related to performance are covered in a subsequent section. In a troubleshooting situation, you should look through and acquaint yourself with all options of the storage engine you use.

InnoDB options. We will start with options of InnoDB storage engine.

`innodb_autoinc_lock_mode`

This option defines which locking mode InnoDB will use when inserting into auto-increment fields. There are three modes: `traditional` (which was used before version 5.1), `consecutive` (the default starting with 5.1), and `interleaved`. The safest is `consecutive`. The two others can be used for better performance, and `traditional` can also be used for backward compatibility.

I won't describe the differences between these lock types here, because the MySQL Reference Manual contains detailed information about how each of them works.

One thing you should keep in mind, though: if your application sets autoincrement values in a fashion that surprises you, check this mode and experiment with how different values affect autoincrementing. I actually don't recommend switching from the safe consecutive mode to any other mode, but in a few environments this can be acceptable.

innodb_file_per_table

By default, InnoDB saves table and index data in a shared tablespace. Using this option, you can tell it to save the index and data for each table in separate files. The shared tablespace is still used for table definitions. This option takes effect only on tables created after it is set; tables created earlier continue to use the shared tablespace.

Using this variable is actually a good practice because it helps InnoDB tables operate more effectively. Besides letting you watch the actual space occupied by a table, it also lets you create partial backups using MySQL Enterprise Backup or even restore a table on a different MySQL installation using the method described in Chris Calender's blog at *http://www.chriscalender.com/?p=28*.

innodb_table_locks

This variable defines how InnoDB handles table lock requests made by LOCK TABLES statements. By default (when it is set) it returns immediately and locks the table internally. When turned off (set to 0), it honors LOCK TABLE statements, so the thread does not return from LOCK TABLES ... WRITE until all locks are released.

innodb_lock_wait_timeout

This is the number of seconds that InnoDB waits for a row lock before giving up. After innodb_lock_wait_timeout seconds, it returns the error "ERROR 1205 (HY000): Lock wait timeout exceeded; try restarting transaction" to the client. I frequently see situations where people set this variable to very large values to prevent their queries from failing as often, only to experience worse problems because many stalled transactions lock each other. Try to handle lock wait errors at the application level, and don't set this value too high. The best value for this option depends on your application and should be about the amount of time your normal transaction takes. The default value of this variable, 50 seconds, can be too big for applications that need to return results almost immediately. This is true for the majority of web shops.

innodb_rollback_on_timeout

When a query is aborted due to a lock wait error, only the last statements rolled back, and the whole transaction is not aborted yet. You can change this behavior if you set this option to 1. In this case the transaction will be rolled back immediately after a lock wait timeout.

innodb_use_native_aio

This option, introduced in InnoDB Plugin 1.1, specifies whether InnoDB should use the native AIO interface on Linux or use its own implementation, called "simulated AIO." If innodb_use_native_aio is set, InnoDB dispatches I/O requests to the kernel. This improves scalability because modern kernels can handle more parallel I/O requests than simulated AIO.

This option is on by default and should not be changed during normal operation. It can be turned off if you experience issues on operating systems with asynchronous I/O subsystems that prevent InnoDB from starting. A typical error message informing you to turn this option off is `error while loading shared libraries: libaio.so.1: cannot open shared object file: No such file or directory`.

innodb_locks_unsafe_for_binlog

This variable defines how InnoDB uses gap locking for searches and index scans. With the default value (set to 0), gap locking is enabled. If set to 1, the option disables gap locking for most operations. It works similar to the `READ COMMITTED` transaction isolation level, but is less tunable and should be avoided. Even if it allows you to handle problems with locking, it creates new problems when parallel transactions insert new rows into the gaps. So `READ COMMITTED` is recommended instead if you want to get that behavior. This variable cannot be set at session level, so it affects all transactions.

MyISAM options. We will discuss only two options here and return to the rest in the next section.

myisam_data_pointer_size

Sets the default pointer size used when creating MyISAM tables without specifying the `MAX_ROWS` parameter. The default value is 6, and the allowed range is 2 to 7. The larger the pointer, the more rows a table can have. The default value, 6, allows you to create tables that take up 256TB. If you get a `"Table is full"` error when using MyISAM tables, this means the pointer size is too small for your table data (see the sidebar "How Big Can the Table Be?").

How Big Can the Table Be?

You can use *myisamchk -dvi* to check exactly how big the table can become with a particular pointer size and how many rows it can store if the `FIXED` row format is used:

```
mysql> CREATE TABLE t1(f1 INT, f2 VARCHAR(255)) ENGINE=MyISAM;
Query OK, 0 rows affected (0.16 sec)

mysql> SET GLOBAL myisam_data_pointer_size=2;
Query OK, 0 rows affected (0.00 sec)

mysql> \q
Bye

C:\Program Files\MySQL\MySQL Server 5.5>.\bin\mysql -uroot test
Welcome to the MySQL monitor.  Commands end with ; or \g.
Your MySQL connection id is 3
Server version: 5.5.13-enterprise-commercial-advanced
MySQL Enterprise Server - Advanced Edition (Commercial)
```

```
Copyright (c) 2000, 2010, Oracle and/or its affiliates. All rights reserved.

Oracle is a registered trademark of Oracle Corporation and/or its
affiliates. Other names may be trademarks of their respective
owners.

Type 'help;' or '\h' for help. Type '\c' to clear the current input statement.

mysql> CREATE TABLE t2(f1 INT, f2 VARCHAR(255)) ENGINE=MyISAM;
Query OK, 0 rows affected (0.13 sec)

mysql> \q
Bye

C:\Program Files\MySQL\MySQL Server 5.5>.\bin\myisamchk.exe -dvi
"C:\ProgramData\MySQL\MySQL Server 5.5\Data\test\t1"

MyISAM file:           C:\ProgramData\MySQL\MySQL Server 5.5\Data\test\t1
Record format:         Packed
Character set:         utf8_general_ci (33)
File-version:          1
Creation time:         2011-11-02 14:43:40
Status:                checked,analyzed,optimized keys,sorted index pages
Data records:                     0  Deleted blocks:             0
Datafile parts:                   0  Deleted data:               0
Datafile pointer (bytes):         6  Keyfile pointer (bytes):    3
Datafile length:                  0  Keyfile length:          1024
Max datafile length: 281474976710654  Max keyfile length: 17179868159
Recordlength:                   774

table description:
Key Start Len Index    Type                    Rec/key       Root  Blocksize

C:\Program Files\MySQL\MySQL Server 5.5>.\bin\myisamchk.exe -dvi
"C:\ProgramData\MySQL\MySQL Server 5.5\Data\test\t2"

MyISAM file:           C:\ProgramData\MySQL\MySQL Server 5.5\Data\test\t2
Record format:         Packed
Character set:         utf8_general_ci (33)
File-version:          1
Creation time:         2011-11-02 14:44:35
Status:                checked,analyzed,optimized keys,sorted index pages
Data records:                     0  Deleted blocks:             0
Datafile parts:                   0  Deleted data:               0
Datafile pointer (bytes):         2  Keyfile pointer (bytes):    3
Datafile length:                  0  Keyfile length:          1024
Max datafile length:          65534  Max keyfile length:   17179868159

Recordlength:                   774

table description:
Key Start Len Index    Type                    Rec/key       Root  Blocksize
```

myisam_recover_options

This option tells the MySQL server to check, each time it opens a MyISAM table,
whether the table is corrupted or was not closed properly. If the check fails, MySQL

runs CHECK TABLE on it and, if needed, repairs it. Possible values are OFF, DEFAULT (not the default for this option, but denoting a recovery method without backup, forcing a quick check), BACKUP (creates a backup of the table data's *.MYD* file), FORCE (instructs the server to run a recovery action, even if there is a risk of losing one or more rows from the *.MYD* file), and QUICK (tells the server not to run a recovery action if there are no deleted blocks in the table). You can use two or more options at the same time. The most popular value for this variable, if set, is BACKUP,FORCE because it fixes all errors and is safe because it creates a backup file. By default, this option is turned off.

Connection-related options

The most important of these options from a troubleshooting standpoint concern time-outs. I'll also discuss some options related to security that commonly cause (or solve) problems.

Timeouts. You are already acquainted with innodb_lock_wait_timeout, which interrupts a query that is waiting for a row lock.

A similar option is lock_wait_timeout, which applies to metadata locks. This lock is set for all operations that acquire the metadata lock: DML (Data Manipulation Language statements, such as INSERT, UPDATE, and DELETE), DDL, LOCK TABLES, and so on. Its default value is 3153600 seconds, which is 1 year. So by default, MDL locks effectively never die. However, you can change this value to anything, starting from 1 second. It is a dynamic variable that can be changed at the session level.

There is also a set of timeout variables that are independent from queries you run and that limit waiting times for result sets, client data, or authorization packets. These are:

connect_timeout
> The timeout used when the MySQL server and client exchange authorization packets. Starting with version 5.1, the default value is 10 seconds.

interactive_timeout
> How much time to wait for activity from an interactive client before killing the connection, i.e., how long the server will wait to read the next command. The term "interactive client" is used for clients that directly run queries sent by a human. For instance, the MySQL command-line client, *mysql*, is interactive, whereas a web application is not by default. When writing an application, you should explicitly specify if you want it to be considered interactive.

wait_timeout
> How much time to wait for activity from any client before killing the connection. If a client is interactive and the value of interactive_timeout is different from wait_timeout, interactive_timeout applies.

`net_read_timeout`

> How much time to wait for an answer from a client writing to the MySQL server. For example, this timeout applies if the client is executing a large insert.

`net_write_timeout`

> How much time to wait for an answer from a client that is reading from the server. For example, when a client sends a `SELECT` query and is reading its result, this timeout kills the connection if the client fails to read data that is waiting for this amount of time. If a client needs to do some job before processing results, check whether that job lasts longer than this timeout.

The symptom of hitting most of these limits is a `"MySQL server has gone away"` error or a `"Lost connection to MySQL server during query"` error. The exception is `connect_timeout`. If you hit this limit, you will get the error `"Lost connection to MySQL server at 'reading authorization packet'"`. You could get a similar error when the slave I/O thread cannot connect to the master.

If you hit one of the limits described earlier, don't just increase them blindly; search for the actual reason for the problem. If a timeout is caused by a flaky network, you should fix the network rather than increasing the timeout. Here is a course of action that can be used when you suspect a timeout problem: Temporarily increase the `*timeout` variable, and rerun the application. If the timeout happens less frequently under these conditions, you can confirm that a timeout is the problem, but search for the real cause of the error. This can be a long-running application, slow access to a huge table, or a flaky network.

Security-related options. These options control permissions and other aspects of MySQL server security.

`skip-grant-tables`

> Another issue with client authorization kicks in when the client lacks the proper user permissions when connecting to the server. We discussed this problem a bit in "Permission Issues" on page 49. Here I just want to mention how to save yourself if you forget a password. You need to start the server with the `skip-grant-tables` option, edit the privilege tables in the `mysql` database manually, and then run the query `FLUSH PRIVILEGES`. After that, new privileges are in effect. Don't forget to restart the server without the `skip-grant-tables` option. Otherwise, anybody can connect to your server after the restart. To do the operation safely, include the option `skip_networking` along with `skip-grant-tables`, so that only local connections are allowed during the time when there are no restrictions on access to the MySQL server.

`safe-user-create`

> Does not allow the creation of users using the `GRANT` statement, unless the user adding the grant has the `INSERT` privilege into the `mysql.user` table.

secure_auth

Does not allow clients earlier than version 4.1 to connect to modern servers. Version 4.1 was chosen because a new security model was added to the connection protocol at that time.

secure_file_priv

Restricts the LOAD_FILE function and the LOAD DATA and SELECT … INTO OUTFILE statements to using only the specified directory.

Performance-Related Options

Here I'll offer a short overview of options that affect performance. Again, I am not describing all of them, but just those that are used most frequently. In contrast with options from the previous section, these options don't lead to different results.[2]

First I will discuss options that affect server behavior as a whole, then some engine-specific options.

Buffers and maximums

The first group of options controls the amount of memory used internally by the server and certain upper limits on memory usage.

join_buffer_size

This is the minimum size of the buffer allocated for joins that use plain index scans, and range scans, and joins that do not use indexes. The buffer is allocated for each full join between two tables. Thus, a query joining two tables allocates one buffer, a query joining three tables allocates two buffers, and so on. This can be used as a session variable and can be set for a particular join.

To find out whether you need to increase join_buffer_size, you can check the Select_scan status variable, which contains the number of joins that do a full scan of the first table, as well as Select_full_range_join, which contains the number of joins that use a range search. The values of these status variables will not change if you change the value of join_buffer_size, so you can use them only to find out if you need a large join_buffer_size, not to measure the effectiveness of a change to that value.

net_buffer_length

The size of a buffer that the server creates right after a client connects to hold the request and the result. This size is increased to max_allowed_packet when needed. You usually don't need to change the default value (16384 bytes), but you should keep the value in mind when setting the max_connections option.

---

2. One exception is the optimizer parameters in EXPLAIN statements.

---

query_prealloc_size

This buffer is allocated for statement parsing and execution. The buffer is not freed between statements. It makes sense to increase this buffer if you run complex queries, so that *mysqld* does not have to spend time allocating memory during query execution. Increase it to the size in bytes of your largest query.

read_buffer_size

Each thread that does a sequential scan allocates this buffer for each table scan.

read_rnd_buffer_size

This controls the size of the buffer that holds read results between sorting them and sending them to the client. A large value can improve the performance of queries that include ORDER BY.

sort_buffer_size

Each thread that needs to do a sort allocates this buffer for it. To find out whether you need to increase the size of this buffer, check the Sort_merge_passes status variable. You can also check the values of Sort_range, Sort_rows, and Sort_scan to find out how many sorting operations you do.

These status variables show only the number of sort operations. To find out which size to use for the buffer, you need to check how many rows one or another query can sort and multiply it by the row size. Or simply try the different values until Sort_merge_passes stops growing.

The sort_buffer_size buffer is allocated too often, so having a large global value can decrease performance rather than increase it. Therefore, it is better not to set this option as a global variable, but increase it when needed using SET SESSION.

sql_buffer_result

When this variable is set, the server buffers the results of each SELECT in temporary tables. This can help to release table locks earlier when a client requires a lot of time to retrieve results. After results are stored in the temporary table, the server can release the locks on the original table, making it accessible to other threads while the first client is still retrieving results.

To find out whether a query is spending a lot of time sending its result set, run SHOW PROCESSLIST and check the amount of time the query is in the state "Sending data."

A status of "Sending data" in SHOW PROCESSLIST output means a thread is reading and processing rows, then sending data to the client. As you see, this is more complicated than the words imply, and does not necessarily mean a query is stuck sending data.

thread_cache_size

The number of threads that should be cached for future use. When a client disconnects, usually its threads are destroyed. If this option is set to a positive value, that number of threads will be put in a cache upon disconnect. This option does not dramatically improve performance on systems with a good thread implementation, but still can be useful if an application uses hundreds of connections.

thread_stack

The stack size for each thread. If set too small, this value limits the complexity of SQL statements, the recursion depth of stored procedures, and other memory-consuming actions on the server. The default value (192KB on 32-bit systems and 256KB on 64-bit systems) works fine for most installations. Increase this variable if you start getting error messages like "Thread stack overrun".

tmp_table_size

The maximum size of the internal temporary table in memory. By default, the server sets this to the minimum of max_heap_table_size and tmp_table_size. Increase this variable if you have enough memory and the status variable Cre ated_tmp_disk_tables is increasing. Having all results that require a temporary table in memory can improve performance a lot.

query_cache_size

The size of the buffer where the MySQL server stores queries and their results. Increasing the value can increase performance because after the query is inserted into the cache, subsequent executions of the same query will take results from the cache, eliminating the work of query parsing, optimization, and execution. But don't set this variable too large, because when the query needs to be removed from the cache—i.e., when you have modified data in the table—the mutex contention can block parallel queries. This is especially true on multicore machines and highly concurrent environments when more than eight user sessions access the query cache concurrently. Reasonable values for this variable are less than 100 MB, although you can set it much larger if you aren't frightened by a possible sudden slow down.

 Best practice can be to set query_cache_size to a reasonably small value and periodically defragment it using the query **FLUSH QUERY CACHE**, rather than increasing this value.

To determine whether the query cache is being used effectively, check the status variables Qcache_free_blocks, Qcache_free_memory , Qcache_hits, Qcache_inserts, Qcache_lowmem_prunes, Qcache_not_cached, Qcache_queries_in_cache, and Qcache_total_blocks.

table_definition_cache

The number of table definitions that are stored in the cache. When you have a lot of tables, you can increase this value. Tune it if necessary to keep `Opened_table_definitions` smaller than or equal to `Open_table_definitions` since the most recent table flush (`FLUSH TABLES` query).

table_open_cache

The number of table descriptors that are stored in the cache. Try to tune this option so that `Opened_tables` remains smaller than or equal to `Open_tables`.

Options that control the optimizer

These variables can be set at the session level, so you can experiment with how they affect particular queries.

optimizer_prune_level

If this variable is on, the optimizer prunes less effective plans discovered by intermediate searches. If the variable is off, the optimizer uses an exhaustive search. The default value is 1 (on). Change the option if you suspect the optimizer is not choosing the best plan for your query.

optimizer_search_depth

The maximum depth of the search performed by the optimizer. The larger this value, the more likely it is that the optimizer can find the best plan for a complex query. The price for raising the value is the time spent by the optimizer while searching for a plan. If set to 0, the server automatically picks a reasonable value. The default is 62 (the maximum value).

optimizer_switch

This variable controls various optimizer features. I will touch on them only slightly here. Intelligent use of this variable requires knowledge of how the optimizer works and a lot of experimentation.

index_merge

Enables or disables index merge optimization. This optimization retrieves rows from several merge scans and merges their results into one. This is shown as "Merge" in the `Type` column of `EXPLAIN` output.

index_merge_intersection

Enables or disables the index merge intersection access algorithm. This algorithm is used when a `WHERE` clause contains several range conditions that use a key and are combined with the `AND` keyword. An example is:

```
key_col1 < 10 AND key_col2 = 'foo'
```

Even though the `key_col2 = 'foo'` comparison involves a single value, the optimizer treats it as a range condition, as explained in the MySQL Reference Manual in the section "The Range Access Method for Single-Part Indexes" (*http://dev.mysql.com/doc/refman/5.5/en/range-access-single-part.html*).

index_merge_union

Enables or disables the index merge union access algorithm. This algorithm is used when a `WHERE` clause contains several range conditions that use a key and are combined with the `OR` keyword. An example is:

```
key_col1 = 'foo' OR (key_col2 = 'bar' AND key_col3 = 'baz')
```

index_merge_sort_union

Enables or disables the index merge sort union access algorithm. This algorithm is used when a `WHERE` clause contains several range conditions that use a key and are combined with the `OR` keyword, but where the index merge union access algorithm is not applicable. An example is:

```
(key_col1 > 10 OR key_col2 = 'bar') AND key_col3 = 'baz'
```

max_join_size

Prevents the optimizer from executing `SELECT` statements that it estimates will exceed certain limits (for instance, examining more than `max_join_size` rows). This option is useful while debugging when you want to find which queries do not use indexes.

max_length_for_sort_data

When doing `ORDER BY` optimization on conditions where indexes cannot be used, MySQL uses a filesort algorithm. There are two variations of this algorithm. The original algorithm reads all matched rows and stores pairs of keys and row pointers in a buffer whose size is limited to `sort_buffer_size`. After the values in the buffer are sorted, the algorithm reads rows from the table a second time, but in sorted order. The disadvantage of this algorithm is that rows must be read twice.

The modified approach reads the whole row into the buffer, then sorts the keys and retrieves rows from the buffer. The problem with this approach is that the result set is usually larger than `sort_buffer_size`, so disk I/O operations make the algorithm slower for large data sets. The `max_length_for_sort_data` variable limits the size of the pairs for this algorithm, so the original algorithm is used if the total size of the extra columns in the pairs exceeds this limit.

High disk activity together with low CPU activity is a signal that you need to lower the value of this variable.

Check the "ORDER BY Optimization" part of the MySQL Reference Manual (*http://dev.mysql.com/doc/refman/5.5/en/order-by-optimization.html*) for further details.

max_seeks_for_key

Sets the threshold, in terms of the number of rows that a table scan must check, for when to use a key instead of a table scan. Setting this option to a small value, such as 100, can force the optimizer to prefer index lookups over table scans.

max_sort_length

Sets the number of initial bytes taken from a `BLOB` or `TEXT` value when doing a sort. Latter bytes are ignored.

Engine-related options

The variables in this section affect the performance of a specific storage engine. As elsewhere in this book, we consider only InnoDB and MyISAM options.

InnoDB options. We will start with options of InnoDB storage engine as before.

`innodb_adaptive_hash_index`

Disables or enables (default) InnoDB adaptive hash indexes. In most cases it is good to have this option on, but there are a few known exceptions when an adaptive hash index can decrease performance, for example, when the number of similar query results is huge and this index takes 30% or more of the buffer pool. This information is shown in the InnoDB monitor output. I will not describe all of them here, because considerations may change as InnoDB evolves, but I recommend you search the Web for actual test cases if you suffer from bad performance.

`innodb_additional_mem_pool_size`

This pool holds information about the data dictionary and internal data structures. In general, the more tables you have, the larger this option should be. But because InnoDB writes messages into the error log when this pool is too small, you should wait to see these messages before tweaking the value.

`innodb_buffer_pool_size`

The size of the memory that InnoDB allocates to store data, indexes, table structures, adaptive hash indexes, and so on. This is the most important option for InnoDB performance. You can set it to up to 80% of your physical RAM. Ideally, the buffer would be large enough to contain all your actively used InnoDB tables, along with extra space. Take other buffers into account, too, and find a good balance.

Status variables matching the pattern `Innodb_buffer_pool_%` show the current state of the InnoDB buffer pool.

`innodb_buffer_pool_instances`

This option sets the number of instances that the buffer pool should be split into. Each instance has its own free lists, flush lists, lists of objects stored using least recently used algorithms, and other data structures, and is protected by its own mutex. Setting this variable greater than 1 can improve concurrency on large systems. The size of each instance is `innodb_buffer_pool_size` divided by `innodb_buffer_pool_instances`, and should be at least 1GB. This option does not take effect if `innodb_buffer_pool_size` is less than 1GB.

`innodb_buffer_pool_instances` splits the buffer pool mutex, so if you have eight or more concurrent sessions that access the InnoDB buffer pool concurrently, set it at least to 4, then up to 16. The number depends on the value of `innodb_buffer_pool_size` and the RAM available on your box.

`innodb_checksums`

By default, InnoDB uses checksum validation on all pages read from disk. This lets it immediately identify whether a datafile was corrupted due to a broken disk or some other intervention. Usually you should keep this feature on, but in rare cases when you don't care about data (for instance, a read-only slave that is not used as a backup), you can get a performance improvement by turning it off.

`innodb_commit_concurrency`
The number of threads that can commit at the same time. The default value is 0 (unlimited).

`innodb_thread_concurrency`
The number of threads that can run concurrently inside of InnoDB. Don't mix this value up with the number of connection threads the MySQL server creates. The default value is 0: infinite concurrency or no concurrency checking.

Although more threads running in parallel generally means higher performance, you can experience mutex contentions if you run many concurrent user sessions in parallel. Usually you should not worry about this variable if you don't have more than 16 concurrent user sessions. If you have more, you need to monitor for mutex locks by querying the Performance Schema or running a `SHOW ENGINE INNODB MUTEX` query.

If mutex contentions appear, try to limit this variable to 16 or 32. Alternatively, place the *mysqld* process into a task set on Linux or a processor set on Solaris, and limit it to fewer cores than the whole box has. This is the best course of action on a system with more than eight cores. Alternatively, you can use the Thread Pool Plugin (see sidebar).

The Thread Pool Plugin

Since version 5.5.16, commercial distributions of MySQL include the Thread Pool Plugin.

By default, the MySQL server creates a new thread for each user connection. If a lot of user connections are created, many threads are running in parallel and context switching overhead becomes high. This can lead to resource contention. For example, for InnoDB this increases the time needed for holding mutexes.

The Thread Pool Plugin provides an alternative way to handle threads. It places all connection threads in groups, the number of which is limited by the variable `thread_pool_size`, and makes sure only one thread per group is executed at any time.[3] This model reduces overhead and greatly improves performance.

You will find more details about the Thread Pool Plugin in the MySQL Reference Manual (*http://dev.mysql.com/doc/refman/5.5/en/thread-pool-plugin.html*).

`innodb_concurrency_tickets`
When a thread is permitted to enter InnoDB, it receives this number of *concurrency tickets*, which permit it to leave and re-enter InnoDB until it uses up these tickets.

---

3. This is not a hard limit, and sometimes more than one thread per group is executing.

The default is 500. After using up its tickets, a thread is placed into a queue of threads waiting to receive a new group of tickets.

innodb_doublewrite

By default, InnoDB stores data twice: first to the doublewrite buffer, and then to datafiles. Like innodb_checksums, this safety option can be turned off to get increased performance on installations where data safety is not the first priority.

 When set, the variable innodb_doublewrite prevents InnoDB data corruption. Therefore, do not switch it off until absolutely necessary.

The Innodb_dblwr_writes and Innodb_dblwr_pages_written status variables show the number of doublewrite operations and the number of pages written, respectively.

innodb_flush_log_at_trx_commit

Defines when changes are written to the logfile and flushed to disk. If set to 1 (the default), changes are written and flushed at each transaction commit. For better performance, you can change this value to 0 (write to log and flush once per second, and do nothing on transaction commit) or 2 (write to file at each commit, but flush once per second). Note that only option 1 is ACID-compliant.

The Innodb_os_log_fsyncs status variable stores the number of fsync() operations done to the logfile. Innodb_os_log_pending_fsyncs contains the number of pending fsync() writes. Innodb_log_writes and Innodb_os_log_pending_writes contain the number of writes and pending writes, respectively.

innodb_flush_method

By default, fdatasync() is used to flush datafiles and fsync() is used to flush logfiles to disk. This value can be changed to one of the following:

O_DSYNC

The operating system uses O_SYNC to open and flush the logfiles, and fsync() to flush the datafiles.

O_DIRECT

The operating system uses O_DIRECT to open the datafiles and fsync() to flush them.

Changing the value of innodb_flush_method can either improve or slow down performance, so test it carefully in your environment.

innodb_io_capacity

An upper limit to the I/O activity performed by the background InnoDB task. The default value of 200 is a good choice for most modern systems, but it can be tuned based on the number of I/O operations the system can perform simultaneously. Increasing this value makes sense on fast storage.

`innodb_log_buffer_size`

The size of the buffer that InnoDB uses to write to the logfiles on disk. When the buffer is full, operations should wait for it to be flushed before continuing. Increasing this variable can save disk I/O operations, but this makes sense only if you have big transactions.

The `Innodb_log_waits` status variable contains the number of times this buffer was too small for the number of necessary I/O operations.

`innodb_log_file_size`

The size of each logfile. Large logfiles reduce checkpoint activity and save disk I/O. However, large logfiles can drastically slow recovery after a crash.[4] Sensible values range from 1 MB up to, but less than, `innodb_buffer_pool_size/log_files_in_group`. The combined size of all logfiles must be less than 4GB.

Best practice is to store InnoDB logfiles, datafiles, and, if used, binary logfiles on different disks, so if one of these devices die, you will not lose all of them at once.

`innodb_open_files`

This variable is meaningful only when you use `innodb_file_per_table`. `innodb_open_files` is the number of *.ibd* files that InnoDB can open at the same time. The default value is 300. It makes sense to increase it to the total number of InnoDB tables.

`innodb_read_io_threads`

The number of I/O threads available for InnoDB read operations. These operations handle read-ahead: I/O requests that asynchronously prefetch a group of pages into the InnoDB buffer pool, then purge and insert buffer operations. The default value is 4.

`innodb_write_io_threads`

The number of I/O threads available for InnoDB to write dirty pages from the buffer. The default is 4.

`innodb_stats_method`

How the server treats NULLs when collecting statistics on index values. This affects the cardinality of the index, and therefore the query plans created by the optimizer.

`innodb_stats_on_metadata`

When this variable is enabled (default), InnoDB updates its statistics at each metadata statement, such as `SHOW TABLE STATUS` or `SHOW INDEX`, or when any connection issues a query on the `INFORMATION_SCHEMA` tables `TABLES` or `STATISTICS`, which select information about an InnoDB table. If this variable is enabled, these queries have the same effect on table statistics as if you had run `ANALYZE TABLE` after each query. You can disable this variable if the server calls such statements

---

4. This is not 100% true anymore, because the InnoDB Plugin 1.0.7 introduced improvements that speed up crash recovery.

frequently or selects databases with a large number of tables. But when the variable is disabled, table statistics can become out of date.

innodb_stats_sample_pages

The number of sampled index pages used by the MySQL Optimizer to calculate index distribution statistics, such as when `ANALYZE TABLE` is called. Increase this variable (the default is 8) if you suspect that the cardinality is being calculated improperly. But note that increasing this variable can increase the time needed to open a table if innodb_stats_on_metadata is enabled.

MyISAM options. In this section, we will discuss options which can affect performance of MyISAM storage engine.

myisam_max_sort_file_size

The maximum temporary file size that MyISAM can use when it re-creates a MyISAM index. The default value is 2GB. If this value is exceeded, MySQL will use a key cache, which can slow down index creation. The temporary file is a disk file, so it's limited only by disk space.

myisam_use_mmap

When this variable is set, the server uses memory mapping when reading and writing MyISAM tables. The default behavior is using system calls for these operations. Although myisam_use_mmap usually improves performance a lot, there are couple of known bugs, so test your application after setting this variable.

myisam_mmap_size

The maximum amount of memory that can be used for memory mapping of compressed MyISAM files. The defaults are large: 4294967295 on 32-bit systems and 18446744073709547520 on 64-bit systems. You can decrease this value to avoid swapping if you use many compressed MyISAM tables.

myisam_sort_buffer_size

The size of the buffer allocated when sorting or creating MyISAM indexes during `REPAIR TABLE`, `CREATE INDEX`, or `ALTER TABLE` operations.

myisam_stats_method

How the server treats NULLs when collecting statistics on index values. This affects the cardinality of the index, and therefore the query plans created by the optimizer.

bulk_insert_buffer_size

The size of a special tree-like cache that MyISAM uses for bulk inserts: `INSERT … SELECT`, `INSERT … VALUES (…), (…)`, … and `LOAD DATA INFILE` statements.

key_buffer_size

Index blocks for MyISAM tables are buffered and shared between threads. This variable controls the size of that buffer. You can create multiple key buffers. Search for this variable description and read about the key cache in the MySQL Reference Manual.

preload_buffer_size
>   The size of the buffer that is allocated to preload indexes.

Calculating Safe Values for Options

When you try to optimize server performance by increasing buffers or maximums, it is crucial to think globally about memory use. Large buffers can crash the MySQL server with an "Out of memory" error. In this section I offer formulas that will help you calculate whether you are exceeding available memory. I will not describe the options themselves in this part. You can refer to previous sections or to the MySQL Reference Manual for more detailed descriptions. Calculations depend on when an option is allocated and whether it is shared, so I divide them into relevant categories in this section.

Options set for the whole server

These options are global, affecting all connections and queries. Some are allocated at server startup, whereas others take effect later, such as the query cache, which is initially zero and grows until it reaches its maximum value. It can take a bit of time until the MySQL server reaches all the limits and fully allocates all the memory you allow. Therefore, you should calculate the amount of RAM *mysqld* can acquire and add up all the buffer sizes to make sure you don't exceed it.

The following is the list of memory buffers allocated for the whole server:

- query_cache_size
- innodb_additional_mem_pool_size
- innodb_buffer_pool_size
- innodb_log_buffer_size
- key_buffer_size

Use the following formula to calculate how much RAM in megabytes you need to allocate these buffers:

```
SELECT (@@query_cache_size + @@innodb_additional_mem_pool_size +
@@innodb_buffer_pool_size + @@innodb_log_buffer_size + @@key_buffer_size)/(1024*1024);
```

The server also has options that limit the number of file descriptors and how many threads can be cached. You can skip them for this calculation because the amount of memory they allocate is just the size of a pointer on the system multiplied by the quantity of items allocated, a total that is small enough to be ignored on modern systems. I just list them here for reference:

- thread_cache_size
- table_definition_cache
- table_open_cache

- innodb_open_files

Thread options

These options are allocated on a per-thread basis. So, the server can allocate max_connections*sum(thread options). Set max_connections and these options to make sure that the total amount of physical RAM - max_connections*sum(thread options) - options for whole server is greater than zero. Leave some RAM for options in the third group and a bit more for background operations, which cannot be controlled by variables.

Here is the list of thread options:

- net_buffer_length
- thread_stack
- query_prealloc_size
- binlog_cache_size
- binlog_stmt_cache_size

Use the following formula to calculate how much RAM in megabytes you need in order to allocate them:

```
SELECT @@max_connections * (@@global.net_buffer_length + @@thread_stack +
@@global.query_prealloc_size + @@binlog_cache_size + @@binlog_stmt_cache_size) /
(1024 * 1024)
```

Or, if you are on a version older than 5.5.9 (the version in which the variable bin log_stmt_cache_size was introduced):

```
SELECT @@max_connections * (@@global.net_buffer_length + @@thread_stack +
@@global.query_prealloc_size + @@binlog_cache_size) / (1024 * 1024)
```

Buffers allocated for a specific operation

These buffers are allocated as needed when the server has to carry out a particular operation. It is hard to calculate the exact amount of RAM they can allocate. Analyze your queries to find out which require a lot of resources, and calculate something like the following:

```
(buffer size) * (number of buffers allocated for particular kind of query)
    * (number of such queries that can be executed in parallel)
```

Do this for all variables, and calculate the sum of the results.

It is good practice to keep these options small, so long as they are adequate for most queries. Then, if a particular query needs more memory, just increase the variable's value for that session. For example, if you need to set max_join_size really high for a statistics query that you run once per week, there is no sense to set it globally; set it just before running the query. Even with this precaution, don't forget about memory usage as a whole.

Some of these options are allocated once per thread. These are:

- read_rnd_buffer_size
- sort_buffer_size
- myisam_mmap_size
- myisam_sort_buffer_size
- bulk_insert_buffer_size
- preload_buffer_size

Others can be allocated more than once per thread. These are:

- join_buffer_size
- read_buffer_size
- tmp_table_size

You can use the following formula to calculate the maximum amount of memory in megabytes that the MySQL server can allocate for such options:

```
set @join_tables = YOUR_ESTIMATE_PER_THREAD;
set @scan_tables = YOUR_ESTIMATE_PER_THREAD;
set @tmp_tables = YOUR_ESTIMATE_PER_THREAD;

SELECT @@max_connections * (@@global.read_rnd_buffer_size +
@@global.sort_buffer_size + @@myisam_mmap_size +
@@global.myisam_sort_buffer_size + @@global.bulk_insert_buffer_size +
@@global.preload_buffer_size + @@global.join_buffer_size * IFNULL(@join_tables,
1) + @@global.read_buffer_size * IFNULL(@scan_tables, 1) +
@@global.tmp_table_size * IFNULL(@tmp_tables, 1)) / (1024 * 1024)
```

Remove from this formula those options that are not suitable for your environment.

To wrap up this chapter, here is a comprehensive formula that calculates the maximum amount of RAM in megabytes that your MySQL installation can use:

```
set @join_tables = YOUR_ESTIMATE_PER_THREAD;
set @scan_tables = YOUR_ESTIMATE_PER_THREAD;
set @tmp_tables = YOUR_ESTIMATE_PER_THREAD;

SELECT (@@query_cache_size + @@innodb_additional_mem_pool_size +
@@innodb_buffer_pool_size + @@innodb_log_buffer_size + @@key_buffer_size +
@@max_connections * (@@global.net_buffer_length + @@thread_stack +
@@global.query_prealloc_size + @@global.read_rnd_buffer_size +
@@global.sort_buffer_size + @@myisam_mmap_size +
@@global.myisam_sort_buffer_size + @@global.bulk_insert_buffer_size +
@@global.preload_buffer_size + @@binlog_cache_size +
@@binlog_stmt_cache_size + @@global.join_buffer_size * IFNULL(@join_tables,
1) + @@global.read_buffer_size * IFNULL(@scan_tables, 1) +
@@global.tmp_table_size * IFNULL(@tmp_tables, 1))) / (1024 * 1024)
```

Or, for versions older than 5.5.9:

```
set @join_tables = YOUR_ESTIMATE_PER_THREAD;
set @scan_tables = YOUR_ESTIMATE_PER_THREAD;
```

```
set @tmp_tables = YOUR_ESTIMATE_PER_THREAD;

SELECT (@@query_cache_size + @@innodb_additional_mem_pool_size +
@@innodb_buffer_pool_size + @@innodb_log_buffer_size + @@key_buffer_size +
@@max_connections * (@@global.net_buffer_length + @@thread_stack +
@@global.query_prealloc_size + @@global.read_rnd_buffer_size +
@@global.sort_buffer_size + @@myisam_mmap_size +
@@global.myisam_sort_buffer_size + @@global.bulk_insert_buffer_size +
@@global.preload_buffer_size + @@binlog_cache_size +
@@global.join_buffer_size * IFNULL(@join_tables,1) + @@global.read_buffer_size *
IFNULL(@scan_tables, 1) + @@global.tmp_table_size * IFNULL(@tmp_tables, 1))) /
(1024 * 1024)
```

Please note that the formulas work only if the values are small enough. If they are large, you either need to convert each variable to megabytes or cast them as UNSIGNED INTEGER. Even casting to UNSIGNED INTEGER won't help if any variable can exceed the maximum unsigned integer value, which is 18446744073709547520. I didn't take these possible overflows into account, because I wanted the formulas to be readable and clear. It also makes sense to remove some of the variables from the calculation if you don't use those buffers or features. For example, instead of using the default value of myisam_mmap_size, use the maximum size of the MyISAM tables that one thread can use instead.

## CHAPTER 4

MySQL's Environment

The MySQL server is not alone in the environment where it runs. Even if it works in a dedicated environment, you still have to consider the hardware resources and operating system (OS) limits. In shared environments, the MySQL server is also affected by other processes. Tuning operating systems for MySQL is a huge topic about which a separate book could be written. Here I won't go deep, but show some starting points from a troubleshooting perspective. MySQL runs in various environments, which is a great advantage for MySQL, but also something that makes it hard to get specific in this chapter. So I decided to show you *what* you need to care about, and leave it up to you to consult the manual for your OS to determine *how* to handle tuning.

Physical Hardware Limits

A common usage mistake is to have unrealistic expectations for performance. One can expect that the MySQL server needs to be tuned while forgetting the latency of hardware components. Therefore, it is important to understand what can cause the latency.

The following hardware resources affect the MySQL server:

- RAM
- CPU
- Number of cores
- Disk I/O
- Network bandwidth

Let's discuss each of them in a bit of detail.

RAM

Memory is a very important resource for MySQL. The server works fast when it does not swap. Ideally, it should fit in RAM. Therefore, it is important to configure buffers in such a way that they stay within the limits of physical memory. I provided guidelines for this in "Effects of Options" on page 35 and in Chapter 3, particularly in "Calculating Safe Values for Options" on page 142.

 You can check whether *mysqld* is not swapping by checking *vmstat* on Linux/Unix or the Windows Task Manager on Windows.

Here is an example of swapping on Linux. Important parts are in bold. For a server that is not swapping, all these values should be equal to zero:

```
procs -----------memory---------- ---swap-- -----io---- -system-- ----cpu----
 r  b   swpd   free   buff  cache   si   so    bi    bo   in   cs us sy id wa
 1  0   1936 296828   7524 5045340    4   11   860     0  470  440  4  2 75 18
 0  1   1936 295928   7532 5046432   36   40   860   768  471  455  3  3 75 19
 0  1   1936 294840   7532 5047564    4   12   868     0  466  441  3  3 75 19
 0  1   1936 293752   7532 5048664    0    0   848     0  461  434  5  2 75 18
```

In those sections, we discussed how configuration variables can affect memory usage. The basic rule is to calculate the maximum realistic amount of RAM that will be used by the MySQL server and to make sure you keep it less than the physical RAM you have. Having buffers larger than the actual memory size increases the risk of the MySQL server crashing with an "Out of memory" error.

- The previous point can be stated the other way around: if you need larger buffers, buy more RAM. This is always a good practice for growing applications.

- Use RAM modules that support extended error correction (EEC), so if a bit of memory is corrupted, the whole MySQL server does not crash.

A few other aspects of memory use that you should consider are listed in a chapter named "How MySQL Uses Memory" in the MySQL Reference Manual (*http://dev .mysql.com/doc/refman/5.5/en/memory-use.html*). I won't repeat its contents here, because it doesn't involve any new troubleshooting techniques.

One important point is that when you select a row containing a BLOB column, an internal buffer grows to the point where it can store this value, and the storage engine does not return the memory to RAM after the query finishes. You need to run FLUSH TABLE to free the memory.

Another point concerns differences between 32-bit and 64-bit architectures. Although the 32-bit ones use a smaller pointer size and thus can save memory, these systems also contain inherent restrictions on the size of buffers due to addressing limits in the operating system. Theoretically, the maximum memory available in a 32-bit system is 4GB per process, and it's actually less on many systems. Therefore, if the buffers you want to use exceed the size of your 32-bit system, consider switching to a 64-bit architecture.

Processors and Their Cores

MySQL's performance does not scale linearly with increasing CPU speed. This does not mean you can't make use of a fast CPU, but don't expect performance will scale by increasing CPU speed in the same way it can increase by adding more RAM.

However, the number of cores is important when you set options that affect internal thread concurrency. There is no sense in increasing the values of such options if you don't have enough cores. This can be easily demonstrated using the benchmark utility named *sysbench*.[1] Table 4-1 shows the results of a small test on a machine with four cores. I used the OLTP *sysbench* test with 16 threads.

Table 4-1. Time spent executing an event with different innodb_thread_concurrency values

innodb_thread_concurrency	Execution time
1	7.8164
2	4.3959
4	2.5889
8	2.6708
16	3.4669
32	3.4235

As you can see, the test runs faster up until I start eight threads, and stops improving at higher values.

Disk I/O

Fast disks are very important for MySQL performance. The faster the disk, the faster the I/O operations.

Regarding disks, you should pay attention to disk read latency—how much time each read access takes—and fsync latency—how long each fsync takes.

Recent solid state disks (SSDs) work well, but don't expect miracles from them yet, because most storage engines are optimized to do read and writes for hard disks.

The same issue applies to network storage. It is possible to store data and logfiles in network filesystems and storage, but these installations may be slower than local disks. You need to check is how fast and reliable your storage is. Otherwise, don't be surprised if you experience data corruption because of network failure.

You can determine whether your disk I/O is overloaded using *iostat* on Linux/Unix. The average queue length of the requests issued to the device should not be high in

---

1. I discuss *sysbench* in "SysBench" on page 212.

normal use. On Windows you can use *perfmon* for the same purpose. Here is an example output of *iostat*:

```
$iostat -x 5
Linux 2.6.18-8.1.1.el5 (blade12)        11/11/2011      _x86_64_

avg-cpu:  %user   %nice %system %iowait  %steal   %idle
           1.27    0.00    0.32    0.65    0.00   97.79

Device:    rrqm/s wrqm/s  r/s   w/s  rsec/s  wsec/s avgrq-sz avgqu-sz await
cciss/c0d0   0.02   7.25  0.50  6.34  14.35  108.73   17.98     0.48   69.58
dm-0         0.00   0.00  0.52 13.59  14.27  108.70    8.72     0.09    6.59

svctm  %util
2.22   1.52
1.08   1.52

avg-cpu:  %user   %nice %system %iowait  %steal   %idle
          38.69    0.00    6.43   47.84    0.00    8.64

Device:    rrqm/s  wrqm/s  r/s     w/s rsec/s   wsec/s avgrq-sz avgqu-sz  await
cciss/c0d0   0.00 5362.40 0.20   713.80   1.60 51547.20   72.20   138.40 193.08
dm-0         0.00    0.00 0.00  6086.00   0.00 48688.00    8.00  1294.74 227.04

svctm %util
1.40 99.88
0.16 99.88

<skipped>

Device:    rrqm/s   wrqm/s  r/s      w/s rsec/s   wsec/s avgrq-sz avgqu-sz  await
cciss/c0d0   0.00 10781.80 0.00    570.20   0.00 84648.00  148.45   143.58 248.72
dm-0         0.00     0.00 0.00 11358.00   0.00 90864.00    8.00  3153.82 267.57

svctm  %util
1.75 100.02
0.09 100.02

avg-cpu:  %user   %nice %system %iowait  %steal   %idle
           8.90    0.00   11.30   75.10    0.00    5.60

Device:    rrqm/s   wrqm/s  r/s      w/s rsec/s   wsec/s avgrq-sz avgqu-sz  await
cciss/c0d0   0.00 11722.40 0.00    461.60   0.00 98736.00  213.90   127.78 277.04
dm-0         0.00     0.00 0.00 12179.20   0.00 97433.60    8.00  3616.90 297.54

svctm %util
2.14 98.80
0.08 98.80

avg-cpu:  %user   %nice %system %iowait  %steal   %idle
          23.55    0.00   23.95   46.19    0.00    7.11

Device:    rrqm/s  wrqm/s  r/s     w/s rsec/s   wsec/s avgrq-sz avgqu-sz  await
cciss/c0d0   0.00 4836.80 1.00   713.60   8.00 49070.40   68.68   144.28 204.08
dm-0         0.00    0.00 1.00  5554.60   8.00 44436.80    8.00  1321.82 257.28
```

```
svctm  %util
1.40 100.02
0.18 100.02
```

This output was taken when *mysqld* was idle and then started an active I/O job. You can see how `avgqu-sz` is growing. Although this is far from problematic, I decided to put this example here to show how disk I/O activity changes while *mysqld* is doing its job.

And aside from speed, remember that the storage can lose data; partial page writes are still possible. If you use InnoDB, use the doublewrite buffer by setting `innodb_double write` to secure your data. Also, is very important to plan battery backups for your disks because these can prevent data loss in case of power failure.

Network Bandwidth

Clients almost always connect to the MySQL server over a network, so it is important to run your MySQL server in a fast network.

In addition to network bandwidth, round-trip time (RTT) and the number of round-trips are important. RTT is a time needed for a client to send a network packet, then receive an answer from the server. The longer distance between the machines, the higher the RTT is.

Network bandwidth and RTT are the reasons why it is recommended to place the MySQL client and the server in the same local network when possible.

Local networks are recommended for replication as well. You can connect to slaves over the Internet instead of a local intranet, but expect delays and even errors due to corruption in the relay log data. Such errors should be fixed automatically after bug #26489 (*http://bugs.mysql.com/bug.php?id=26489*) is fixed and if you use the `relay-log-recovery` option starting with version 5.5 and binary log checksums starting with version 5.6. But the master and slave will still spend time resending packets due to network failures.

Example of the Effect of Latencies

To finish this part of the chapter, I will show you small example of how hardware latencies affect a trivial `UPDATE` query. We will use an InnoDB table with `autocommit` turned on. We will also turn on the binary logfile.

```
UPDATE test_rrbs SET f1 = md5(id*2) WHERE id BETWEEN 200000 AND 300000;
```

This simple query could experience latencies when:

The client sends a command to the server that takes a half of RTT.
The `WHERE` clause of the `UPDATE` is executed, and *mysqld* reads the disk.
mysqld does an `fsync` call to prepare for the transaction because `autocommit` is on.

mysqld does an `fsync` call to write into a binary logfile.

mysqld does an `fsync` call to commit changes.

The client receives the result from the server, which is another aspect of RTT.

Operating System Limits

Other limits on MySQL are set by operating systems. For example, I saw a case when a server failed because the Linux host specified `vm.overcommit_ratio = 50`. This option specifies the percentage of the system's total virtual memory that can be allocated via `malloc()`; attempts to allocate more memory by a process will fail. Fifty percent is the default value for many Linux installations. So when `mysqld` allocates about 50% of existing RAM and then tries to allocate more, it fails. In a multitasking setup, such an option may be useful because it protects other critical processes from a greedy MySQL server, but it's absolutely ridiculous in a dedicated server.

Another important Unix option is `ulimit`, which restricts various resources for users.[2] When you set resources using the `ulimit` command or another system utility, remember that the MySQL server runs as a simple user and is subject to the same limits as everyone else.

"Server-related options" on page 117 mentioned how OS restrictions affect the `open_files_limit` variable, and I'll show an example here. Suppose the server's `ulimit` on open files (the `-n` option) is set to 1024, the default on many systems. If you try to start *mysqld* with `--open-files-limit=4096`, it would not override the operating system limit.

```
$ulimit -n
1024

$./bin/mysqld --defaults-file=support-files/my-small.cnf --basedir=.
--datadir=./data --socket=/tmp/mysql_ssmirnova.sock --port=33051 --log-error
--open-files-limit=4096 &
[1] 31833

$./bin/mysql -uroot -S /tmp/mysql_ssmirnova.sock -e "SELECT
@@open_files_limit"
+--------------------+
| @@open_files_limit |
+--------------------+
|               1024 |
+--------------------+
```

This option is very important if you have many tables, and a value that's too small can lead to a slowdown because the MySQL server has to spend time opening and closing

---

2. Although the proper way to set operating system resource limits is to use your specific platform tools, it is still worth mentioning the built-in shell command `ulimit` due to its ease of use and availability for every user. It can either show all current restrictions if run as `ulimit -a` or set soft limits for the current user.

tables, or it may even reject connection attempts if the server can't open new tables due to lack of resources.

I won't describe how to tune OS limits in detail here, because this information is specific to each OS. I haven't mentioned Windows, but rest assured it has limits too.

When you suspect that the OS is limiting your MySQL server, first check the resources described earlier: RAM, CPU, and network bandwidth. Check whether *mysqld* is using less than the hardware offers. Usually, performance problems occur when RAM or CPU are limited. Also check the number of open files allowed.

If you find that *mysqld* can and should use more resources, check various aspects of operating system tuning. For example, the OS's kernel options or user defaults might set no limit on the amount of RAM available, but might specifically limit the user running *mysqld*. This is a common case when overall OS limits are huge or even not set, while defaults for user accounts are small.

If MySQL is using limited resources, you may sometimes wonder whether it is in trouble because of lack of resources or just isn't using them because its load is low at the moment. When the server is in trouble, it either prints messages to the error logfile or starts performing poorly. Another telltale sign is when you try to increase an option, but it does not increase. The earlier open_files_limit example illustrated this situation. In such cases, you will either find messages in the error logfile if you set the option at startup or see a warning when you set the option dynamically. It's also a good idea to check the real value of the suspected variable.

Effects of Other Software

Everything we've discussed so far is important when the MySQL server runs in any environment. Ideally, it should run in a dedicated environment and use all physical resources the machine has. But some sites use MySQL in shared environments. This includes shared hosting, where many instances of the *mysqld* server are running on behalf of different customers, and systems simultaneously running *mysqld* with client applications and other processes.

When you tune a MySQL installation in such configurations, you need to check two additional things: how many resources other processes use in their normal operations and how many resources they allocate at critical times.

Under normal loads, you can guess how many resources are left after other programs reserve theirs, and set MySQL's options appropriately. Critical loads are usually surprising and can lead to sudden, mysterious MySQL errors or even crashes. There is no universal rule about what to do in these situations. Just remember that third-party software can affect a MySQL installation, analyze the potential load, and take action to compensate for the effects.

Thus, if you anticipate that some other application has a critical load at time *X*, measure its resource use under the load and adjust MySQL server options accordingly. In such environments, it makes sense to limit resources at the OS level or use virtualization. In contrast to previous sections, I am advising here to add restrictions rather than remove them.

The worst case occurs when an unusually heavy load cannot be predicted. You learn about it only when you hit a problem. So if MySQL starts failing when it should not, always remember the effects of concurrent processes, check OS logs, and see whether other applications can affect MySQL's access to resources. It is also valuable to install software that monitors the activity of all processes running on the same box together with your MySQL installation.

- A good method to ascertain whether the MySQL server was affected by another OS process is to run a problematic query in an isolated environment. This is the same method recommended in "How Concurrency Affects Performance" on page 76.

## CHAPTER 5

Troubleshooting Replication

I already touched on replication issues in previous chapters, showing how the problems discussed in each chapter can affect replicated environments. This chapter focuses on issues specific to replication itself. These are mostly replication failures due to errors or slowdowns, such as a slave that lags several hours behind the master.

MySQL's replication is asynchronous. This means the master does not care whether data on the slave is consistent. Although circular multiple master replication can be set up, in a practical sense it is a chain of servers, with each of them serving as a slave and a master at the same time.

MySQL Multiple Master Setup

To illustrate the concept behind MySQL multiple master replication, let's consider Figure 5-1.

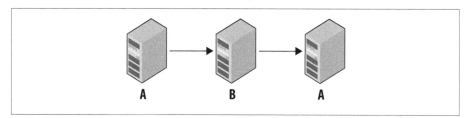

Figure 5-1. Two servers that replicate each other

Here server **A** is a master of its slave **B**, and at the very same time, server **B** is a master of slave **A**.

You can add as many servers as you wish to such chains (Figure 5-2).

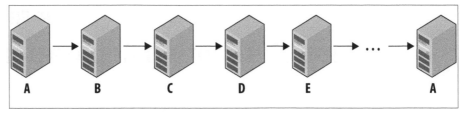

Figure 5-2. Circular replication with multiple servers

To troubleshoot such setups, you need to take a single master/slave pair (Figure 5-3).

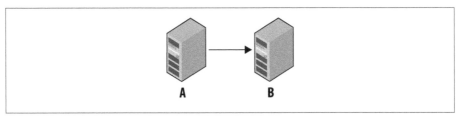

Figure 5-3. Focusing on one direction in multimaster replication

Then work it out like any simple replication setup. Then take another pair, and so on. I won't describe this specific case in detail, but just touch on it later in the section "Circular Replication and Nonreplication Writes on the Slave" on page 168.

Since version 5.5, MySQL packages include a semi-synchronous replication plug-in. If this plug-in is turned on, the master will wait for a confirmation from one of its slaves that it received and successfully applied each event. This is still not synchronous replication, because the master does not know whether the slave has the same data after applying the event (I discussed this possibility in "Statement-Based Replication Issues" on page 87). Furthermore, if many slaves are connected to the same master, there is no guarantee that data is replicated on all of the slaves.

Troubleshooting semi-synchronous replication is the same as troubleshooting asynchronous replication. The only difference is the effect of its specific options. So I won't describe issues specific to semi-synchronous replication. If you encounter problems with it, just follow the methods described in Chapter 3.

The MySQL slave runs two threads related to replication: the I/O thread, which handles all the traffic with the master, and the SQL thread, which reruns the events themselves to replicate results on the slave. These threads experience different problems that should be solved using different techniques, so I discuss each in its own section in this chapter.

Displaying Slave Status

Before we start troubleshooting threads, I'll present an excellent source of replication state information: the `SHOW SLAVE STATUS` query for slaves.

The following examples were taken when running a slave without errors and a slave whose master has stopped to show how errors would look. I'll discuss the output in chunks.

```
mysql> SHOW SLAVE STATUS\G
*************************** 1. row ***************************
               Slave_IO_State: Connecting to master
```

This is the status of the I/O thread. For a running slave, it usually contains `Waiting for master to send event`:

```
               Slave_IO_State: Waiting for master to send event
                  Master_Host: 127.0.0.1
                  Master_User: root
                  Master_Port: 4041
                Connect_Retry: 60
              Master_Log_File: mysqld511-bin.000007
```

The `Master_Log_File` field shows the name of the master binary logfile. If the slave had an I/O error, the field would be empty.

```
          Read_Master_Log_Pos: 106
```

106 is the position in the master's binary log that was read.

```
               Relay_Log_File: mysqld512-relay.000097
```

`Relay_Log_File` is the name of the relay logfile, a file on the slave that contains the information transferred from the master's binary log.

```
                Relay_Log_Pos: 255
```

255 is the current position in the relay logfile.

```
        Relay_Master_Log_File: mysqld511-bin.000007
             Slave_IO_Running: Yes
```

`Slave_IO_Running` indicates the basic state of the I/O thread, i.e., whether it is running. This can be either `Yes` or `No`.

```
            Slave_SQL_Running: Yes
```

This time, we see the running status of the SQL thread. Again, it can be either `Yes` or `No`.

```
              Replicate_Do_DB:
          Replicate_Ignore_DB:
           Replicate_Do_Table:
       Replicate_Ignore_Table:
      Replicate_Wild_Do_Table:
  Replicate_Wild_Ignore_Table:
                   Last_Errno: 0
                   Last_Error:
```

```
            Skip_Counter: 0
   Exec_Master_Log_Pos: 106
```

The 106 in `Exec_Master_Log_Pos` represents the position in the master binary log that was just executed. This can be different from `Read_Master_Log_Pos` if the slave is behind the master.

```
        Relay_Log_Space: 106
        Until_Condition: None
         Until_Log_File:
          Until_Log_Pos: 0
      Master_SSL_Allowed: No
      Master_SSL_CA_File:
      Master_SSL_CA_Path:
        Master_SSL_Cert:
      Master_SSL_Cipher:
         Master_SSL_Key:
   Seconds_Behind_Master: 2
```

`Seconds_Behind_Master` shows how far the slave lags behind the master. It contains the number of seconds between the last executed event on the slave and the last event from the master binary log that was replicated into the relay logfile. Ideally this value should be zero. If the slave is not connected to a master, this field contains `NULL`.

```
   Master_SSL_Verify_Server_Cert: No
```

Here is output from the stopped slave again:

```
           Last_IO_Errno: 2013
```

`Last_IO_Errno` is either the number of the most recent error on the I/O thread or zero if there has been no error since the slave started.

```
   Last_IO_Error: error connecting to master 'root@127.0.0.1:4041'
   - retry-time: 60  retries: 86400
```

These two rows contain the text of the most recent I/O error. In this case, they contain information about why the I/O thread failed.

```
          Last_SQL_Errno: 0
```

`Last_SQL_Errno` is either the number of the most recent error on the SQL thread or zero if there has been no error since the slave started.

```
           Last_SQL_Error:
```

Again, the text of last SQL error. Although there is no error in this example, these two rows can contain information about why the SQL thread failed.

Now that you are familiar with the output of `SHOW SLAVE STATUS`, we can go on to troubleshooting.

Problems with the I/O Thread

Common I/O errors include:

- The slave cannot connect to the master.
- The slave connects to master, but repeatedly disconnects.
- The slave is far behind master.

When an I/O error happens, the slave status that we saw in the previous section becomes `Slave_IO_Running: No` and the reason appears in the `Last_IO_Errno` and `Last_IO_Error` fields. The error logfile also contains messages about I/O thread failures if `log_warnings` is set to 1 (the default).

When the slave cannot connect, the first thing to check is whether the replication user has the correct permissions on the master. The replication user (the user you specify as `master_user` in the `CHANGE MASTER` query that begins replication) must have the `REPLICATION SLAVE` privilege on the master. If it does not, just grant such a privilege to this user on the master.

Once you are sure the replication user has the correct permissions, you need to check the network. Use the *ping* utility to find out whether the master host can be reached. Here is an example:

```
$ping 192.168.0.4
PING 192.168.0.4 (192.168.0.4): 56 data bytes
64 bytes from 192.168.0.4: icmp_seq=0 ttl=64 time=0.113 ms
64 bytes from 192.168.0.4: icmp_seq=1 ttl=64 time=0.061 ms
^C
--- 192.168.0.4 ping statistics ---
2 packets transmitted, 2 packets received, 0% packet loss
round-trip min/avg/max/stddev = 0.061/0.087/0.113/0.026 ms
```

If *ping* fails to connect to the master host, this clearly locates the problem in the network and you need to fix it. You can also use *telnet* to check whether the MySQL server itself is reachable. Specify the host and port of the master as arguments for the `telnet` command:

```
$telnet 192.168.0.4 33511
Trying 192.168.0.4...
Connected to apple.
Escape character is '^]'.
>
5.1.59-debug-log}O&i`(D^,#!\o8h%zYO$`;D^]
telnet> quit
Connection closed.
```

In this example, the MySQL server was reachable: `5.1.59-debug-log}O&i`(D^,#!\o8h %zYO$`;D^]` is its welcome string. If *ping* works but *telnet* cannot connect to the server, you need to find out whether the MySQL server is running and whether the port is accessible, that is, whether the slave host can open the master port and whether the master host allows the slave host to connect to this port.

If the preceding tests succeed but the replication IO thread is still stopped, connect using the MySQL command-line client to be sure you can connect to the master using the credentials of the replication user. Here is an example where I successfully establish a connection and determine that the replication user has the right privileges:

```
$mysql -h 127.0.0.1 -P 33511 -urepl -preplrepl
Welcome to the MySQL monitor.  Commands end with ; or \g.
Your MySQL connection id is 6783
Server version: 5.1.59-debug-log Source distribution

Copyright (c) 2000, 2011, Oracle and/or its affiliates. All rights reserved.

Oracle is a registered trademark of Oracle Corporation and/or its
affiliates. Other names may be trademarks of their respective
owners.

Type 'help;' or '\h' for help. Type '\c' to clear the current input statement.

mysql> SELECT user(), current_user();
+----------------+----------------+
| user()         | current_user() |
+----------------+----------------+
| repl@localhost | repl@localhost |
+----------------+----------------+
1 row in set (0.13 sec)

mysql> SHOW GRANTS\G
*************************** 1. row ***************************
Grants for repl@localhost: GRANT REPLICATION SLAVE ON
*.* TO 'repl'@'localhost' IDENTIFIED BY PASSWORD
'*17125BDFB190AB635083AF9B26F9E8F00EA128FE'
1 row in set (0.00 sec)
```

SHOW GRANTS here shows the parameters through which the slave's replication user can replicate data from the master.

When the slave can connect to the master but repeatedly disconnects, use your operating system tools to check the network. You can use tcpdump or netstat to watch traffic, or even send a large file through the network and watch progress to be sure the network is stable. The goal is to determine whether the connection between the master and slave is being interrupted.

If a connection to the master is established, netstat should print something like:

```
$netstat -a
Active Internet connections (including servers)
Proto Recv-Q Send-Q  Local Address       Foreign Address         (state)
tcp4      0      0   apple.60344         master.mysql.com.33051 ESTABLISHED
```

tcpdump would print packets:

```
$tcpdump -i en1 host master.mysql.com and port 33051
tcpdump: verbose output suppressed, use -v or -vv for full protocol decode
listening on en1, link-type EN10MB (Ethernet), capture size 96 bytes
22:28:12.195270 IP master.mysql.com.33051 > apple.60344: P
1752426772:1752426864(92) ack 1474226199 win 91 <nop,nop,timestamp 1939999898
649946687>
```

```
22:28:12.195317 IP apple.60344 > master.mysql.com.33051: . ack 92 win 65535
<nop,nop,timestamp 649946998 1939999898>
^C
2 packets captured
37 packets received by filter
0 packets dropped by kernel
```

This example was taken when I issued a query on the master, and it was successfully replicated.

When the slave is far behind the master, this can be a symptom of a slow network or a load that's too heavy on the slave. We will return to overloaded slaves later in this chapter when discussing the SQL thread.

To check whether the network is slow, use `tcpdump` or send large files and watch the times in which packets are transferred. Also check whether MySQL is using all of the bandwidth available to the system on each side. If bandwidth usage is above 80%, you may need to buy faster network hardware. If it isn't using all of the available bandwidth, check whether other software is using the same network interface and affecting the MySQL server. If other software is getting in the way, move it to a different host or at least a different hardware network interface.

Another error related to the I/O thread is relay log corruption. You would most likely see it as an SQL thread error:

```
Last_SQL_Errno: 1594
Last_SQL_Error: Relay log read failure: Could not parse relay log event
entry. The possible reasons are: the master's binary log is corrupted (you can
check this by running 'mysqlbinlog' on the binary log), the slave's relay log is
corrupted (you can check this by running 'mysqlbinlog' on the relay log), a
network problem, or a bug in the master's or slave's MySQL code. If you want to
check the master's binary log or slave's relay log, you will be able to know
their names by issuing 'SHOW SLAVE STATUS' on this slave.
```

I'm discussing this problem in this section instead of the SQL thread section because the real cause of the error could be a failure in the I/O thread that corrupted the relay log earlier. What could be happening is that the SQL thread has encountered the corruption while trying to execute events in the relay log.

In case of such an error, the first thing to do is follow the directions in the error message: check the master's binary log and the slave's relay log for corruption using the *mysqlbinlog* utility. *mysqlbinlog* converts binary logfiles into a human-readable format. Simply call it like this:

```
$mysqlbinlog /Users/apple/Applications/mysql-5.1/data511/mysqld511-bin.005071
/*!40019 SET @@session.max_insert_delayed_threads=0*/;
/*!50003 SET @OLD_COMPLETION_TYPE=@@COMPLETION_TYPE,COMPLETION_TYPE=0*/;
DELIMITER /*!*/;
# at 4
#110904 16:50:00 server id 511  end_log_pos 106          Start: binlog v 4,
server v 5.1.59-debug-log created 110904 16:50:00
BINLOG '
CIJjTg//AQAAZgAAAGoAAAAAAQANS4xLjU5LWR1YnVnLWxvZwAAAAAAAAAAAAAAAAAAAAAAAAAA
```

```
AAAAAAAAAAAAAAAAAAAAAAAAAEzgNAAgAEgAEBAQEEgAAUwAEGggAAAAICAgC
'/*!*/;
# at 106
#110904 16:50:14 server id 511   end_log_pos 192          Query    thread_id=7251
exec_time=0      error_code=0
use test/*!*/;
SET TIMESTAMP=1315144214/*!*/;
SET @@session.pseudo_thread_id=7251/*!*/;
SET @@session.foreign_key_checks=1, @@session.sql_auto_is_null=1,
@@session.unique_checks=1, @@session.autocommit=1/*!*/;
SET @@session.sql_mode=0/*!*/;
SET @@session.auto_increment_increment=1, @@session.auto_increment_offset=1/*!*/;
/*!\C latin1 *//*!*/;
SET
@@session.character_set_client=8,@@session.collation_connection=8,@@session.
collation_server=33/*!*/;
SET @@session.lc_time_names=0/*!*/;
SET @@session.collation_database=DEFAULT/*!*/;
create table t1(f1 int)
/*!*/;
# at 192
#110904 16:50:20 server id 511   end_log_pos 260          Query    thread_id=7251
exec_time=0      error_code=0
SET TIMESTAMP=1315144220/*!*/;
BEGIN
/*!*/;
# at 260
# at 301
#110904 16:50:20 server id 511   end_log_pos 301          Table_map: `test`.`t1`
mapped to number 21
#110904 16:50:20 server id 511   end_log_pos 335          Write_rows: table id 21
flags: STMT_END_F

BINLOG '
HIJjThP/AQAAKQAAAC0BAAAAABUAAAAAAAEABHR1c3QAAnQxAAEDAAE=
HIJjThf/AQAAIgAAAE8BAAAAABUAAAAAAAEAAf/+AQAAAA==
'/*!*/;
# at 335
#110904 16:50:20 server id 511   end_log_pos 404          Query    thread_id=7251
exec_time=0      error_code=0
SET TIMESTAMP=1315144220/*!*/;
COMMIT
/*!*/;
# at 404
#110904 16:50:36 server id 511   end_log_pos 451          Rotate to
mysqld511-bin.005072  pos: 4
DELIMITER ;
# End of log file
ROLLBACK /* added by mysqlbinlog */;
/*!50003 SET COMPLETION_TYPE=@OLD_COMPLETION_TYPE*/;
```

In this example I used a valid binary logfile. If the file was corrupted, *mysqlbinlog* will
mention it explicitly:

```
$mysqlbinlog --verbose --start-position=260 --stop-position=335 \
/Users/apple/Applications/mysql-5.1/data511/mysqld511-bin.000007.corrupted
```

```
/*!40019 SET @@session.max_insert_delayed_threads=0*/;
/*!50003 SET @OLD_COMPLETION_TYPE=@@COMPLETION_TYPE,COMPLETION_TYPE=0*/;
DELIMITER /*!*/;
ERROR: Error in Log_event::read_log_event(): 'Found invalid event in binary
log', data_len: 102, event_type: 15
ERROR: Could not read a Format_description_log_event event at offset 4; this
could be a log format error or read error.
DELIMITER ;
# End of log file
ROLLBACK /* added by mysqlbinlog */;
/*!50003 SET COMPLETION_TYPE=@OLD_COMPLETION_TYPE*/;
```

I used the row binary log format here to show how row events look when printed. If
binlog_format='statement' is used, all events are printed as SQL statements. You can
see the SQL representation of row events by using the --verbose option:

```
$mysqlbinlog --verbose --start-position=260 --stop-position=335 \
/Users/apple/Applications/mysql-5.1/data511/mysqld511-bin.005071
/*!40019 SET @@session.max_insert_delayed_threads=0*/;
/*!50003 SET @OLD_COMPLETION_TYPE=@@COMPLETION_TYPE,COMPLETION_TYPE=0*/;
DELIMITER /*!*/;
# at 4
#110904 16:50:00 server id 511  end_log_pos 106          Start: binlog v 4,
server v 5.1.59-debug-log created 110904 16:50:00
BINLOG '
CIJjTg//AQAAZgAAAGoAAAAAAQANS4xLjU5LWRlYnVnLWxvZwAAAAAAAAAAAAAAAAAAAAAAAAAA
AAAAAAAAAAAAAAAAAAAAAAAAEzgNAAgAEgAEBAQEEgAAUwAEGggAAAAICAgC
'/*!*/;
# at 260
# at 301
#110904 16:50:20 server id 511  end_log_pos 301          Table_map: `test`.`t1`
mapped to number 21
#110904 16:50:20 server id 511  end_log_pos 335          Write_rows: table id 21
flags: STMT_END_F

BINLOG '
HIJjThP/AQAAKQAAAC0BAAAAABUAAAAAAAEABHRlc3QAAnQxAAEDAAE=
HIJjThf/AQAAIgAAAE8BAAAAABUAAAAAAAEAAf/+AQAAAA==
'/*!*/;
### INSERT INTO test.t1
### SET
###   @1=1
DELIMITER ;
# End of log file
ROLLBACK /* added by mysqlbinlog */;
/*!50003 SET COMPLETION_TYPE=@OLD_COMPLETION_TYPE*/;
```

In addition to the --verbose option, I used --start-position and --stop-position to
show how to limit *mysqlbinlog* output to particular positions if the logfile is large.

You can pipe *mysqlbinlog* output into the MySQL client and have it execute the queries.
This works for SBR and Row-Based Replication (RBR), and is useful when you want
to debug how binary log events are applied to the slave.

If there is a problem with the master logfile, find out why it happened. First, restart replication manually. Restore events from `Exec_Master_Log_Pos` to the latest possible position, and apply them manually. Then, wait until `Seconds_Behind_Master` is 0, and compare the tables on the master and slave.

If a lot of changes are corrupted and finding which rows are modified is practically impossible, you probably need to back up the master, then load the backup on the slave and restart replication. You can replay replication for a single table. Figure out the last point in the binary log where the data was correctly replicated, then set the `replicate-wild-ignore-table` option and run:

```
START SLAVE [SQL_THREAD] UNTIL
    MASTER_LOG_FILE = 'log_name', MASTER_LOG_POS = log_pos
START SLAVE [SQL_THREAD] UNTIL
    RELAY_LOG_FILE = 'log_name', RELAY_LOG_POS = log_pos
```

where `log_pos` is the position of the last correct change of that table in either the master binary file or relay logfile. After the slave reaches this position and stops, remove the option `replicate-wild-ignore-table` and restart the server.

How to Check Whether Tables Are Consistent

There are few ways to check whether tables on a master and a slave are consistent. Here is quick overview of them. Use one or another depending on the problem you hit.

CHECKSUM TABLE
:   As should be clear from the name, this query returns a table checksum. This MySQL statement does not require additional installation and is always available.

    ```
    mysql> CHECKSUM TABLE test;
    +--------------+------------+
    | Table        | Checksum   |
    +--------------+------------+
    | test.test    | 4220395591 |
    +--------------+------------+
    1 row in set (0.43 sec)
    ```

    When you want to check whether the tables on the master and slave have the same data, run the query on both servers and compare results. Make sure that `Seconds_Behind_Master` is zero and that there is no write activity on the same table on the master while `CHECKSUM TABLE` is running.

mysqldiff
:   This is a tool from the MySQL WB Utilities bundle that comes with the MySQL Workbench installation. The tool reads the definition of database objects and compares their definitions using a `diff`-like method to determine whether two objects are same. Here is an example of its use for troubleshooting replication:

    ```
    $mysqldiff --server1=root@127.0.0.1:33511 --server2=root@127.0.0.1:33512 \
    test.t1:test.t1
    # server1 on 127.0.0.1: ... connected.
    # server2 on 127.0.0.1: ... connected.
    # Comparing test.t1 to test.t1                                      [PASS]
    Success. All objects are the same.
    ```

---

pt-table-checksum

> This is part of the Percona Toolkit (*https://launchpad.net/percona-toolkit*) and the most powerful tool among those discussed here. It connects to a master and a slave and compares whether tables have the same structure and the same data. To do this, the tool creates a table that stores a checksum from the master table. After this value is replicated, a second run of *pt-table-checksum* checks the data on a slave.

> Here is an example of checking replication:

```
$pt-table-checksum --replicate=test.checksum --create-replicate-table
h=127.0.0.1,P=33511,u=root --databases book
DATABASE TABLE CHUNK HOST      ENGINE  COUNT  CHECKSUM TIME WAIT STAT  LAG
book     t1      0 127.0.0.1 MyISAM      5  42981178    0 NULL NULL NULL
book     ts      0 127.0.0.1 MyISAM     65  aeb6b7a0    0 NULL NULL NULL
```

> This command calculates and saves checksums for each table in the book database. Once the slave is up, we can check whether the tables are the same:

```
$pt-table-checksum --replicate=test.checksum --replicate-check=2
h=127.0.0.1,P=33511,u=root --databases book
Differences on P=33512,h=127.0.0.1
DB    TBL   CHUNK CNT_DIFF CRC_DIFF BOUNDARIES
book  ts        0      -5        1 1=1
```

> The tool prints the differences it finds, if any. Here we can see that data in the ts table is different on the master and slave, whereas data in t1 is same.

Whatever tool you use, you need to be sure that no change was replicated since the last check was taken on the master. The easiest way to do this is to write-lock the tables you are currently examining.

mysqldiff and *pt-table-checksum* can do more than what I described here, but the uses I showed are the most important to help diagnose replication failures.

If you haven't found any problem with the master binary log or find that the relay log is corrupt, it can be a symptom of either a network issue or disk corruption. In both cases, you can reposition the relay log on the slave to the Exec_Master_Log_Pos position and restart it using sequence of queries STOP SLAVE; CHANGE MASTER master_log_pos=Exec_Master_Log_Pos_Value, master_log_file ='Relay_Master_Log_File_Value'; START SLAVE, and the relay log will be re-created. If the corruption was a singular occurrence, replication will be up and running again.

But don't just clean up and ignore whatever could have caused the problem. Check your logs for disk and network problems.

To find out whether the cause was a disk problem, examine the operating system's logfiles and use tools to check the disk for bad segments. If you find any, fix the disk. Otherwise, you can expect similar failures again.

Network problems can cause corruption in older versions of MySQL. Before versions 5.0.56 and 5.1.24, relay logs could often be corrupted by unstable networks. In versions

5.0.56 and 5.1.24, bug #26489 (*http://bugs.mysql.com/bug.php?id=26489*) was fixed, and now this problem is quite rare. Since version 5.6.2, replication checksums were also inserted. This solves the rest of the corruption problems caused by network breakage.

These fixes do not automatically recover corrupted relay logs, but prevent them from becoming corrupted due to either a problem on the master or a network issue. Since version 5.5, the `relay-log-recovery` option is available, which turns on automatic recovery when the slave restarts.

But even if you use newer versions of MySQL with these fixes, you should check the network. The earlier you find problems with a network, the sooner you can fix them. Even with automatic recovery, resolving network issues takes time and can slow down replication.

In this section, we've had to consider some SQL thread errors, even though the causes were on the I/O thread. In the next section, I will discuss SQL thread problems that are not related to the I/O thread.

Problems with the SQL Thread

As I already mentioned in "Statement-Based Replication Issues" on page 87, each slave has a single SQL thread, so all its errors can be tested in a single-threaded MySQL client. Even if you run the multithreaded slave preview, you can always ask it to use a single thread when you're trying to reproduce an error. If reducing activity to one SQL thread fails to make the problem go away, use the following techniques to fix logic errors on the single thread, then switch to multiple threads again.

It's easy to re-create a query that caused a slave to fail: just run it using the MySQL command-line utility.

When you get an SQL error on the slave, it stops. `SHOW SLAVE STATUS` shows the SQL thread error that caused the problem:

```
Last_SQL_Errno: 1146
Last_SQL_Error: Error 'Table 'test.t1' doesn't exist' on query.
Default database: 'test'.
Query: 'INSERT INTO t1 VALUES(1)'
```

The error message usually contains the text of the SQL query and the reason why it failed. In this case, the error message explains everything (I dropped the `t1` table on the slave to create this example), but in case of doubt, you can try to run same query in the MySQL command-line client and see the results:

```
mysql> INSERT INTO t1 VALUES(1);
ERROR 1146 (42S02): Table 'test.t1' doesn't exist
```

The error in this example makes it clear what you need to do to solve the problem: create the table.

```
mysql> CREATE TABLE t1(f1 INT);
Query OK, 0 rows affected (0.17 sec)
```

After the table is created, we can restart the slave SQL thread:

```
mysql> STOP SLAVE SQL_THREAD;
Query OK, 0 rows affected, 1 warning (0.00 sec)

mysql> SHOW WARNINGS;
+-------+------+-------------------------------+
| Level | Code | Message                       |
+-------+------+-------------------------------+
| Note  | 1255 | Slave already has been stopped |
+-------+------+-------------------------------+
1 row in set (0.00 sec)

mysql> START SLAVE SQL_THREAD;
Query OK, 0 rows affected (0.10 sec)

mysql> SHOW SLAVE STATUS\G
*************************** 1. row ***************************
               Slave_IO_State: Waiting for master to send event
               <skipped>
            Slave_IO_Running: Yes
           Slave_SQL_Running: Yes
               <skipped>
                  Last_Errno: 0
                  Last_Error:
               <skipped>
               Last_IO_Errno: 0
               Last_IO_Error:
              Last_SQL_Errno: 0
              Last_SQL_Error:
1 row in set (0.00 sec)
```

Now the problem is solved and the slave runs successfully again.

When Data Is Different on the Master and Slave

If you have errors that cannot be solved so easily, check whether the table definition is the same on the master and slave. You should also check whether both tables had the same data before the problematic query ran.

 MySQL replication allows you to have different definitions for a table on the master and slave. If you run such a setup, analyze how the same query runs on these different tables. Also check whether using different storage engines and indexes can affect the final result.

When the SQL thread stops, a very common reason is that the slave's tables differ from the master. I won't describe all the reasons for these errors here, but the most common are:

- The problems we saw in Example 2-1 and elsewhere with concurrent transactional updates that don't preserve the consistency of data.
- `INSERT ON DUPLICATE KEY UPDATE`, which, if run on the slave along with other updates in other connections in a different order from the master, can update the wrong rows and skip rows that were updated on the master.
- Running concurrent inserts on a MyISAM table on the master without taking into account the existence of a slave.
- Use of nondeterministic functions.[1]

It is also important to remember that a slave is not crash-proof, so if *mysqld* crashed, restarting it can repeat the transaction executed just before the crash and thus leave the slave with different data from the master. A similar issue happens when the slave fails while in the middle of updating a nontransactional table, such as MyISAM.

Circular Replication and Nonreplication Writes on the Slave

If you write to a slave outside of replication, you have to care about data consistency. Two good ways to avoid problems are to make sure the writes affect different objects from the changes being replicated and to always use primary keys with different sequences on the master and slave. You can ensure different primary key values by using `AUTO_INCREMENT`, giving each master a different starting point with the `auto_increment_offset` option, and setting `auto_increment_increment` to the number of servers in the replication setup.

Circular replication, where each master is a slave of another master,[2] can be affected by the same issue because such a setup does not prevent writes on the slave that can conflict with the data being replicated.

MySQL allows you to create circular replication setups, but does not guarantee data consistency for such setups due to their asynchronous replication design. You need to take care of data consistency yourself. Therefore, from a troubleshooting perspective, debugging errors caused by circular replication are the same as any other replication problem. In a bidirectional setup, remember that servers can be both masters and slaves of each other. So when you meet an error, determine which of them is playing the master role and which the slave's, then act correspondingly. You will probably need to test replication with one server playing just the master role and the other the slave's, then swap roles.

To illustrate this technique, let's take a simple multimaster setup from "MySQL Multiple Master Setup" on page 155 (Figure 5-4).

---

1. A deterministic function is one that returns the same result each time it runs with the same input parameters. `CONCAT('Hello, ', 'world!')` is deterministic, whereas `NOW()` is not.
2. Such replication can be also called "multimaster replication" or "bidirectional replication."

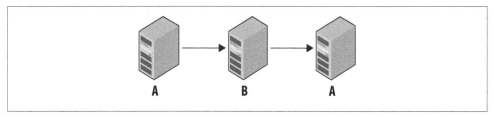

Figure 5-4. Two servers that replicate each other

If you meet a problem in such a setup, take a pair (as in Figure 5-5) and solve the problem as if it were simple master-slave replication. Stop all updates on B while you are working on the problem.

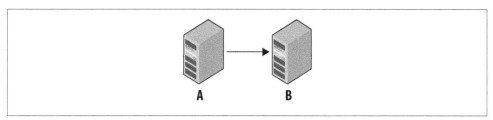

Figure 5-5. Focusing on one direction in multimaster replication

After the problem is solved, temporarily stop updates on A and turn them on on B, so you have a simple setup like the one shown in Figure 5-6.

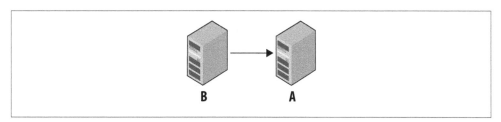

Figure 5-6. Reversing direction in multimaster replication

If this setup is still experiencing problems, solve them here, too, and then start updates on A again, so you have same circular multimaster setup.

At this point, it is good to analyze why the problem occurred in the first place and fix it before restarting updates on both servers.

The same method would work for any number of servers in the circle.

When setting up circular replication, you need to clearly split queries so that changes from one master don't interfere with another. Errors can break replication or cause data inconsistency. I won't describe best practices here, but you can find a detailed overview of how to set up multimaster replication in Chapter 4, "Replication for High Availability," of *MySQL High Availability* by Charles Bell et al. (O'Reilly).

- Good design is crucial to creating a trouble-free circular multimaster replication setup.

Incomplete or Altered SQL Statements

If an error message does not show the full query and the error log does not contain the full query either (which can happen if the query is larger than 1,024 bytes), you need to run the *mysqlbinlog* utility on either the master binary log or the slave's relay log to get the full version of the query as the slave got it, and then analyze why it failed.

That can help with statement-based replication, which logs and sends queries in the original human-readable SQL. But what do you do if row format was used? Row events are the same events as queries and can be run through any MySQL client. Use *mysqlbinlog* with the `--verbose` option to get the SQL representation of row events.

- Always use the same query on the slave that was executed when the master binary log event was applied. Using the *mysqlbinlog* utility to check what query ran will save you time. The binary log sometimes contains a query that is a bit different from what was originally executed on the master, and side effects could be introduced. If you ignore such a side effect, you could spend hours trying to repeat a problem that just can't be found by running the query as the master ran it.

Different Errors on the Master and Slave

Another status message that can be confusing is "Query caused different errors on master and slave..." The message usually contains the error. Most confusing is when such a message says there was no error on the slave—"Error on slave: 'no error' (0)."— but there was one on the master. This can happen, for example, if an error was caused by a trigger on the master but the update on the master table succeeded. The query on the original table will be written to the binary logfile with a note containing the error number for the failed trigger. In this case, if the trigger successfully finished on the slave or the slave's table does not have a trigger at all, the query on the slave will return no error, and thus you will get such a message.

To quickly fix this issue, skip the error using SET GLOBAL SLAVE_SKIP_COUNTER=1; and continue replication. Don't forget to find the real cause of the problem to prevent the same error from recurring.

If a problem occurred on the master due to a deadlock in a trigger, fix the slave manually because the master and slave tables can contain different data. To do this, you need to find out which tables contain different data and update the slave to match the master.

Configuration

Another important thing to check is the configuration options of the master and slave. Ideally they should be the same, but sometimes there are good reasons, such as different hardware or the kind of load, to make them different. When they are different and you starting receive SQL errors that cannot be easily explained, check the options that can change server behavior. I described some of them in Chapter 3.

Just as for the single-server setup, when I recommended you run `mysqld` with the `--no-defaults` option to know whether it is affected by your custom options, here I recommend copying the master's options into the slave configuration, so that the slave has exactly the same options as the master. Adjust only those options that differ between servers, such as `server_id`, which must always be unique. Determine whether the problem is still reproducible. If it is not, you can feel confident that a configuration variable is the reason for the failure. At that point you need only to find the troublesome variable using the techniques described in "Haste Makes Waste" on page 114, and adjust it correspondingly.

- Always compare the options on the master and slave for differences.

When the Slave Lags Far Behind the Master

"Problems with the I/O Thread" on page 158 discussed the situation when `Seconds_Behind_Master` grows large because the network is flaky. Another reason for huge delays is when the slave performs more slowly than the master.

The slave can be slower than the master if it has slower hardware, smaller buffers, or its own read load that competes with the replicated load for resources. Another possible cause of slowness is when a master executes queries in parallel, but the slave executes all the binary log events in a single thread, one after another.

The first thing you need to do when a slave lags behind the master is to find what is causing this behavior and how it can be improved.

Slow hardware is an easy case and can be solved by buying faster hardware. But before spending the money, analyze whether the master is using all its hardware and whether performance-related options on the slave are optimized. For example, if the master runs in a shared environment and the slave is on a dedicated but slower server, you have a chance to improve its speed. Calculate how many resources the master actually uses and how much the slave's performance can be improved by tuning configuration parameters.

If the hardware is the same on both servers, or the slave runs on an even faster machine but still lags behind, check differences in performance-related options. Analyze their effect, and tune the slave correspondingly. Configuring the same options on the master and slave is a good start. In this case, you can be sure that the options are good for replicated events, so you should adjusting only those options on the slave that can improve a concurrent load.

The hardest case to solve is a slave whose slowness is caused by performing operations in a single thread while the master executes them in parallel. The only thing you can do in this case, besides trying the multithreaded slave preview, is to upgrade the hardware on the slave and tune performance-related options as much as possible.

In all these cases, you also should analyze the effect of queries that run on the slave concurrently with the slave SQL thread. I described concurrency troubleshooting in Chapter 2.

## CHAPTER 6

Troubleshooting Techniques and Tools

I have discussed many troubleshooting techniques and tools earlier in this book. Some of them were explained thoroughly, and in other cases I only touched on aspects of their use. This chapter adds details left out of previous chapters. I have tried to avoid repetition. Many techniques and tools depend on each other, so they are combined in this chapter.

There are too many tools to describe them all, so here I stick to those that I find absolutely necessary. They are mostly command-line tools that either come with the MySQL distribution or are provided as separate packages. I include a few descriptions of third-party tools, again command-line utilities. I did this not because I don't like third-party tools, but to let you know about the great tools that come with MySQL and that you therefore always have. One of the advantages of MySQL tools is that they are always available, which is very important for our customers. Some companies have rules that prevent their employees from downloading a third-party tool. Therefore, when doing customer support, we always prefer tools that come with the MySQL distribution.

For similar reasons, I don't describe graphical tools here. The command-line tools pose no special requirements, such as the X Window System or a particular operating system, whereas graphical tools are more demanding.

Finally, I know MySQL's tools much better than their analogs in other packages. If you find more powerful third-party tools, use them. But knowing what can be done with simple tools is always useful.

The Query

In Chapter 1 we learned how a single query can affect performance across the whole server and how to find which one is misbehaving. Here I'll add a few words about this type of problem.

A problematic query fired by an application can be found by checking the error logs, through the use of output functions in the application that automatically logs queries sent to the MySQL server, using a library written for such a purpose in the application, and in the general query logfile. Here I want to discuss how such logging can be tuned.

The general query log is missing some useful information that can help you debug your query, such as query execution time, information about errors and warnings, and the result set. Information about query execution time can be used to find slow queries. Of course, you can log all this special data using a custom library or by simply adding output functions everywhere in your application. But before you start tuning the application, you can still use a built-in resource: the slow query log.

Slow Query Log

The slow query log contains queries that run longer than `long_query_time` seconds. The default value of this variable is 10, but you can decrease it. In fact, by setting the value to zero, you can log all queries. Since version 5.1, you can turn logging to the slow log on and off dynamically as needed, just as for the general query log. You can also redirect output to a table, so it can be queried like any other.

For performance tuning, find the slowest queries, check them one by one in isolation, and then change the query statement or make other necessary changes, such as to indexes. You can start from the default `long_query_time`, then decrease it bit by bit to zero to find more and more queries. This method reveals the slowest queries first.

By default, this option does not log administrative statements and fast queries that don't use indexes, but you can log such queries by setting the `log-slow-admin-statements` and `log_queries_not_using_indexes` options, respectively.

One disadvantage of the slow query log is that you can't omit queries that you think don't need to be optimized. Writing the log to a table can help you screen out what you don't need to see because you can use WHERE clauses, grouping, and sorting to focus down on the queries that you think are important.

---

mysqldumpslow

The `mysqldumpslow` utility prints the contents of the slow query log in a kind of summary format. It groups queries, so if two queries are literally the same but use different parameters, they are printed once, together with the number of execution times. This means the utility treats queries such as SELECT * FROM t2 WHERE f1=1 and SELECT * FROM t2 WHERE f1=2 as the same because the actual value of the parameter f1 usually does not affect query execution time. This is especially convenient if you want to find slow queries that use a similar pattern in an application that runs thousands of them.

```
$mysqldumpslow /Users/apple/Applications/mysql-5.1/data512/mysqld512-apple-slow.log

Reading mysql slow query log from
/Users/apple/Applications/mysql-5.1/data512/mysqld512-apple-slow.log
```

```
Count: 3  Time=0.03s (0s)  Lock=0.03s (0s)  Rows=0.7 (2), root[root]@localhost
  SELECT * FROM t2 WHERE f1=N

Count: 1  Time=0.03s (0s)  Lock=0.00s (0s)  Rows=1.0 (1), root[root]@localhost
  select @@version_comment limit N

Count: 1  Time=0.02s (0s)  Lock=0.03s (0s)  Rows=3.0 (3), root[root]@localhost
  SELECT * FROM t2

Count: 3  Time=0.00s (0s)  Lock=0.00s (0s)  Rows=0.3 (1), root[root]@localhost
  select TEXT from test where ID=N

Count: 1  Time=0.00s (0s)  Lock=0.00s (0s)  Rows=3.0 (3), root[root]@localhost
  select * from t2
```

Note that although the utility is smart enough to group similar queries using different parameters, it treats queries that differ syntactically only in insignificant ways—such as using a different letter case or having different whitespace—as different queries.

Tools That Can Be Customized

Usually, just finding slow queries is not enough. You'll want to know such things as which error or warning was returned and how many rows were updated or selected. There are three ways to get this information: through your application, by writing a plug-in, or by using a proxy.

An application can use the methods described in "Getting Information About a Query" on page 16 to receive and log information; I won't offer details or examples, because they depend so much on your programming language and other context. If you are interested in query execution time, just measure it in the application before and after a `mysql_query` or `mysql_real_query` call. The advantage of this method is that it is very tunable. The disadvantage is that you need to modify the application, which isn't possible for people using third-party software.

If you want to write a MySQL server plug-in for auditing purposes, refer to the section "Writing Audit Plugins (*http://dev.mysql.com/doc/refman/5.5/en/writing-audit-plugins .html*)" in the MySQL Reference Manual. Once installed, a MySQL server plug-in becomes part of the MySQL server and can be accessed through SQL queries. Besides this advantage, the solution is completely independent from the application, does not need any changes to existing code, and can be used by multiple applications. The disadvantage is that it must be compiled for a specific version of the MySQL server and installed, which is not good if you distribute your plug-in to a wide audience.

The third solution is to use a scriptable proxy. A proxy is a daemon that sits between the server and client and can be configured independently from both the server and the client. Because it gets all traffic, you can do whatever you want with it. The advantages of this method are that you are completely independent from both the server and client, so you don't need to change anything that you have inherited from other people. The disadvantage is that the proxy adds an additional layer of processing, so it will slow

down the application and create a new single point of failure between the client and
server.

MySQL Proxy

MySQL Proxy is a scriptable daemon that supports the MySQL protocol and sits
between the MySQL server and the application. The application should be configured
in such a way that all queries go through the proxy. This generally just means setting
the proper hostname and port.

MySQL Proxy supports the Lua scripting language. It allows query and result set
rewriting, logging, load balancing, and much more. Here I'll discuss only logging
because that's what will help you debug slow queries.

For auditing purposes, you need to write a Lua script that saves the necessary information. A sample script that can imitate general query log behavior and, in addition,
save query execution time can look like:

```lua
function read_query( packet )
        if packet:byte() == proxy.COM_QUERY then
                print(os.date("%d%m%y %H:%M:%S") .. "\t"
                .. proxy.connection.server.thread_id
                .."\tQuery\t" .. packet:sub(2))

                proxy.queries:append(1, packet )
                return proxy.PROXY_SEND_QUERY
        end
end

function read_query_result(inj)
        print("Query execution time: " .. (inj.query_time / 1000) .. "ms,\t"
        .. "Response time: " .. (inj.response_time / 1000) .. "ms,\t"
        .. "Total time: " .. ((inj.query_time + inj.response_time) / 1000) .. "ms")
end
```

Call the script as follows:

```
$mysql-proxy --admin-username=admin --admin-password=foo \
--admin-lua-script=./lib/mysql-proxy/lua/admin.lua \
--proxy-address=127.0.0.1:4040 --proxy-backend-addresses=127.0.0.1:3355 \
--proxy-lua-script=`pwd`/general_log.lua
```

The results will look like:

```
$mysql-proxy --admin-username=admin --admin-password=foo \
--admin-lua-script=./lib/mysql-proxy/lua/admin.lua \
--proxy-address=127.0.0.1:4040 --proxy-backend-addresses=127.0.0.1:3355 \
--proxy-lua-script=`pwd`/general_log.lua
031111 01:51:11    20    Query    show tables
Query execution time: 376.57ms, Response time: 376.612ms, Total time: 753.182ms
031111 01:51:19    20    Query    select * from t1
Query execution time: 246.849ms,    Response time: 246.875ms, Total time: 493.724ms
031111 01:51:27    20    Query    select * from t3
Query execution time: 689.772ms,    Response time: 689.801ms, Total time: 1379.573ms
031111 01:51:39    20    Query    select count(*) from t4
Query execution time: 280.751ms,    Response time: 280.777ms, Total time: 561.528ms
```

You can adapt this script to your needs. MySQL Proxy has access to the query and result set both before and after its execution, which allows you to save much more information than a simple general logfile: errors, warnings, number of affected rows, query execution time, and even the full result set.

A lot of useful scripts can also be found at MySQL Forge (*http://forge.mysql.com/search .php?k=proxy*).

The MySQL Command-Line Interface

MySQL command-line client, also known as MySQL CLI, is the first tool you should use for testing most situations.

When queries do not work properly, the first suspect is a bug in the application. But every query can be affected by numerous issues, especially client and server options. So if you think you're sending the correct query but getting wrong results, test it in the MySQL CLI. This is the easiest and fastest way to confirm your guess.

When members of MySQL Support Bugs Verification Group suspect client bugs or (most often) misconfigurations, we always ask for queries that we can test in the MySQL CLI. Here I'll explain briefly why this is important and why other tools do not suit the first round of troubleshooting so well.

 Besides the regular client options, which affect every MySQL client application, Connector/J and Connector/ODBC have their own APIs and configurations. Queries can also be affected by conversion rules carried out by these interfaces. Therefore, if you use one of them, it becomes critical to test a problematic query in the MySQL CLI.

To test an application that gets results that are different from what you expect, start the MySQL CLI with the `--column-type-info` option, which prints information about data types:

```
$mysql --column-type-info test
Reading table information for completion of table and column names
You can turn off this feature to get a quicker startup with -A

Welcome to the MySQL monitor.  Commands end with ; or \g.
Your MySQL connection id is 415
Server version: 5.1.60-debug Source distribution

Copyright (c) 2000, 2011, Oracle and/or its affiliates. All rights reserved.

Oracle is a registered trademark of Oracle Corporation and/or its
affiliates. Other names may be trademarks of their respective
owners.

Type 'help;' or '\h' for help. Type '\c' to clear the current input statement.
```

```
mysql> SELECT * FROM t1;
Field     1:  `f1`
Catalog:      `def`
Database:     `test`
Table:        `t1`
Org_table:    `t1`
Type:         LONG
Collation:    binary (63)
Length:       11
Max_length:   2
Decimals:     0
Flags:        NOT_NULL PRI_KEY AUTO_INCREMENT NUM PART_KEY

Field     2:  `f2`
Catalog:      `def`
Database:     `test`
Table:        `t1`
Org_table:    `t1`
Type:         BLOB
Collation:    latin1_swedish_ci (8)
Length:       65535
Max_length:   32
Decimals:     0
Flags:        BLOB


+----+----------------------------------+
| f1 | f2                               |
+----+----------------------------------+
|  1 | f9f760a2dc91dfaf1cbc95046b249a3b |
|  2 | e81077a403cc27525fdbb587451e7935 |
|  3 | a003a1256c0178e0c4d37a063ad1786b |
|  4 | 2447565c49917f2daeaac192614eabe8 |
|  6 | 6bfb21c57cc3a8de22dc4dbf635fdc77 |
|  7 | 2d9f5350ba5b914a8f4abf31b5ae975c |
|  8 | 57e87a3c55d053b5ab428f5da7f6ba28 |
|  9 | ad2ede5e02ce1da95dcd8f71426d5e7b |
| 13 | 65400ab09cdc725ec5bafe2ac4f5045d |
| 14 | 48f1b1e99041365a74444f75a6689d64 |
| 15 | 1f6c558fe2c492f1da2ebfb42d9f53dc |
| 16 | ff931f7ac8c8035a929dc35fee444332 |
| 17 | f26f6b6e8d16ae5603cf8c02409f4bb5 |
| 18 | 239ca93bf7b5fd82a53e731004cba761 |
| 19 | 1f985d1fe9efa14453a964e2c4657ab5 |
| 20 | 1d599460b91f2d892c024fe5a64f7d6d |
+----+----------------------------------+
16 rows in set (0.09 sec)
```

This output tells you basic meta-information about the field, such as its data type and collation—information that may be changed by configuration options or application settings. By running it in the MySQL CLI, you can see what the query would normally do on the server, and you can guess there's a problem if the information received by the server from the application is different. Let's examine this output line by line.

```
mysql> SELECT `name` FROM `t1`;
Field   1:  `name`
```

The preceding output shows the name of a field.

```
Catalog:    `def`
```

The catalog name, which is always def.

```
Database:   `test`
```

The database currently being used.

```
Table:      `t1`
```

The table name, but the output shows the alias of the table when you use a syntax such as select *field_name* from *table_name* as *alias_name*.

```
Org_table:  `t1`
```

The original table name, which is useful to know if the previous line showed an alias.

```
Type:       VAR_STRING
```

The preceding line shows the field type.

```
Collation:  latin1_swedish_ci (8)
```

The collation.

```
Length:     255
```

The field length as defined in the table's definition.

```
Max_length: 5
```

The length of the largest value in the field, in the result set that was returned.

```
Decimals:   0
```

The number of decimals in the field, if it is an integer type.

```
Flags:
```

Field flags, if any. For instance, a primary key field will have the flags PRI_KEY and AUTO_INCREMENT.

```
+-------+
| name  |
+-------+
| sveta |
+-------+
1 row in set (0.00 sec)
```

The result set of the query.

What if your favorite MySQL client is something other than the MySQL CLI? You can test there, but remember that it may introduce side effects. This is particularly true of GUI clients. For example, if the client uses JDBC, it is affected by its configuration, which wouldn't affect the MySQL CLI. Other clients have preconfigured character sets, such as MySQL Workbench, which supports only UTF-8. Such a setup prevents you from testing another character set. Some clients (Workbench again) disconnect and reconnect after each query. Others can be affected by small thread buffers, which is common for web-based clients. Sometimes you can reconfigure the client, but when in doubt, it's much easier to switch to the command line and try the query in the MySQL CLI.

One of the strengths of the MySQL CLI is that it's very transparent in regard to options: you can always see and tune its configuration. Like every piece of software, admittedly, the MySQL CLI could have a bug. But the tool is in regular, heavy use by millions of users and actively used internally at Oracle, so the chances that you'll be affected by a bug in it is very low.

 All of the connectors in their unconfigured state, with the exception of Connector/PHP, start with `character_set_client` set to `UTF8` and `character_set_results` set to NULL. This is actually a "debugging" mode regarding charsets and is not recommended in a command-line client.

The reason behind this behavior is to let the driver logic determine the best way of displaying and storing results to or from the client and to avoid "double-conversion" bugs, which are rather common, by preventing the server from converting textual results into charset results. However, this trick does not work on ad-hoc queries, such as `SHOW CREATE TABLE`, where it should treat `BINARY` as `UTF8`, or `SELECT varbinary_col FROM some_table`, where it really should be binary, or with `SELECT CONCAT(char_field1, 1) AS a` where a will have `BINARY` flag set.

Thus, all of the connectors have some sort of workaround in their connection options that tells the driver to treat function results as `UTF8` instead of `BINARY` strings. Also, even though each connector has its own default encoding, they issue `SET NAMES UTF8`. This is mostly to avoid the default behavior of the *libmysqlclient* library, which sets all character-set-related variables to `latin1`.

- If you think a query should run fine but it is giving you unexpected results, before you consider the possibility of a bug in the MySQL server code, try the query in the MySQL CLI.

I love automation. When I create tests for bug reports, I use a script that runs MySQL Test Framework tests (see "MySQL Test Framework" on page 216) in a bunch of MySQL server distributions. This helps me to test a problem in many versions with single a command.

But once this habit played a bad joke on me. I tested one of the bug reports and could not repeat it. I spent a lot of time communicating with the reporter and tried many options without any luck. I relied entirely on our test suite and didn't suspect that the client could be introducing side effects. Then my colleague tried the test case in the MySQL CLI and got the absolute same results as the original reporter. The bug was confirmed and fixed.

This experience shows how dangerous it is to ignore possible client differences and how important it is to try the MySQL CLI before anything else.

Effects of the Environment

I already discussed some effects of environments such as concurrent threads, the operating system, hardware, concurrently running software, and the MySQL server and client options in this book. But a query, even if it is running in a single client connected to a dedicated MySQL server, can also be affected by the context in which it is run.

When you call a query from a stored procedure, function, trigger, or event, these contexts can override current session options with their own defaults. Therefore, if you encounter a problem you can't explain, try the same query outside of the routine. If the results are different, check the routine's character set and SQL mode. Examine the body of the routine to check whether all necessary objects exist and whether a variable that can affect the query was set. Another environment variable that matters is `time_zone`, which affects the results of time functions such as `NOW()` and `CURDATE()`.

- If a query does not work properly, check the environment in which it was called.

Sandboxes

A *sandbox* is an isolated environment for running an application, where it cannot affect anything outside of that environment. Throughout this book, I've been encouraging you to "try" various configuration options and changes to databases. But some such "tries" can slow down the application or even crash the application or the database. This is not what most users want. Instead, you can use a sandbox to isolate the system you're testing in its own environment, where anything you do wrong doesn't matter.

In the MySQL world, Giuseppe Maxia introduced this term by creating a tool named the MySQL Sandbox. I will describe the MySQL Sandbox and how it can be helpful a bit later, but here I want to briefly show some variants of sandboxes.

The simplest way to safely test queries on a table is to make a copy, so that the original table is secured and can be used by the application as usual while you are be experimenting with the copy. You also won't have to worry about reverting changes that you inadvertently make:

```
CREATE TABLE test_problem LIKE problem;
INSERT INTO test_problem SELECT * FROM problem;
```

One good thing with this solution is that you can copy just part of the data, using WHERE to limit the number of rows. For example, suppose you are testing a complex query and are sure that it is correctly executing one of its WHERE clauses. You can limit your test table to items meeting that condition when you create it, and then have a smaller table on which to test the query:

```
INSERT INTO test_problem SELECT FROM problem WHERE condition]
```

You can then simplify the query as well by removing that condition. This can save a lot of time when the original table is huge. This technique is also useful when the WHERE clause worked properly but a GROUP BY grouping or ORDER BY sort is wrong.

If a query accesses more than one table or you just want to test queries on different tables, it makes sense to create a whole separate database:

```
CREATE DATABASE sandbox;
USE sandbox;
CREATE TABLE problem LIKE production.problem;
INSERT INTO problem SELECT * FROM production.problem [WHERE ...]
```

In this case, you will have an environment absolutely reproducing your production database, but you won't harm anything, even if you damage rows in the copy.

These two methods are good for query rewriting and similar problems. But if the server crashes or uses a lot of resources, it's best not to test anything on it. Instead, set up a development server just for testing purposes and copy the data from the production server. This also can help if you are planning an upgrade or want to check whether a particular bug is fixed in a newer version of MySQL.

When you create an application in the first place, you can just upgrade the MySQL server on your development machine. But if the application has been running for a long time and you need to test how a particular MySQL version affects actual data, such an upgrade in a sandbox can be hard to create manually. In this case, the MySQL Sandbox is the best choice.

To create the installation in the first place, you need to have a MySQL package without an installer (such as those that end with *tar.gz* for Linux), of the desired version and a copy of MySQL Sandbox, available for download from *https://launchpad.net/mysql -sandbox*. Create the sandbox from the MySQL package with a command such as the following:

```
$make_sandbox mysql-5.4.2-beta-linux-x86_64-glibc23.tar.gz
unpacking /mysql-5.4.2-beta-linux-x86_64-glibc23.tar.gz
...
```

```
The MySQL Sandbox,  version 3.0.05
(C) 2006,2007,2008,2009 Giuseppe Maxia
installing with the following parameters:
upper_directory  = /users/ssmirnova/sandboxes
...
........ sandbox server started
Your sandbox server was installed in
$HOME/sandboxes/msb_5_4_2
```

Once installed, you should stop the server and change the configuration file so it corresponds to your production configuration, then restart it and load a backup of your production databases. Now you are ready to test safely. This method is very useful when you need to quickly check an application on several versions of MySQL, for example, to determine whether a bug is fixed.

You can have as many sandboxes as you want and test different aspects of MySQL and your databases without additional effort. You can even create a replication sandbox—a sandbox that contains a master server along with as many slave servers as you choose:

```
$make_replication_sandbox mysql-5.1.51-osx10.4-i686.tar.gz

installing and starting master
installing slave 1
installing slave 2
starting slave 1
... sandbox server started
starting slave 2
....... sandbox server started
initializing slave 1
initializing slave 2
replication directory installed in $HOME/sandboxes/rsandbox_5_1_51

$cd $HOME/sandboxes/rsandbox_5_1_51

$./m
Welcome to the MySQL monitor.  Commands end with ; or \g.
Your MySQL connection id is 4
Server version: 5.1.51-log MySQL Community Server (GPL)

Copyright (c) 2000, 2010, Oracle and/or its affiliates. All rights reserved.
This software comes with ABSOLUTELY NO WARRANTY. This is free software,
and you are welcome to modify and redistribute it under the GPL v2 license

Type 'help;' or '\h' for help. Type '\c' to clear the current input statement.

master [localhost] {msandbox} ((none)) > \q
Bye

$./s1
Welcome to the MySQL monitor.  Commands end with ; or \g.
Your MySQL connection id is 5
Server version: 5.1.51-log MySQL Community Server (GPL)
```

Type 'help;' or '\h' for help. Type '\c' to clear the current input statement.

```
slave1 [localhost] {msandbox} ((none)) > SHOW SLAVE STATUS\G
*************************** 1. row ***************************
               Slave_IO_State: Waiting for master to send event
                  Master_Host: 127.0.0.1
                  Master_User: rsandbox
                  Master_Port: 26366
                Connect_Retry: 60
              Master_Log_File: mysql-bin.000001
          Read_Master_Log_Pos: 1690
               Relay_Log_File: mysql_sandbox26367-relay-bin.000002
                Relay_Log_Pos: 1835
        Relay_Master_Log_File: mysql-bin.000001
             Slave_IO_Running: Yes
            Slave_SQL_Running: Yes
              Replicate_Do_DB:
          Replicate_Ignore_DB:
           Replicate_Do_Table:
       Replicate_Ignore_Table:
      Replicate_Wild_Do_Table:
  Replicate_Wild_Ignore_Table:
                   Last_Errno: 0
                   Last_Error:
                 Skip_Counter: 0
          Exec_Master_Log_Pos: 1690
              Relay_Log_Space: 2003
              Until_Condition: None
               Until_Log_File:
                Until_Log_Pos: 0
           Master_SSL_Allowed: No
           Master_SSL_CA_File:
           Master_SSL_CA_Path:
              Master_SSL_Cert:
            Master_SSL_Cipher:
               Master_SSL_Key:
        Seconds_Behind_Master: 0
Master_SSL_Verify_Server_Cert: No
                Last_IO_Errno: 0
                Last_IO_Error:
               Last_SQL_Errno: 0
               Last_SQL_Error:
1 row in set (0.00 sec)

slave1 [localhost] {msandbox} ((none)) > \q
Bye

$./stop_all
executing "stop" on slave 1
executing "stop" on slave 2
executing "stop" on master
```

Once the sandbox is running, experiment with its options.

One gorgeous advantage of using the MySQL Sandbox for a single server is when you need to compare many environments. If you are working with only one version of software on one type of system, you can just load production data from a backup of MySQL onto your development machine. With replication, this would not work, because you will need at least two MySQL instances. And a replication sandbox can dramatically save time, even if you don't care about versions or custom environments, because it takes only a couple of minutes to install and set up as many MySQL instances as you need.

 Tools from Workbench Utilities set can help to create a sandbox copy of your production database.

mysqldbcopy
    Copies a database, either creating a new database on the same server under a different name or placing the database on a different server with the same name or a different one

mysqlreplicate
    Configures and starts replication among two servers

mysqlserverclone
    Starts a new instance of a running server

Errors and Logs

Another important troubleshooting technique sounds simple: read and analyze information from the server. This is a very important step. In Chapter 1, I discussed tools that can help you get and analyze information, along with examples. Here I want to add details I skipped before.

Error Information, Again

Error messages are key and should never be ignored. You can find information about errors in the MySQL Reference Manual at *http://dev.mysql.com/doc/refman/5.5/en/error -handling.html*. This page lists client and server error messages, but omits messages specific to a storage engine. Nor does it explain errors that come from the operating system. Strings of information describing operating system errors can be derived through the *perror* utility (see "Retrieving Error Strings Through perror" on page 19).

Another very important tool is the *mysqld* error logfile, which contains information about table corruption, server crashes, replication errors, and much more. Always have it turned on, and analyze it when you encounter a problem. A log from an application cannot always replace the MySQL server error log, because the latter can contain problems and details not visible to the application.

Crashes

I discussed crashes and a general troubleshooting sequence applicable to them in "When the Server Does Not Answer" on page 39. Start by using the techniques described in the previous section: look in the error logfile, and analyze its content. This works in most cases, but this section discusses what to do if the error log does not contain enough information to help you troubleshoot the crash.

The latest versions of the MySQL server can print a backtrace, even in release builds. Therefore, if the error logfile does not contain a backtrace, check whether the *mysqld* binary is stripped.[1] (On Unix-style systems, the `file` command will report whether an executable file is stripped.) If it is, replace the *mysqld* binary with the one that came with your MySQL distribution. If you built it yourself, compile a version with symbols for use in testing.

- Check whether the *mysqld* binary contains symbols, e.g., is not stripped.

In some cases you may need to run a debug binary. This is a file named *mysqld-debug*, located in the *bin* directory under the MySQL installation root.

The debug binary contains assertions that can help to catch the problem at an earlier stage. In this case, you probably will get a better error message because the error will be caught when the server does something wrong, rather than when a memory leak occurs. Using the release binary, you don't get an error message until the memory leak actually leads to a crash.

The price for using debug binary is a performance decrease.

If the error logfile does not have enough information about the crash to help you find the source of the problem, try the two methods that follow. In any case, always work from evidence, as I did when discussing the backtrace from the error logfile in "When the Server Does Not Answer" on page 39. Don't just make intuitive guesses, because if you try to solve a problem using a wrong guess, you can introduce even more problems.

- Always test. Any guess can be wrong.

Core file

Core files contain the memory image of a process and are created (if the operating system is configured to do so) when a process terminates abnormally. You can obtain a core file by starting the MySQL server with the `core` option, but first you should make sure the operating system allows the file to be created.

To debug using a core file, you need to be acquainted with the MySQL source code. The "MySQL Internals" page on MySQL Forge (*http://forge.mysql.com/wiki/MySQL*

---

1. I have seen setups where the customers manually stripped the *mysqld* binary to achieve better performance, so I considered it important to include this in the book.

_Internals) is good start. I also recommend the book *Expert MySQL* by Dr. Charles A. Bell (Apress). You can also find useful information in the books *Understanding MySQL Internals* by Sasha Pachev (O'Reilly) and *MySQL 5.1 Plugin Development* by Andrew Hutchings and Sergei Golubchik (Packt). At some point, of course, you have to dive into the MySQL source code itself.

I won't describe how to deal with core files here in detail, because that would require a whole book about the MySQL source code, but I will show a small example.

To enable the creation of core files, start *mysqld* with the `core` option and adjust the operating system to allow core files of unlimited size to be created. Different operating systems use different tools to control the creation of core files. For example, Solaris uses *coreadm*, whereas on my Mac OS X Tiger box I have to edit */etc/hostconfig*. On Windows, you should have debugging symbols for both *mysqld* and the operating system. On Unix-style systems, the simplest method is the `ulimit -c` command, which should be set to `unlimited`, but consult your OS manual to find out if you need a configuration change somewhere else too.

After the core file is created, you can access its content using a debugger. I use `gdb` here, but this is not required; use your favorite debugger.

```
$gdb ../libexec/mysqld var/log/main.bugXXXXX/mysqld.1/data/core.21965
```

The command line contains the name of the `gdb` command followed by the path to the *mysqld* executable file and the path to core file itself.

```
GNU gdb (GDB) 7.3.1
Copyright (C) 2011 Free Software Foundation, Inc.
License GPLv3+: GNU GPL version 3 or later
<http://gnu.org/licenses/gpl.html7gt;
This is free software: you are free to change and redistribute it.
There is NO WARRANTY, to the extent permitted by law.  Type "show copying"
and "show warranty" for details.
This GDB was configured as "i686-pc-linux-gnu".
For bug reporting instructions, please see:
<http://www.gnu.org/software/gdb/bugs/7gt;...
Reading symbols from /users/ssmirnova/build/mysql-5.1/libexec/mysqld...done.
[New LWP 21984]
[New LWP 21970]
[New LWP 21972]
[New LWP 21974]
[New LWP 21965]
[New LWP 21973]
[New LWP 21967]
[New LWP 21971]
[New LWP 21968]
[New LWP 21969]

warning: Can't read pathname for load map: Input/output error.
[Thread debugging using libthread_db enabled]
Core was generated by `/users/ssmirnova/build/mysql-5.1/libexec/mysqld
--defaults-group-suffix=.1 --de'.
Program terminated with signal 11, Segmentation fault.
```

```
#0  0x00832416 in __kernel_vsyscall ()
(gdb)
```

The backtrace is the first thing we need:

```
(gdb) bt
#0  0x00832416 in __kernel_vsyscall ()
#1  0x008ce023 in pthread_kill () from /lib/libpthread.so.0
#2  0x085aa6ad in my_write_core (sig=11) at stacktrace.c:310
#3  0x0824f412 in handle_segfault (sig=11) at mysqld.cc:2537
#4  7lt;signal handler called>
#5  0x084bce68 in mach_read_from_2 (b=0xfffffffe 7lt;Address 0xfffffffe out of
bounds>) at ../../storage/innobase/include/mach0data.ic:68
#6  0x084cfdd6 in rec_get_next_offs (rec=0x0, comp=1) at
../../storage/innobase/include/rem0rec.ic:278
#7  0x084e32c9 in row_search_for_mysql (buf=0x284d7b0 "\371\001", mode=2,
prebuilt=0xb732de68, match_mode=1, direction=0) at row/row0sel.c:3727
#8  0x08476177 in ha_innobase::index_read (this=0xb281d660, buf=0xb281d7b0
"\371\001", key_ptr=0xb2822198 "", key_len=0, find_flag=HA_READ_KEY_EXACT) at
handler/ha_innodb.cc:4443
#9  0x0838f13c in handler::index_read_map (this=0xb281d660, buf=0xb281d7b0
"\371\001", key=0xb2822198 "", keypart_map=0, find_flag=HA_READ_KEY_EXACT) at
handler.h:1390
#10 0x082dd38f in join_read_always_key (tab=0xb28219e8) at sql_select.cc:11691
#11 0x082da39f in sub_select (join=0xb2822468, join_tab=0xb28219e8,
end_of_records=false) at sql_select.cc:11141
#12 0x082da79f in do_select (join=0xb2822468, fields=0xb2834954, table=0x0,
procedure=0x0) at sql_select.cc:10898
#13 0x082f1bef in JOIN::exec (this=0xb2822468) at sql_select.cc:2199
#14 0x082090db in subselect_single_select_engine::exec (this=0xb28358a0) at
item_subselect.cc:1958
<skipped>
```

From this output, you already have a bit of information. If you want to learn more about using core files, turn to man core, debugger documentation, the MySQL internals manual, the books I mentioned, and the source code.

General log file

Another way to catch what is going on is to use the two solutions I mentioned in "Tools That Can Be Customized" on page 175: the general logfile and the use of a proxy solution. As the concept is similar here, I'll show how to catch errors with the general query log and let you deduce proxy solutions on your own if you decide to use one. I'll use the example from "When the Server Does Not Answer" on page 39 again, but in this case I'll run it on my MacBook. The error log contains:

```
091002 16:49:48 - mysqld got signal 10 ;
This could be because you hit a bug. It is also possible that this binary
or one of the libraries it was linked against is corrupt, improperly built,
or misconfigured. This error can also be caused by malfunctioning hardware.
We will try our best to scrape up some info that will hopefully help diagnose
the problem, but since we have already crashed, something is definitely wrong
and this may fail.
```

```
key_buffer_size=8384512
read_buffer_size=131072
max_used_connections=1
max_connections=100
threads_connected=1
It is possible that mysqld could use up to
key_buffer_size + (read_buffer_size + sort_buffer_size)*max_connections = 225784
K
```

This build does not print backtrace information. If I'm in a situation where I can't use the debug version of MySQL server, how can I know what is going on?

Here is the place where the general query log can help again. MySQL writes each query to this log before executing it. Therefore, we can find information about a crash in this log. First, set up logging:

```
mysql> SET GLOBAL general_log=1;
Query OK, 0 rows affected (0.00 sec)
mysql> SET GLOBAL log_output='table';
Query OK, 0 rows affected (0.00 sec)
```

Wait until the crash happens again, and then check the contents of the general log:

```
mysql> SELECT argument FROM mysql.general_log ORDER BY event_time
desc \G
*************************** 1. row ***************************
argument: Access denied for user 'MySQL_Instance_Manager'@'localhost'
(using password: YES)
*************************** 2. row ***************************
argument: select 1 from `t1` where `c0` <> (SELECT geometrycollectionfromwkb(`c3`)
FROM `t1`)
```

The second row in this output is the query that crashed the server.

- Use the general query log if the error log does not contain enough information about the server crash.

The only situation in which this technique would not help is when the crash happens while the MySQL server is writing into the general query log, or even before it. You can try logging to a file instead of a table if this happens. Proxy and application-side solutions are not affected by this issue.

Information-Gathering Tools

Information directs all troubleshooting. It is very important to know what is happening in the server process. I have discussed ways to get this information throughout this book, but here I will add some missing details about the tools discussed.

Information Schema

INFORMATION_SCHEMA is a schema that provides information about database metadata. All SHOW queries are now mapped to SELECT statements from INFORMATION_SCHEMA tables.

You can query INFORMATION_SCHEMA tables like any other table; this is their great advantage over other tools. The only problem is that INFORMATION_SCHEMA tables are not optimized to work fast, so queries on them can be slow, especially on tables that contain information about many objects.

I won't describe each and every table here, because the MySQL Reference Manual contains a great deal of detail about their structure (see *http://dev.mysql.com/doc/ref man/5.6/en/information-schema.html*). Instead, I'll show a few queries to demonstrate the sort of useful information you can get from the INFORMATION_SCHEMA. You'll still need the user manual for details. I put the link to the 5.6 MySQL Reference Manual here because I mention a few tables introduced in this version.

To get an idea of what can be done with INFORMATION_SCHEMA, let's start by extracting an overview of how many tables in each storage engine are in current use. I'm excluding the mysql database from the list because all its tables always use the MyISAM storage engine.

```
mysql> SELECT count(*), engine FROM tables WHERE table_schema !=
'mysql' GROUP BY engine;
+----------+--------------------+
| count(*) | engine             |
+----------+--------------------+
|      255 | InnoDB             |
|       36 | MEMORY             |
|       14 | MyISAM             |
|       17 | PERFORMANCE_SCHEMA |
+----------+--------------------+
4 rows in set (4.64 sec)
```

This information can be useful if, for example, you want to choose a strategy for a daily backup.[2]

Another example is to get a list of the foreign keys that reference a particular table. This can be useful if you get error 150, Foreign key constraint is incorrectly formed, when accessing the parent table and have absolutely no idea which children it is linked to:

```
mysql> SELECT KU.CONSTRAINT_SCHEMA, KU.CONSTRAINT_NAME,
KU.TABLE_SCHEMA, KU.TABLE_NAME FROM TABLE_CONSTRAINTS AS TC JOIN
KEY_COLUMN_USAGE AS KU ON(TC.CONSTRAINT_NAME=KU.CONSTRAINT_NAME AND
TC.CONSTRAINT_SCHEMA=KU.CONSTRAINT_SCHEMA) WHERE CONSTRAINT_TYPE='FOREIGN KEY'
AND REFERENCED_TABLE_SCHEMA='collaborate2011' AND REFERENCED_TABLE_NAME='items'
and REFERENCED_COLUMN_NAME='id'\G
*************************** 1. row ***************************
CONSTRAINT_SCHEMA: collaborate2011
  CONSTRAINT_NAME: community_bugs_ibfk_1
    TABLE_SCHEMA: collaborate2011
      TABLE_NAME: community_bugs
```

2. MySQL supports different kinds of backups and ways to do them. When planning backups, you need to take into account their effect on tables, such as locking, which depends on the storage engine you use. I will touch on backups in "Backups" on page 221.

```
*************************** 2. row ***************************
CONSTRAINT_SCHEMA: collaborate2011
  CONSTRAINT_NAME: customers_bugs_ibfk_1
     TABLE_SCHEMA: collaborate2011
       TABLE_NAME: customers_bugs
*************************** 3. row ***************************
CONSTRAINT_SCHEMA: collaborate2011
  CONSTRAINT_NAME: items_links_ibfk_1
     TABLE_SCHEMA: collaborate2011
       TABLE_NAME: items_links
*************************** 4. row ***************************
CONSTRAINT_SCHEMA: collaborate2011
  CONSTRAINT_NAME: mysql_issues_ibfk_1
     TABLE_SCHEMA: collaborate2011
       TABLE_NAME: mysql_issues
*************************** 5. row ***************************
CONSTRAINT_SCHEMA: collaborate2011
  CONSTRAINT_NAME: oracle_srs_ibfk_1
     TABLE_SCHEMA: collaborate2011
       TABLE_NAME: oracle_srs
5 rows in set (9.58 sec)
```

In this output, you can see that five tables reference the table items as a parent. So if a query that runs on the items table fails with error 150, you can quickly find all its children and fix the data, causing the query to execute without that problem.

Now that you have an idea of what INFORMATION_SCHEMA tables are, we can switch to specifics.

InnoDB Information Schema Tables

We already discussed the INNODB_TRX, INNODB_LOCKS, and INNODB_LOCK_WAITS tables in "INFORMATION_SCHEMA Tables" on page 99 in the context of concurrency troubleshooting. Here I'll also give a quick overview of other tables.

INNODB_TRX provides a lot of detail about currently running transactions. You can use it even when locking and concurrency are not an issue, but in the context of locking problems, you can do such things as find transactions that run for long time (replace '00:30:00' with a relevant time for your situation):

```
SELECT TRX_ID, TRX_MYSQL_THREAD_ID FROM INNODB_TRX
WHERE TIMEDIFF(NOW(),TRX_STARTED) > '00:30:00';
```

You can find out which threads are waiting on locks:

```
SELECT TRX_ID, TRX_MYSQL_THREAD_ID, TRX_REQUESTED_LOCK_ID, TRX_WAIT_STARTED
FROM INNODB_TRX
WHERE TRX_STATE = 'LOCK WAIT';
```

or are waiting on a lock longer than a specific time:

```
SELECT TRX_ID, TRX_MYSQL_THREAD_ID, TRX_REQUESTED_LOCK_ID, TRX_WAIT_STARTED
FROM INNODB_TRX
WHERE TIMEDIFF(NOW(),TRX_WAIT_STARTED) > '00:30:00';
```

To get an overview of how large your transactions are, retrieve the number of rows locked (TRX_ROWS_LOCKED), the size of lock structures in memory (TRX_LOCK_MEMORY_BYTES), or the rows modified (TRX_ROWS_MODIFIED):

```
SELECT TRX_ID, TRX_MYSQL_THREAD_ID, TRX_ROWS_MODIFIED
FROM INNODB_TRX ORDER BY TRX_ROWS_MODIFIED DESC;
```

You can also check the transaction isolation level, whether foreign key checks are turned on, and other information.

 Note that transactions appear in INNODB_TRX only after they open an InnoDB table. Exceptions are transactions started with START TRANSACTION WITH CONSISTENT SNAPSHOT, which has the same effect as a START TRANSACTION query followed by a SELECT from every InnoDB table.

Tables whose names begin with INNODB_CMP show how well InnoDB uses compression. Thus, INNODB_CMP and INNODB_CMP_RESET contain status information about compressed tables, whereas INNODB_CMPMEM and INNODB_CMPMEM_RESET contain status information about compressed pages in the InnoDB buffer pool.

The only extra feature added by the _RESET versions of these calls is that they reset statistics in all INNODB_CMP tables to zero after being queried. Therefore, if you want repeatable statistics, query the _RESET tables, and if you want statistics since startup, query only INNODB_CMP and INNODB_CMPMEM.

Since version 5.6.2, tables beginning with INNODB_SYS and an INNODB_METRICS table also exist. The INNODB_SYS tables contain information about how InnoDB tables are stored in the internal dictionary and replace the InnoDB Table Monitor. A great explanation and some examples of their use can be found at the InnoDB Team blog (*http://blogs .innodb.com/wp/2011/04/information-schema-system-table/*). The INNODB_METRICS table contains all the data related to performance and resource usage counters in a single place. To get these statistics, you need to enable a module. It's worth studying these counters because they can help you analyze what happens inside the InnoDB storage engine. Again, an explanation and examples are at the InnoDB Team blog (*http://blogs .innodb.com/wp/2011/04/information-schema-system-table/*).

InnoDB Monitors

We already discussed InnoDB Monitors in "SHOW ENGINE INNODB STATUS and InnoDB Monitors" on page 96. Here is a summary of that section and a few extra useful details.

To enable InnoDB monitors, create InnoDB tables named innodb_monitor, innodb_lock_monitor, innodb_table_monitor, and innodb_tablespace_monitor. These enable periodical writes to STDERR output from standard, lock, table, and tablespace monitors, respectively.

It doesn't matter which structure you define for these tables or what database you add them to, so long as they use the InnoDB storage engine.[3]

The monitors are turned off on shutdown. To re-enable them on startup, you need to re-create the tables. Put DROP and CREATE statements into your init-file option if you want them created automatically.

The standard monitor contains something similar to the output that follows, which comes from version 5.5 of MySQL. I'll break up the output with explanations.

```
mysql> SHOW ENGINE INNODB STATUS\G
*************************** 1. row ***************************
  Type: InnoDB
  Name:
Status:
=====================================
110910 14:56:10 INNODB MONITOR OUTPUT
=====================================
Per second averages calculated from the last 7 seconds
-----------------
BACKGROUND THREAD
-----------------
```

As the last text in the preceding output shows, this output concerns work done by the main background thread.

```
srv_master_thread loops: 95 1_second, 89 sleeps, 7 10_second, 36 background, 36 flush
```

The numbers count activity from InnoDB startup. The five numbers in the preceding output show, respectively, the number of iterations of the "once per second" loop, calls to sleep by the "once per second" loop, iterations by the "once per 10 seconds" loop, iterations of the loop named "background_loop" that runs background operations when there is currently no user activity, and iterations of the loop bounced by the "flush_loop" label. All these loops are run by the master thread, which does purge and other background operations.

```
srv_master_thread log flush and writes: 116
```

This shows how many times the log was written and flushed.

```
----------
SEMAPHORES
----------
```

Here begins information about internal semaphores. We touched on these a bit in Chapter 2. High numbers here can show slow disk I/O or high InnoDB contention. In the latter case, you could try decreasing innodb_thread_concurrency to see whether it causes an improvement. Note that these numbers are taken since the most recent

---

3. innodb_monitor, innodb_lock_monitor, innodb_table_monitor, and innodb_tablespace_monitor are not supposed to be used as real tables, but instead provide a method to tell InnoDB to write debugging output into STDERR. Although you can use them as any other table, be prepared for their content to disappear after server restart.

InnoDB startup, so information here about waits does not mean that there are actual waits. You need to query the Performance Schema or check the mutex status to identify whether waits are occurring at the moment.

```
OS WAIT ARRAY INFO: reservation count 519, signal count 476
```

This begins a section showing global wait array information. The first number is a count of cell reservations since the array was created, and the second shows how many times an object has been signaled.

```
Mutex spin waits 212, rounds 6360, OS waits 169
```

The preceding line shows the number of spin waits on mutex calls, the number of iterations of a spin loop, and the number of waits for OS system calls.

```
RW-shared spins 171, rounds 5130, OS waits 171
```

This line shows the number of spin waits on rw-latches that resulted during shared (read) locks, the number of iterations of a spin loop, and the number of waits for OS system calls.

```
RW-excl spins 55, rounds 5370, OS waits 151
```

This line shows the number of spin waits on rw-latches that resulted during exclusive (write) locks, the number of iterations of a spin loop, and the number of waits for OS system calls.

```
Spin rounds per wait: 30.00 mutex, 30.00 RW-shared, 97.64 RW-excl
```

This shows, for each mutex, the number of iterations of a spin loop per wait for OS system calls.

The following is an example of how values in this section change during the execution of an UPDATE query:

```
SEMAPHORES
----------
OS WAIT ARRAY INFO: reservation count 1197, signal count 1145
--Thread 6932 has waited at trx0rec.c line 1253 for 0.00 seconds the semaphore:
X-lock (wait_ex) on RW-latch at 03CD2028 created in file buf0buf.c line 898
a writer (thread id 6932) has reserved it in mode  wait exclusive
number of readers 1, waiters flag 0, lock_word: ffffffff
Last time read locked in file buf0flu.c line 1292
Last time write locked in file ..\..\..\mysqlcom-pro-5.5.13\storage\innobase\trx\
trx0rec.c line 1253
Mutex spin waits 1163, rounds 33607, OS waits 659
RW-shared spins 248, rounds 7440, OS waits 248
RW-excl spins 47, rounds 8640, OS waits 280
Spin rounds per wait: 28.90 mutex, 30.00 RW-shared, 183.83 RW-excl
```

The preceding output was taken when the query started executing and tried to reserve a mutex.

```
----------
SEMAPHORES
----------
```

```
OS WAIT ARRAY INFO: reservation count 1324, signal count 1246
--Thread 5680 has waited at buf0buf.c line 2766 for 0.00 seconds the semaphore:
Mutex at 038BE990 created file buf0buf.c line 1208, lock var 1
waiters flag 1
Mutex spin waits 1248, rounds 36397, OS waits 745
RW-shared spins 252, rounds 7560, OS waits 252
RW-excl spins 53, rounds 9750, OS waits 310
Spin rounds per wait: 29.16 mutex, 30.00 RW-shared, 183.96 RW-excl
```

This was taken a bit later when the mutex defined in the file *buf0buf.c* at line 2766 was created.

In the semaphores section, you should examine whether values become large and if many operations are waiting for mutexes for a long time.

```
------------
TRANSACTIONS
------------
```

We thoroughly discussed the transactions section in "Transactions" on page 63, so here I'll only touch on a few things.

```
Trx id counter 4602
```

The preceding line is the number of the next transaction.

```
Purge done for trx's n:o < 4249 undo n:o < 0
```

This shows that all transactions with numbers less than 4249 were purged from the history list, which contains entries used to provide consistent reads for running transactions that accessed the same tables as the transactions in the list, but before their modification at commit time. The second number shows how many records with an undo number less than 4249 were purged from the history.

```
History list length 123
```

This is the length of the history list (undo log records for committed transactions that are not purged). If this value grows large, you can expect a performance decrease. There is no linear relation, because purge performance also depends on the total size of the transaction data this list keeps, so it's difficult to give a precise example of a large value that will cause a performance decrease. A large value in this list can also mean you have long-running transactions that aren't closed, because entries from here are removed only when no transaction refers to an entry.

```
LIST OF TRANSACTIONS FOR EACH SESSION:
---TRANSACTION 4601, not started, OS thread id 33716224
MySQL thread id 6906, query id 123 localhost root
show engine innodb status
```

The preceding lines start a list of all currently running transactions. I described this in detail in "Transactions" on page 63, so I won't repeat the explanation here.

```
--------
FILE I/O
--------
```

This starts a section about internal InnoDB threads that perform various I/O operations. You can use this to find out how many I/O operations InnoDB performs. The rates show how effective they are.

```
I/O thread 0 state: waiting for i/o request (insert buffer thread)
I/O thread 1 state: waiting for i/o request (log thread)
I/O thread 2 state: waiting for i/o request (read thread)
I/O thread 3 state: waiting for i/o request (read thread)
I/O thread 4 state: waiting for i/o request (read thread)
I/O thread 5 state: waiting for i/o request (read thread)
I/O thread 6 state: waiting for i/o request (write thread)
I/O thread 7 state: waiting for i/o request (write thread)
I/O thread 8 state: waiting for i/o request (write thread)
I/O thread 9 state: waiting for i/o request (write thread)
```

These show the current status of internal InnoDB threads. The thread name is in parentheses on each line.

```
Pending normal aio reads: 1 [1, 0, 0, 0] , aio writes: 9 [6, 0, 3, 0] ,
 ibuf aio reads: 0, log i/o's: 0, sync i/o's: 1
Pending flushes (fsync) log: 0; buffer pool: 0
```

This is information about pending operations. **aio** is an abbreviation for asynchronous input-output.

```
7204 OS file reads, 10112 OS file writes, 711 OS fsyncs
```

These show total statistics since InnoDB startup.

```
21.71 reads/s, 16384 avg bytes/read, 78.13 writes/s, 3.00 fsyncs/s
```

These show total statistics since the most recent display.

```
-------------------------------------
INSERT BUFFER AND ADAPTIVE HASH INDEX
-------------------------------------
```

As the name says, this starts a section about the insert buffer and adaptive hash statistics. Use this information to find out how effective they are.

```
Ibuf: size 1, free list len 0, seg size 2, 1724 merges
```

These are, respectively, the current size of the insert buffer index tree in pages, the length of the free list, the number of allocated pages in the file segment containing the insert buffer tree and header, and the number of pages that were merged.

```
merged operations:
 insert 15, delete mark 1709, delete 0
```

This shows the number of operations merged for index pages, divided up by type.

```
discarded operations:
 insert 0, delete mark 0, delete 0
```

This shows the number of operations discarded without merging because the tablespace or index was deleted.

```
Hash table size 195193, node heap has 1 buffer(s)
```

This shows the number of cells in the adaptive hash index table and the number of reserved buffer frames.

```
0.00 hash searches/s, 40.71 non-hash searches/s
```

This shows the number of successful adaptive hash index lookups and the number of searches down the B-tree when the adaptive hash index could not be used. These statistics are reset each time they are queried.

```
---
LOG
---
```

This starts a section of information about activity in the InnoDB log.

```
Log sequence number 2055193301
Log flushed up to   2055180837
Last checkpoint at  2054187263
```

These show the current log sequence number (LSN), the number up to which the LSN logfile was flushed, and the LSN of the most recent checkpoint. This information allows you to calculate the age of the checkpoint through the subtraction Log flushed up to - Last checkpoint at, or 993574 in this example. You need to make sure the checkpoint ages do not approach 77% of the value innodb_log_file_size * innodb_log_files_in_group, because at that ratio InnoDB considers the difference between the current log LSN and the LSN of the older page in the buffer pool to be too great and starts aggressive flushing. This can lead to a database freeze.

```
0 pending log writes, 0 pending chkp writes
357 log i/o's done, 1.29 log i/o's/second
```

These show the number of pending log writes, pending checkpoint writes, I/O operations since InnoDB started, and I/O operations per second since the most recent display.

```
----------------------
BUFFER POOL AND MEMORY
----------------------
```

This indicates the start of information about InnoDB buffer pool and memory usage. Use this to evaluate how effectively the InnoDB buffer pool is used.

```
Total memory allocated 49938432; in additional pool allocated 0
```

The preceding line shows the total amount of memory allocated and how much is allocated in the additional pool.

```
Dictionary memory allocated 23269
```

This shows the space in bytes occupied by the data dictionary table and index objects.

```
Buffer pool size   3008
Free buffers       0
```

This shows the size of the buffer pool in pages and the number of free buffers in it. Here you can see that the buffer is full, and it makes sense to increase it. In this case it was set to the default value on my machine, so I have room for an increase.

```
Database pages      3007
Old database pages 1090
Modified db pages   860
```

The InnoDB buffer pool stores objects in a list that uses the least recently used (LRU) algorithm with a midpoint insertion strategy. When a new block needs to be added, InnoDB puts it into the middle of the list. The least recently used block is removed from the list to free room for the new one. These statistics show the length of the current InnoDB buffer LRU queue, the length of the old LRU queue, and the number of pages that need to be flushed.

 The InnoDB midpoint insertion strategy actually manages two lists: a sublist of new (young) blocks that were accessed recently and a sublist of old blocks that were not accessed recently. Blocks from the old blocks sublist are candidates for eviction.

```
Pending reads 2
Pending writes: LRU 0, flush list 10, single page 0
```

The first line shows the number of pending read operations. The second shows the number of pages waiting to be flushed through the LRU algorithm, the number of pages waiting to be flushed in the BUF_FLUSH_LIST, and the number of pages waiting to be flushed in the BUF_FLUSH_SINGLE_PAGE list.[4]

```
Pages made young 3508, not young 0
16.71 youngs/s, 0.00 non-youngs/s
```

The first line shows the number of pages made young, followed by the number of those that were not made young, because they were first accessed recently. The second line shows rates per second since the most recent display of these values.

```
Pages read 7191, created 1871, written 9384
21.43 reads/s, 5.57 creates/s, 74.13 writes/s
```

The first line shows the number of read operations, the number of pages created in the pool but not yet read, and the number of write operations. The second line shows rates per second of these values.

```
No buffer pool page gets since the last printout
```

In one of my test outputs, I had not accessed the buffer pool since the most recent display. If I had, more information would be printed in the preceding output.

```
Buffer pool hit rate 937 / 1000, young-making rate 49 / 1000 not 0 / 1000
```

---

4. There are two flush types for this buffer. BUF_FLUSH_LIST flushes via the flush list of dirty blocks, whereas BUF_FLUSH_SINGLE_PAGE flushes single pages.

This line shows three ratios. The first is the ratio of the number of pages read to the number of buffer pool page gets. The second is the ratio of the number of pages made young to buffer pool page gets. The third is the ratio of the number of pages not made young to buffer pool page gets. All of these values are reset each time they are queried.

```
Pages read ahead 0.00/s, evicted without access 0.00/s
```

This is the read-ahead rate and the number of read-ahead pages evicted without access. The measurements are average per-second values since the most recent display.

```
LRU len: 3007, unzip_LRU len: 0
I/O sum[3937]:cur[1], unzip sum[0]:cur[0]
```

The first line shows the length of the LRU list and the unzip_LRU list. The latter is a subset of the common LRU list, holding a compressed file page and the corresponding uncompressed page frame. The second line shows the number of I/O operations and I/O for current intervals for both common LRU and unzip_LRU lists.

```
--------------
ROW OPERATIONS
--------------
```

The row operations section begins information about the main thread.

```
1 queries inside InnoDB, 0 queries in queue
1 read views open inside InnoDB
```

The first line shows how many queries are currently executing and how many are in the `innodb_thread_concurrency` queue. The second line shows the number of read views.

```
Main thread id 4192, state: flushing buffer pool pages
```

The preceding line shows the ID of the main thread and its state. I took this example on Windows. On Linux, it also prints the thread process number.

```
Number of rows inserted 0, updated 1759, deleted 0, read 1765
0.00 inserts/s, 5.86 updates/s, 0.00 deletes/s, 5.86 reads/s
```

The first line shows the number of rows inserted, updated, deleted, and read since InnoDB startup. The second line shows rates per second since the most recent display. Knowing which kind of queries you perform most often can help you set options for InnoDB effectively.

```
------------------------------
END OF INNODB MONITOR OUTPUT
==============================

1 row in set (0.00 sec)
```

I discussed the InnoDB Lock Monitor in "SHOW ENGINE INNODB STATUS and InnoDB Monitors" on page 96 in detail, so I won't say any more about it here.

Two monitors are left to discuss: the InnoDB Tablespace Monitor and the InnoDB Table Monitor.

The InnoDB Table Monitor prints the contents of the internal InnoDB dictionary. You can use this monitor to see how InnoDB stores a table, for example, if you suspect it is corrupted. Sample output looks like:

```
===========================================
110911 15:27:40 INNODB TABLE MONITOR OUTPUT
===========================================
--------------------------------------
TABLE: name collaborate2011/customers_bugs, id 1110, flags 1, columns 5, indexes 3,
appr.rows 0
  COLUMNS: iid: DATA_INT DATA_BINARY_TYPE len 4; bugid: DATA_INT
  DATA_BINARY_TYPE len 4; DB_ROW_ID: DATA_SYS prtype 256 len 6; DB_TRX_ID:
  DATA_SYS prtype 257 len 6; DB_ROLL_PTR: DATA_SYS prtype 258 len 7;
  INDEX: name GEN_CLUST_INDEX, id 2960, fields 0/5, uniq 1, type 1
   root page 3, appr.key vals 0, leaf pages 1, size pages 1
  FIELDS:  DB_ROW_ID DB_TRX_ID DB_ROLL_PTR iid bugid
  INDEX: name iid, id 2961, fields 2/3, uniq 2, type 2
   root page 4, appr.key vals 0, leaf pages 1, size pages 1
  FIELDS:  iid DB_ROW_ID
  FOREIGN KEY CONSTRAINT collaborate2011/customers_bugs_ibfk_1:
  collaborate2011/customers_bugs ( iid )
             REFERENCES collaborate2011/items ( id )
--------------------------------------
TABLE: name collaborate2011/items, id 1106, flags 1, columns 9, indexes 1,
appr.rows 5137
  COLUMNS: id: DATA_INT DATA_BINARY_TYPE DATA_NOT_NULL len 4; short_description:
  DATA_VARMYSQL len 765; description: DATA_BLOB len 10; example: DATA_BLOB len
  10; explanation: DATA_BLOB len 10; additional: DATA_BLOB len 10; DB_ROW_ID:
  DATA_SYS prtype 256 len 6; DB_TRX_ID: DATA_SYS prtype 257 len 6; DB_ROLL_PTR:
  DATA_SYS prtype 258 len 7;
  INDEX: name PRIMARY, id 2951, fields 1/8, uniq 1, type 3
   root page 3, appr.key vals 5137, leaf pages 513, size pages 545
  FIELDS:  id DB_TRX_ID DB_ROLL_PTR short_description description example
  explanation additional
  FOREIGN KEY CONSTRAINT collaborate2011/community_bugs_ibfk_1: collaborate2011/
  community_bugs ( iid )
             REFERENCES collaborate2011/items ( id )
  FOREIGN KEY CONSTRAINT collaborate2011/customers_bugs_ibfk_1: collaborate2011/
  customers_bugs ( iid )
             REFERENCES collaborate2011/items ( id )
  FOREIGN KEY CONSTRAINT collaborate2011/items_links_ibfk_1: collaborate2011/
  items_links ( iid )
             REFERENCES collaborate2011/items ( id )
  FOREIGN KEY CONSTRAINT collaborate2011/mysql_issues_ibfk_1: collaborate2011/
  mysql_issues ( iid )
             REFERENCES collaborate2011/items ( id )
  FOREIGN KEY CONSTRAINT collaborate2011/oracle_srs_ibfk_1: collaborate2011/
  oracle_srs ( iid )
             REFERENCES collaborate2011/items ( id )
```

This output shows information about the table from Example 1-1 and another from the same database. The output is reasonably self-explanatory and explained in detail in the MySQL Reference Manual (*http://dev.mysql.com/doc/refman/5.5/en/innodb-mon*

---

itors.html#innodb-table-monitor), so I won't describe the fields. I just wanted to put it here so you are acquainted with what it looks like.

The InnoDB Tablespace Monitor displays information about the file segments in the shared tablespace. This information helps you find problems with tablespaces, such as fragmentation or corruption. Note that if you use the `innodb_file_per_table` option, information about individual tablespaces is not displayed by this monitor. Sample output looks like the following:

```
=====================================================
110911 20:33:50 INNODB TABLESPACE MONITOR OUTPUT
=====================================================
FILE SPACE INFO: id 0
size 5760, free limit 5440, free extents 51
not full frag extents 5: used pages 290, full frag extents 3
first seg id not used 857
SEGMENT id 1 space 0; page 2; res 1568 used 1339; full ext 20
fragm pages 32; free extents 0; not full extents 4: pages 27
SEGMENT id 2 space 0; page 2; res 1 used 1; full ext 0
fragm pages 1; free extents 0; not full extents 0: pages 0
SEGMENT id 3 space 0; page 2; res 1 used 1; full ext 0
fragm pages 1; free extents 0; not full extents 0: pages 0
...
```

The meaning of this output is clearly explained in the "InnoDB Tablespace Monitor Output" section of the MySQL Reference Manual (*http://dev.mysql.com/doc/refman/5.5/en/innodb-monitors.html#innodb-tablespace-monitor*), so once again I won't bother to repeat it.

Performance Schema

I already discussed how to use Performance Schema to investigate locking problems in "PERFORMANCE_SCHEMA Tables" on page 100, but it has many other performance-related uses. Here I'll describe a set of tables whose names begin with `SETUP_` and that let you control which events are monitored. Here are some examples of their contents:

```
mysql> SELECT * FROM setup_consumers LIMIT 2;
+----------------------+---------+
| NAME                 | ENABLED |
+----------------------+---------+
| events_waits_current | YES     |
| events_waits_history | YES     |
+----------------------+---------+
2 rows in set (0.00 sec)

mysql> SELECT * FROM setup_instruments LIMIT 2;
+----------------------------------------+---------+-------+
| NAME                                   | ENABLED | TIMED |
+----------------------------------------+---------+-------+
| wait/synch/mutex/sql/PAGE::lock        | YES     | YES   |
| wait/synch/mutex/sql/TC_LOG_MMAP::LOCK_sync | YES | YES   |
```

```
+-----------------------------------------------+---------+-------+
2 rows in set (0.43 sec)

mysql> SELECT * FROM setup_timers;
+------+------------+
| NAME | TIMER_NAME |
+------+------------+
| wait | CYCLE      |
+------+------------+
1 row in set (0.00 sec)
```

System variables control how many events will be stored in history tables.

Tables whose names end with _INSTANCES document which objects are being instrumented. The type of the object is part of the name of each table.

```
mysql> SELECT * FROM FILE_INSTANCES WHERE FILE_NAME LIKE '%ITEMS%'
LIMIT 2\G
*************************** 1. row ***************************
 FILE_NAME: /users/apple/Applications/mysql-trunk/data/collaborate2011/items_links.ibd
EVENT_NAME: wait/io/file/innodb/innodb_data_file
OPEN_COUNT: 1
*************************** 2. row ***************************
 FILE_NAME: /users/apple/Applications/mysql-trunk/data/collaborate2011/items.ibd
EVENT_NAME: wait/io/file/innodb/innodb_data_file
OPEN_COUNT: 1
2 rows in set (0.08 sec)

mysql> SELECT * FROM RWLOCK_INSTANCES LIMIT 2\G
*************************** 1. row ***************************
                     NAME: wait/synch/rwlock/innodb/index_tree_rw_lock
    OBJECT_INSTANCE_BEGIN: 503973272
WRITE_LOCKED_BY_THREAD_ID: NULL
      READ_LOCKED_BY_COUNT: 0
*************************** 2. row ***************************
                     NAME: wait/synch/rwlock/innodb/index_tree_rw_lock
    OBJECT_INSTANCE_BEGIN: 503813880
WRITE_LOCKED_BY_THREAD_ID: NULL
      READ_LOCKED_BY_COUNT: 0
2 rows in set (0.08 sec)

mysql> SELECT * FROM MUTEX_INSTANCES LIMIT 2\G
*************************** 1. row ***************************
                 NAME: wait/synch/mutex/innodb/rw_lock_mutex
OBJECT_INSTANCE_BEGIN: 491583300
   LOCKED_BY_THREAD_ID: NULL
*************************** 2. row ***************************
                 NAME: wait/synch/mutex/innodb/rw_lock_mutex
OBJECT_INSTANCE_BEGIN: 345609668
   LOCKED_BY_THREAD_ID: NULL
2 rows in set (0.00 sec)

mysql> SELECT * FROM COND_INSTANCES LIMIT 2\G
*************************** 1. row ***************************
                 NAME: wait/synch/cond/innodb/commit_cond
OBJECT_INSTANCE_BEGIN: 10609120
```

```
*************************** 2. row ***************************
                 NAME: wait/synch/cond/sql/MYSQL_BIN_LOG::update_cond
OBJECT_INSTANCE_BEGIN: 35283728
2 rows in set (0.00 sec)
```

Tables whose names begin with EVENT_WAITS_ store information about events:

```
mysql> SELECT COUNT(*), EVENT_NAME FROM EVENTS_WAITS_CURRENT GROUP
BY EVENT_NAME;
+----------+-----------------------------------------+
| count(*) | EVENT_NAME                              |
+----------+-----------------------------------------+
|        1 | wait/io/table/sql/handler               |
|        6 | wait/synch/mutex/innodb/ios_mutex       |
|        1 | wait/synch/mutex/innodb/kernel_mutex    |
|        1 | wait/synch/mutex/innodb/log_sys_mutex   |
|        1 | wait/synch/mutex/innodb/rw_lock_mutex   |
|        1 | wait/synch/mutex/innodb/thr_local_mutex |
|        2 | wait/synch/mutex/sql/LOCK_thread_count  |
+----------+-----------------------------------------+
7 rows in set (0.26 sec)
```

I used COUNT here because knowing how many events were executed can help you find how they contribute to your MySQL load.

Tables whose names end in _HISTORY store information about which events happened, and tables whose names end in _SUMMARY contain summaries of these events based on various parameters.

Now I'll give examples of ways to use these tables. For instance, you can find out which instance is used for the most time or locked for the longest time. This can shed some light on aspects of performance that can be improved.

```
mysql> SELECT COUNT(*), (TIMER_END-TIMER_START) AS TIME,
EVENT_NAME FROM EVENTS_WAITS_HISTORY_LONG GROUP BY EVENT_NAME ORDER BY TIME
DESC;
+----------+---------+-----------------------------------------+
| count(*) | time    | EVENT_NAME                              |
+----------+---------+-----------------------------------------+
|     9967 | 3289104 | wait/io/table/sql/handler               |
|       10 | 2530080 | wait/synch/mutex/innodb/log_sys_mutex   |
|        5 | 2439720 | wait/synch/mutex/innodb/kernel_mutex    |
|        2 | 1481904 | wait/synch/mutex/mysys/THR_LOCK::mutex  |
|        2 | 1102392 | wait/synch/rwlock/sql/MDL_lock::rwlock  |
|        1 | 1036128 | wait/synch/rwlock/sql/LOCK_grant        |
|        2 |  789144 | wait/synch/mutex/mysys/THR_LOCK_lock    |
|        2 |  457824 | wait/synch/mutex/sql/LOCK_plugin        |
|        5 |  415656 | wait/synch/mutex/sql/THD::LOCK_thd_data |
|        2 |  343368 | wait/synch/mutex/sql/MDL_map::mutex     |
|        2 |  325296 | wait/synch/mutex/sql/LOCK_open          |
+----------+---------+-----------------------------------------+
11 rows in set (0.26 sec)
```

SHOW [GLOBAL] STATUS

I already discussed status variables related to configuration options in Chapter 3. Here I'll add some information about other status variables. Like server variables, status variables can be global or per-session. When a client connects, the session variables are set to zero. Global variables show the status since server startup or since the most recent FLUSH STATUS query.

When troubleshooting with status variables, don't just look at isolated values, but instead follow them over time. One huge number in itself may not mean anything; perhaps you've just been lucky enough to experience years of uptime. If it's large and growing rapidly, though, you might be seeing symptoms of a problem.

We recommend to our customers to take SHOW GLOBAL STATUS output at intervals of 5 to 10 minutes during critical loads, and to compare the values of variables at different times. This is the easiest way to find meaningful information.

The following list focuses in on particular types of status variables.

Com_* *status variables*

> These contain the number of statements issued of various types. For instance, Com_select shows how many SELECT queries were run, and Com_begin shows how many transactions were started.
>
> Use these variables to get an overview of your load. For example, if you have a large Com_select value with zero values for Com_insert, Com_update, and Com_delete, you can adjust configuration options to favor SELECT queries.

Handler_*, Select_*, *and* Sort_* *variables*

> Handler_* variables show what happens in the table internally when a query is run. For example, Handler_delete shows how many rows were actually deleted. You can use this variable to watch the progress of a DELETE that is currently running on a large table.
>
> Select_* variables show the numbers of the various kinds of joins that are used. Sort_* variables show information about sorts. These can help you find out how effective your queries are in terms of performance.
>
> I discussed these variables in "Queries That Modify Data" on page 36, so I won't spend more time on them here, but they warrant detailed study.

Innodb_* *variables*

> As can be guessed from the name, these variables show the internal status of the InnoDB storage engine. Study them and how they are affected by various InnoDB options if you use this storage engine.

Performance_schema_* *variables*

> The performance schema provides information about those objects for which "instrumentation points" were created in the MySQL server or the storage engine

source code. These variables show how many instrumentations could not be loaded or created.

Ssl_* *variables*

These show statistics about SSL connections.

open *and* *create* *variables*

Variables that contain these keywords show how many objects of various kinds were opened or created.

The purposes of other status variables either can be deduced from their names or can be found in Chapter 3.

Localizing the Problem (Minimizing the Test Case)

I already showed the value of minimizing a test case in "Single Server Example" on page 22, where I reduced an incorrect SELECT to a CREATE TABLE that reproduced the wrong parameters. Here I will discuss the principle of a minimal test case in more general terms.

As an example, take the following huge query[5]:

```
SELECT
IF(TABLE1.FIELD1 = 'R' AND TABLE1.FIELD2 IS NOT NULL AND TABLE1.FIELD3 = '1' AND
TABLE2.FIELD4 = TABLE2.FIELD5 AND TABLE3.FIELD6 = TABLE4.FIELD6, TABLE3.FIELD7,
TABLE4.FIELD7) AS ALIAS1,

IF(TABLE1.FIELD1 = 'R' AND TABLE1.FIELD2 IS NOT NULL AND TABLE1.FIELD3 = '1' AND
TABLE2.FIELD4 = TABLE2.FIELD5 AND TABLE3.FIELD6 = TABLE4.FIELD6, TABLE3.FIELD8,
TABLE4.FIELD8) AS ALIAS2,

SUM(
IF (
(SELECT TABLE5.FIELD7 FROM TABLE4 ALIAS3, TABLE2 ALIAS4, TABLE4 ALIAS5 WHERE
TABLE5.FIELD5 = ALIAS4.FIELD4 AND ALIAS4.FIELD5 = ALIAS5.FIELD5 AND
ALIAS5.FIELD7 = FIELD9 AND TABLE5.FIELD6 = TABLE6.FIELD7 LIMIT 1 ) IS NULL, 0,
TABLE7.FIELD10/TABLE7.FIELD11)
) AS ALIAS11

FROM TABLE4 ,TABLE4 ALIAS6, TABLE8 , TABLE4 ALIAS7, TABLE9 , TABLE7 , TABLE2 ,
TABLE1 FORCE INDEX(FIELD12)
LEFT JOIN TABLE1 ALIAS8 ON TABLE1.FIELD13 = TABLE10.FIELD13
LEFT JOIN TABLE1 ALIAS9 ON ALIAS9.FIELD13 = TABLE10.FIELD2
LEFT JOIN TABLE4 ALIAS10 ON ALIAS10.DFIELD5 = TABLE3.FIELD5

WHERE TABLE1.FIELD14 > DATE_sub(now(), INTERVAL 16 DAY)
and TABLE1.FIELD1 IN ('P', 'R','D')
AND TABLE1.DFIELD5 = TABLE4.FIELD5
AND TABLE1.FIELD15 = TABLE8.FIELD16
AND TABLE6.FIELD7 = TABLE8.FIELD17
```

---

5. This example is based on Community bug #33794 (*http://bugs.mysql.com/bug.php?id=33794*).

```
      AND TABLE4.FIELD18 = TABLE9.FIELD18
      AND TABLE1.FIELD19 = TABLE7.FIELD19
      AND TABLE1.FIELD20 = TABLE2.FIELD21
      AND TABLE4.FIELD6 = TABLE11.FIELD7

      GROUP BY TABLE4.FIELD6, FIELD9;
```

We can isolate the problem into a smaller equivalent:

```
SELECT
IF(T1.F1 = 'R', A1.F2, T2.F2) AS A4,
IF(T1.F1 = 'R' , A1.F3, T2.F3) AS F3,
SUM( IF ( (SELECT A7.F2
FROM T2 A7, T4 A2,  T2 A3
WHERE
A7.F4 = A2.F10
AND    A3.F2 = A4
LIMIT 1 ) IS NULL, 0, T3.F5)) AS A6

FROM T2, T3, T1
JOIN T2 A1 ON T1.F9 = A1.F4

GROUP BY  A4;
```

With this equivalent, it is very easy to test a problem. In the following section I describe how I create such small test cases, then return to use cases.

General Steps to Take in Troubleshooting

Here are the steps I take to localize a problem. They aren't perfectly linear, because there are different paths to take for different problems. But the sequence can serve as a checklist.

Try to identify the actual query that causes the problem.
> I've discussed many ways to determine the query or, in the case of a concurrency issue, the set of queries that cause the problem collectively. Once you obtain the query and its environment, you're halfway done. Either the problem is repeatable, or it has something to do with concurrency and you can investigate those issues.

Check to make sure the query's syntax is correct.
> The easiest way to do this is to run the query in the MySQL CLI. If the query is syntactically incorrect, it will return an error. In either case, once you figure out which part of the syntax is wrong, you have the source of the problem. Otherwise, continue to the next step.

Confirm that the problem is in the query.
> If the problem is a wrong result or a performance issue, check to make sure the problem is repeatable in the MySQL CLI.

> You may notice that I am branching out in various directions while listing steps to follow. These symptoms cannot always be resolved through a single path, because problems differ and the most effective methods to find the cause can vary.

If the query returns wrong data, try to rewrite it to get correct results, i.e., those that you expect to obtain.

If the problem is repeatable with a single query, it always can be rewritten to reflect your needs. This is the time when you can make your query shorter, reduce the data set, and test your changes. When modifying the query, do not make the typical mistake of forcing a single query to produce the final result. A one-query solution to get the necessary result set is not always faster than a sequence of multiple queries.

If a rewrite does not help, check the server options and try to determine whether they're affecting results.

This method can be used together with the previous one. Experienced users know when to suspect the effect of a configuration option. When in doubt, try options after simplifying the query.

If you decide that the query is correct, go backward until you find a statement or action that corrupted the data on which the query is acting.

After you are sure the query is absolutely correct and that no configuration option is affecting its results, there's no longer any sense in blaming the query. Check the data for corruption and find out what was originally responsible. This could be an application or external factors such as physical disk corruption or a modification of database files at the operating system level.

If the problem is not repeatable in the MySQL CLI, examine whether it could be a concurrency issue.

Use all the means from Chapter 2 to find out what is causing the problem. I start from SHOW PROCESSLIST and finish with application-level techniques.

If the problem causes a crash or a hang, check the error log first.

Although information about the latest crash is at the end of the log, use the full file and pay attention to older messages, too. They can contain information about table corruption or similar issues that occurred in the past, thus giving you a better idea about what is going on.

If the error logfile doesn't give you a clue, try to find the last query before the crash.

As described earlier, you can do this using the general query log, application-level logging, or a proxy.

Use mysqld-debug to generate a core file from a failed server, then analyze it.

Connect a debugger to the running process if this is a repeatable hang not a crash.

Analyze and adjust configuration options.

Options can cause a hang or crash too. Analyze every possible option that can have an effect, and adjust them correspondingly.

Use operating system tools to find out which external process could affect mysqld.

After you try everything related to the MySQL server itself and are sure it works properly, check its environment.

This general action plan splits a large, unknown issue into smaller parts that can be analyzed and solved. The execution path need not always be followed in order, because sometimes you find the reason for a problem right away and can go right to the fix. But the order shown works for cases when the cause is hard to determine and you need guidance to find it. I skipped the actual fixes because earlier parts of the book discussed them in detail.

Minimizing the Test Case in Environments with Incomplete Information

Finding the smallest test case for a problem is a general strategy that you can use in many situations, not just SQL applications.

When I started working on this book, I found I had not installed the XML plug-in for my favorite editor. I opened the plug-in manager and found that many plug-ins were out of date.

And here I made a mistake: I downloaded and installed them all.

The exact reason this was a bad idea is that my favorite editor runs in the Java virtual machine, and I need an outdated version of it to run a program required for my daily tasks.

But since last year, the editor and its plug-ins switched to the latest version of Java. So the next time I started the editor, I got a lot of errors about the wrong versions of the plug-in, and finally the program hung.

I did not want to reinstall everything, because I did not want to lose my current settings. And I was sure the source of the problem was one of the plug-ins, not the editor itself. But having installed dozens of plug-ins, I'd have a hard time determining which one prevented the editor from starting.

So I opened the editor's options directory and copied the content of the plug-ins sub-directory to another safe place. I was surprised to see that the editor still did not start.

Next, I determined which files were touched when I had opened the editor the last time, and moved them to another safe place too.

This time, the editor started and re-created its environment. This was good, but I wanted my preferences back.

So I started to add the option files back one by one, restarting the editor after each one, until I found the file that was corrupted. Fortunately, it did not contain the options I wanted to restore, so I just got rid of it and let editor the re-create it.

Now the plug-ins' turn came. I again added them one by one into the directory until I started to get errors. After examining them all, I got my installation working again.

- The principle of a minimal test case can be used even in environments where you have limited information.

Testing Methods

Creating a minimal test case can confirm the problem, but you can do even more with it. The minimal test case makes it easy to pinpoint the reason for the problem. When you look at a JOIN that connects several tables with complicated WHERE conditions, it's hard to say what exactly is wrong. But reducing the query to a couple of tables narrows the possibilities dramatically. Sometimes you fix the problem along the way when minimizing the query.

- Minimizing the test case usually reveals and fixes the problem.

In this section we'll consider what to do if you create the test but can't fix the issue on your own. There can be two reasons for this: a bug in the MySQL code or a misunderstanding of how some feature works. I'll assume you already read the parts of the MySQL Reference Manual pertaining to the problem and found no answer. There are still some resources you can try.

Try the Query in a Newer Version

The reason for trying a newer version of MySQL is that, in case your problem was actually caused by a bug in the server, you may find that it's already fixed. Installing and using a new version of MySQL might sound complicated. But if you followed my advice in "Sandboxes" on page 181 and have a sandbox, it's easy, especially if you use a minimal data set and combine the sandbox with your minimal test case.

Check for Known Bugs

If trying a newer version does not work, you can check the bug databases for known bugs. You could even consider searching for a bug report before you try the new version of MySQL. As you encounter more problems and become more experienced, you'll get a sense of which to do first. One simple rule you can follow is this: if the problem is repeatable with a dataset you can easily create, try a new version of MySQL first; otherwise, search the bug databases first.

You can start the search from the community bug database (*http://bugs.mysql.com*). If you are an Oracle customer, you can use the internal bug database inside the support portal. If you find a case that seems to match your situation, this will tell you whether it was considered a bug and whether it was already fixed.

If it was a bug, either download and test the version where it was fixed or find a workaround until it is fixed. If there is a known workaround, you'll find it as a public comment. Search engines are also useful for finding a workaround.

If the problem was not considered a bug, the bug report will point to the part of the MySQL Reference Manual describing proper usage. We don't explain in detail why one or another feature is not a bug, because that is not the purpose of the MySQL bug database, but learning about the proper behavior of the MySQL software can help you find a solution.

If you don't find a problem in the bug databases, use your favorite search engine to find mentions of similar problems. And if you still cannot find anything wrong in your logic and the problem is repeatable with the latest version of MySQL, it is time to report a bug.

Workarounds

If the previous sections did not help to solve your problem, you can try creating a workaround yourself. Rewrite your query to exclude the parts that cause the problem, and break the query down into smaller queries that execute correctly.

The following example, which is based on bug #47650 (*http://bugs.mysql.com/bug.php ?id=47650*), now fixed, illustrates the concept. First, we'll look at a simple version of the incorrect behavior that triggered the bug report:

```
mysql> CREATE TABLE `t1` (
    ->   `id` BIGINT(20) NOT NULL AUTO_INCREMENT,
    ->   PRIMARY KEY (`id`)
    -> ) ENGINE=MyISAM;
Query OK, 0 rows affected (0.04 sec)

mysql> CREATE TABLE `t2` (
    ->   `id` BIGINT(20) NOT NULL AUTO_INCREMENT,
    ->   `t1_id` BIGINT(20) DEFAULT NULL,
    ->   PRIMARY KEY (`id`)
    -> ) ENGINE=MyISAM;
Query OK, 0 rows affected (0.04 sec)

mysql> INSERT INTO `t1` VALUES
(1),(2),(3),(4),(5),(6),(7),(8);
Query OK, 8 rows affected (0.00 sec)
Records: 8 Duplicates: 0 Warnings: 0
mysql> INSERT INTO `t2` VALUES
(1,1),(2,1),(3,1),(4,2),(5,2),(6,2),(7,3),(8,3);
Query OK, 8 rows affected (0.01 sec)
Records: 8 Duplicates: 0 Warnings: 0

mysql> SELECT t1.id AS t1_id, COUNT(DISTINCT t2.id) AS cnt FROM t1
LEFT JOIN t2 ON t1.id = t2.t1_id
    -> WHERE t1.id = 1 GROUP BY t1.id WITH ROLLUP LIMIT 100;
+-------+-----+
| t1_id | cnt |
+-------+-----+
|     1 |   8 |
|  NULL |   8 |
+-------+-----+
2 rows in set (0.01 sec)
```

Why do we have eight rows where t1_id=1? Only three rows with t1_id = 1 were inserted:

```
mysql> INSERT INTO `t2` VALUES (1,1),(2,1),(3,1),
(4,2),(5,2),(6,2),(7,3),(8,3);
Query OK, 8 rows affected (0.01 sec)
Records: 8 Duplicates: 0 Warnings: 0
```

The problem can be clearly seen if we remove the GROUP BY clause:

```
mysql> SELECT t1.id AS t1_id, t2.id FROM t1 LEFT JOIN t2 ON t1.id =
t2.t1_id WHERE t1.id = 1;
+-------+------+
| t1_id | id   |
+-------+------+
|     1 |    1 |
|     1 |    2 |
|     1 |    3 |
+-------+------+
3 rows in set (0.00 sec)
```

This listing shows that the data is correct and that GROUP BY causes the problem.

At first glance, the only way to solve the problem is to break the query up into several queries. But there may be another workaround that we can try, knowing something about the optimizer. The query execution plan can change if GROUP BY uses an index, so let's try adding one:

```
mysql> ALTER TABLE t2 ADD INDEX(t1_id);
Query OK, 8 rows affected (0.05 sec)
Records: 8 Duplicates: 0 Warnings: 0
```

Now the problem is solved:

```
mysql> SELECT t1.id AS t1_id, COUNT(DISTINCT t2.id) AS cnt FROM t1 LEFT JOIN t2
ON t1.id = t2.t1_id WHERE t1.id = 1 GROUP BY t1.id WITH ROLLUP LIMIT 100;
+-------+-----+
| t1_id | cnt |
+-------+-----+
|     1 |   3 |
|  NULL |   3 |
+-------+-----+
2 rows in set (0.02 sec)
```

So play around with the SQL to see whether you can avoid the bug. The example I showed doesn't have any general application, but it shows that help can come from subtle changes. It also shows again the advantages of using a sandbox.

Special Testing Tools

When you test a problem that has more than one solution, such as a performance issue or the design of your SQL application, you need to test how each suits your needs. This section offers a quick overview of tools that can help in such testing.

Benchmarking Tools

Benchmarking tools test an application's speed. MySQL benchmarking tools usually test MySQL installations, which is not the same as testing an application, but they can still be useful for testing a particular set of options. If a benchmarking tool allows you to use custom queries written specially for your application, you also can run tests on your own dataset.

The most popular benchmarks for MySQL are *sysbench* and *mysqlslap*. The following subsections describe them.

mysqlslap

mysqlslap is a load emulation client that comes with the MySQL distribution. It makes it easy to test concurrent loads on similar queries. Run it with an SQL script, either from a file or specified as an argument:

```
$ mysqlslap  --socket=/tmp/mysql51.sock --user=root --delimiter=";" \
--create-schema=mstest --create="CREATE TABLE mstest(id INT NOT NULL \
AUTO_INCREMENT PRIMARY KEY, f1 VARCHAR(255)) ENGINE=InnoDB" --query="INSERT INTO \
mstest(f1) VALUES(MD5(RAND())); SELECT f1 FROM mstest;" --concurrency=10 \
--iterations=1000
Benchmark
        Average number of seconds to run all queries: 0.039 seconds
        Minimum number of seconds to run all queries: 0.025 seconds
        Maximum number of seconds to run all queries: 0.173 seconds
        Number of clients running queries: 10
        Average number of queries per client: 2
```

 Note that if you specify the `create` option for *mysqlslap*, the schema specified in the `create-schema` option will be dropped. This will also happen if you use a *mysqlslap* older than 5.1.57 or 5.5.12, even if you don't use the `create` option.

- Use this tool only in a new, empty schema.

SysBench

This benchmark utility, available from Launchpad (*https://launchpad.net/sysbench*), measures the performance of a whole system, testing the CPU, file I/O, OS scheduler, POSIX threads performance, memory allocation, transfer speed, and database server performance. We are interested in the last feature in the list.

In early versions, you can test database server options using only the predefined online transaction processing (OLTP) test, which creates a table and runs a concurrency test on it:

```
$sysbench --test=./sysbench/tests/db/oltp.lua
--mysql-table-engine=innodb --oltp-table-size=1000000
--mysql-socket=/tmp/mysql60.sock --mysql-user=root prepare
sysbench 0.5:  multi-threaded system evaluation benchmark
```

```
Creating table 'sbtest1'...
Inserting 1000000 records into 'sbtest1'

$sysbench --test=./sysbench/tests/db/oltp.lua
--mysql-table-engine=innodb --oltp-table-size=1000000
--mysql-socket=/tmp/mysql60.sock --mysql-user=root --num-threads=16
--max-requests=100000 run
sysbench 0.5:  multi-threaded system evaluation benchmark

Running the test with following options:
Number of threads: 16
Random number generator seed is 0 and will be ignored


Threads started!

OLTP test statistics:
    queries performed:
        read:                       1400154
        write:                      400044
        other:                      200022
        total:                      2000220
    transactions:                   100011 (50.84 per sec.)
    deadlocks:                      0      (0.00 per sec.)
    read/write requests:            1800198 (915.16 per sec.)
    other operations:               200022 (101.68 per sec.)

General statistics:
    total time:                     1967.0882s
    total number of events:         100011
    total time taken by event execution: 31304.4927s
    response time:
        min:                             18.10ms
        avg:                            313.01ms
        max:                          13852.37ms
        approx.  95 percentile:         595.43ms

Threads fairness:
    events (avg/stddev):        6250.6875/22.15
    execution time (avg/stddev):  1956.5308/0.65
```

The preceding output was taken using the latest version of MySQL, which allows you to point *sysbench* to a custom test, but this predefined test behaves similarly to the predefined test used in earlier versions.

Since version 0.5, you can write your own tests using the Lua programming language. The easiest way to start is to take *oltp.lua* as a template. The following simple script shows which functions you must define:

```
$cat sysbench.lua
function prepare()
        local i

        db_connect()
```

```
        print("Creating table 'test'")
        db_query("CREATE TABLE test(id INT NOT NULL AUTO_INCREMENT PRIMARY KEY,
        f1 VARCHAR(255))")
        print("Inserting 1000 rows")
        for i = 1, 1000 do
                db_query("INSERT INTO test(f1) VALUES(1000*rand(1000))")
        end

end

function cleanup()
        print("Dropping table 'test'")
        db_query("DROP TABLE test")
end

function event(thread_id)
        db_query("SELECT * FROM test WHERE f1 = " ..  sb_rand(1, 1000))
end
```

In real benchmarks, you can code more complicated scenarios.

The result of the preceding test looks similar to the default OLTP test:

```
$sysbench
--test=/Users/apple/Documents/web_project/MySQL/examples/sysbench.lua
--mysql-table-engine=innodb
--mysql-socket=/tmp/mysql60.sock --mysql-user=root --num-threads=16
--max-requests=100000 prepare
sysbench 0.5:  multi-threaded system evaluation benchmark

Creating table 'test'
Inserting 1000 rows

$sysbench
--test=/Users/apple/Documents/web_project/MySQL/examples/sysbench.lua
--mysql-table-engine=innodb
--mysql-socket=/tmp/mysql60.sock --mysql-user=root --num-threads=16
--max-requests=100000 run
sysbench 0.5:  multi-threaded system evaluation benchmark

Running the test with following options:
Number of threads: 16
Random number generator seed is 0 and will be ignored


Threads started!

OLTP test statistics:
    queries performed:
        read:                           100001
        write:                          0
        other:                          0
        total:                          100001
    transactions:                       0       (0.00 per sec.)
    deadlocks:                          0       (0.00 per sec.)
```

```
        read/write requests:                100001 (37.08 per sec.)
        other operations:                   0      (0.00 per sec.)

    General statistics:
        total time:                         2697.2491s
        total number of events:             100001
        total time taken by event execution: 43139.9169s
        response time:
            min:                                   7.54ms
            avg:                                 431.39ms
            max:                               2304.82ms
            approx.  95 percentile:             913.27ms

    Threads fairness:
        events (avg/stddev):        6250.0625/27.35
        execution time (avg/stddev): 2696.2448/0.57
```

Gypsy

Gypsy, also available from Launchpad (*https://launchpad.net/gypsy*), is a tool written for load testing by MySQL Support Engineer Shane Bester. We actively use this tool when testing concurrent loads. It's not a benchmarking tool, but an aid to finding locking issues or other problems with concurrency.

Gypsy is scriptable. Its syntax for query files is easy:

```
i|1|DROP TABLE IF EXISTS t1|
i|1|CREATE TABLE t1( id INT, f1 INT, PRIMARY KEY(id)) ENGINE=InnoDB|
i|1|SET GLOBAL SQL_MODE='strict_trans_tables'|
n|100|INSERT INTO t1 SET id = ?, f1 = 1 ON DUPLICATE KEY UPDATE f1 = f1 + 1|tinyint
```

Rows marked with i are part of the initial setup and are run only once. Rows marked with n denote queries that emulate the load. You can run Gypsy as follows:

```
$gypsy --host=127.0.0.1:3351 --user=root --password= --database=test
--queryfile=bug42644.query --threads=2 --duration=100
[INFO]    04:08:15 [0290] 2684407808 - 32-bit version of Gypsy
[INFO]    04:08:15 [0291] 2684407808 - sizeof(long long int) = 8
[INFO]    04:08:15 [0300] 2684407808 - using 1 hosts
[WARN]    04:08:15 [2950] 2684407808 - setting statement on line 1 to non-prepared by
default
[WARN]    04:08:15 [2950] 2684407808 - setting statement on line 2 to non-prepared by
default
[WARN]    04:08:15 [2950] 2684407808 - setting statement on line 3 to non-prepared by
default
[INFO]    04:08:15 [0362] 2684407808 - client library version: 5.0.92
[ALWAYS] 04:08:15 [0376] 2684407808 - server 00: '5.1.60-debug', host:
'127.0.0.1 via TCP/IP',  SSL: 'NULL', protocol: 10, charset: latin1
[ALWAYS] 04:08:15 [0414] 2684407808 - thrd = 2
[INFO]    04:08:15 [0459] 2684407808 - read 4 valid queries from query file
[INFO]    04:08:15 [0556] 2684407808 - spawning data generation thread
[INFO]    04:08:15 [0693] 25182208 - creating new char data for the first time
[INFO]    04:08:15 [0711] 25182208 - refreshing char data
[INFO]    04:08:15 [0718] 25182208 - char data has been generated, char_increment=2
```

```
[INFO]   04:08:15 [0603] 2684407808 - now running for 100 seconds.
[INFO]   04:08:15 [0609] 2684407808 - running initialization queries
[INFO]   04:08:15 [1443] 25183232 - thread 0 connecting to host 0
[INFO]   04:08:15 [1456] 25183232 - thread 0 has 1 alive hosts connected
[WARN]   04:08:16 [2182] 25183232 - thread[00] didn't complete entire query
file. Might need longer --duration=
[INFO]   04:08:16 [0636] 2684407808 - about to create all 'populate' scripts from I_S
[INFO]   04:08:16 [0691] 2684407808 - spawning database stats thread
[ALWAYS] 04:08:16 [0708] 2684407808 - spawning 2 new thread(s)
[INFO]   04:08:16 [1443] 25184256 - thread 0 connecting to host 0
[INFO]   04:08:16 [0957] 25183232 - writing server status variables to
'report_18098_host_00.txt'
[INFO]   04:08:16 [1456] 25184256 - thread 0 has 1 alive hosts connected
[INFO]   04:08:16 [1443] 25188352 - thread 1 connecting to host 0
[INFO]   04:08:16 [1456] 25188352 - thread 1 has 1 alive hosts connected
[INFO]   04:08:17 [0736] 2684407808 - completed spawning new database worker threads
[INFO]   04:08:28 [0777] 2684407808 - 02 threads running, 0030487 successful
queries.  0000000 failed queries (2540.583333 QPS).
[INFO]   04:08:39 [0777] 2684407808 - 02 threads running, 0059212 successful
queries.  0000000 failed queries (2393.750000 QPS).
[INFO]   04:08:50 [0777] 2684407808 - 02 threads running, 0084904 successful
queries.  0000000 failed queries (2141.000000 QPS).
[INFO]   04:09:01 [0777] 2684407808 - 02 threads running, 0110477 successful
queries.  0000000 failed queries (2131.083333 QPS).
[INFO]   04:09:12 [0777] 2684407808 - 02 threads running, 0133212 successful
queries.  0000000 failed queries (1894.583333 QPS).
[INFO]   04:09:23 [0777] 2684407808 - 02 threads running, 0148816 successful
queries.  0000000 failed queries (1300.333333 QPS).
[INFO]   04:09:34 [0777] 2684407808 - 02 threads running, 0165359 successful
queries.  0000000 failed queries (1378.583333 QPS).
[INFO]   04:09:45 [0777] 2684407808 - 02 threads running, 0178743 successful
queries.  0000000 failed queries (1115.333333 QPS).
[ALWAYS] 04:09:56 [0792] 2684407808 - waiting for threads to finish
[INFO]   04:09:56 [0808] 2684407808 - running cleanup queries
[INFO]   04:09:56 [1443] 25188352 - thread 0 connecting to host 0
[INFO]   04:09:56 [1456] 25188352 - thread 0 has 1 alive hosts connected
[WARN]   04:09:56 [2182] 25188352 - thread[00] didn't complete entire query file.
Might need longer --duration=
[INFO]   04:09:56 [0835] 2684407808 - now about to tell stats thread to exit
[INFO]   04:09:56 [0842] 2684407808 - now about to tell data generation thread to exit
[ALWAYS] 04:09:56 [0884] 2684407808 - done!!!
[ALWAYS] 04:09:56 [0885] 2684407808 - press a key to continue!!
```

MySQL Test Framework

The MySQL Test Framework is also called MTR, which is an abbreviation of its main command, *mysql-test-run*. It is a test automation package used by MySQL developers, and is available in all full MySQL packages. In concept, it's similar to unit testing. It involves test cases, each of which is a pair consisting of a test and a result file. Test files contain sets of MySQL queries along with special MTR commands, and result files contain the expected results.

Here's an example of a test file that creates a table, inserts one row, and then selects it:

```
--source include/have_innodb.inc

CREATE TABLE t1(f1 int NOT NULL AUTO_INCREMENT PRIMARY KEY, f2 VARCHAR(255))
ENGINE=InnoDB;
INSERT INTO t1 (f2) VALUES('test');
SELECT f1, f2 FROM t1;
DROP TABLE t1;
```

Let's suppose you've stored this in a file named *book.test* in MTR's *t* subdirectory. If you are sure your version of MySQL works fine, you can automatically record a result file by issuing:

```
$./mtr --record book
Logging: ./mtr  --record book
110915  3:58:38 [Warning] Setting lower_case_table_names=2 because file system
for /tmp/PrqusdwLQa/ is case insensitive
110915  3:58:39 [Note] Plugin 'FEDERATED' is disabled.
110915  3:58:39 [Note] Plugin 'ndbcluster' is disabled.
MySQL Version 5.1.60
Checking supported features...
 - skipping ndbcluster
 - SSL connections supported
 - binaries are debug compiled
Collecting tests...
vardir: /users/apple/bzr/mysql-5.1/mysql-test/var
Checking leftover processes...
Removing old var directory...
Creating var directory '/users/apple/bzr/mysql-5.1/mysql-test/var'...
Installing system database...
Using server port 56970


==============================================================================

TEST                                    RESULT   TIME (ms)
------------------------------------------------------------

worker[1] Using MTR_BUILD_THREAD 300, with reserved ports 13000..13009
main.book                               [ pass ]    124
------------------------------------------------------------
The servers were restarted 0 times
Spent 0.124 of 20 seconds executing testcases

Completed: All 1 tests were successful.
```

The contents of the result file are now:

```
$cat r/book.result
CREATE TABLE t1(f1 INT NOT NULL AUTO_INCREMENT PRIMARY KEY, f2 VARCHAR(255))
ENGINE=InnoDB;
INSERT INTO t1 (f2) VALUES('test');
SELECT f1, f2 FROM t1;
f1      f2
1       test
DROP TABLE t1;
```

When you run the same test without the `--record` option, MTR compares the actual result with the contents of the result file and fails if they are different. You can move the test and result files to another server to test whether execution has changed.

MTR allows you to create suites for separate products starting with version 2.0, which comes with MySQL server 5.1 and higher. So you can create your own testing suites like the following:

```
$./mtr --suite=./suite/book book
Logging: ./mtr  --suite=book book
110915  4:05:29 [Warning] Setting lower_case_table_names=2 because file system
for /tmp/7npx97ZLbz/ is case insensitive
110915  4:05:29 [Note] Plugin 'FEDERATED' is disabled.
110915  4:05:29 [Note] Plugin 'ndbcluster' is disabled.
MySQL Version 5.1.60
Checking supported features...
 - skipping ndbcluster
 - SSL connections supported
 - binaries are debug compiled
Collecting tests...
vardir: /users/apple/bzr/mysql-5.1/mysql-test/var
Checking leftover processes...
Removing old var directory...
Creating var directory '/users/apple/bzr/mysql-5.1/mysql-test/var'...
Installing system database...
Using server port 56998


==============================================================================

TEST                                    RESULT   TIME (ms)
------------------------------------------------------------

worker[1] Using MTR_BUILD_THREAD 300, with reserved ports 13000..13009
book.book                               [ pass ]     72
------------------------------------------------------------
The servers were restarted 0 times
Spent 0.072 of 12 seconds executing testcases

Completed: All 1 tests were successful.
```

Outside of MySQL development, this tool can be useful to automatically check how installations with different options or MySQL versions run a custom query.

You can find more information in the the MTR user guide (*http://dev.mysql.com/doc/ mysqltest/2.0/en/index.html*).

Maintenance Tools

The tools in this section are useful in a day-to-day DBA job, not just when trouble occurs. If you use them regularly, you can avoid most troublesome situations. That's why I'm describing them here: one of my reasons for writing this book was to help you have trouble-free MySQL installations.

These tools have great user guides as well as reference manuals, so I'll just introduce them without details.

Tools from the MySQL distribution

MySQL comes with set of tools that you can find in the *bin* directory of the MySQL installation. Become acquainted with them. They are described in the section of the MySQL Reference Manual about MySQL programs (*http://dev.mysql.com/doc/refman/5.5/en/programs.html*).

Percona Toolkit

This toolkit, available from Percona (*http://www.percona.com/software/percona-toolkit/*), was put together from the Aspersa and Maatkit distributions. It contains a lot of powerful instruments to control the server and its tables.

MySQL WB Utilities

Although they are part of the MySQL Workbench installation, these run from the command line. They are independent from MySQL Workbench and can be run on platforms that don't run MySQL Workbench. The tools are written in the Python language. They work mostly with database structure, not with data, and can help automate processes such as replication setup and grant migration.

Monitoring tools

It is very important to monitor your system for statistics related to its day-to-day operation. Here I describe two tools that can help you monitor a MySQL installation:

MySQL Enterprise Manager

The MySQL team provides MySQL Enterprise Manager (MEM) for monitoring purposes.

MEM is commercial software available for Enterprise customers. It runs as a server on a dedicated machine, along with lightweight agents that should run on the same machine as the one where the monitored MySQL server is running. These agents collect information about both MySQL and the operating system and send it to MEM server. Through a web-based GUI, a DBA can get a graphical overview of what is going on across multiple servers. MEM also suggests improvements in server setup.

You can read about MEM in detail in the book *MySQL High Availability* by Charles Bell et al. (O'Reilly), or in the official documentation (*http://dev.mysql.com/doc/mysql-monitor/2.3/en/index.html*).

dim_STAT

dim_STAT is a tool for monitoring performance of Unix, Linux, and Solaris systems. It collects output received from operating system monitoring tools such as *vmstat*, and *iostat*, has its own plug-ins that collect different statistics, draws graphs, and much more. dim_STAT supports multiple hosts.

dim_STAT also has MySQL add-ons that monitor MySQL and InnoDB usage.

You can examine statistics and see graphs using a web-based GUI. dim_STAT also has a CLI solution that can generate a single graph in PNG format for a given database, collect ID, and time interval.

You can download dim_STAT from *http://dimitrik.free.fr/*.

## CHAPTER 7

Best Practices

This chapter summarizes some best practices that can help you troubleshoot MySQL effectively and safely. They aren't troubleshooting methods or tools in themselves, but they can dramatically affect troubleshooting. These practices were discussed throughout the book but are combined here to emphasize their value.

Backups

Many of the procedures in this book can make changes to databases, which is why I've encouraged you to run tests in a sandbox. You can create your own disaster, however, by making such changes in a production database. Backups can save you in such cases.

A backup is a state to which you can return at any step. If something is damaged during tests or an application failure, you can restore all but the most recent changes to data. Backups are also useful because you can load data from them into a sandbox for testing. If you make a backup at a convenient time, you don't have to wait until load is low on the main server and you can take a new snapshot of a running instance. Without interrupting normal operation, you can just copy the backup to the sandbox and start testing.

Of course, a backup is useful only if it's recent. A backup made a month ago of an application with extensive write operations won't help much. So it's a good idea to make periodical full backups and frequent incremental backups. It's also good to have the binary log turned on so that you have all the changes made at the time a problem occurred.

The books *High Performance MySQL* by Baron Schwartz et al. and *MySQL High Availability* by Charles Bell et al. (both published by O'Reilly) describe how to make backups, including descriptions of when, why, and how, and the available tools to do the backups. The following subsections just give you some considerations to keep in mind when planning backups.

Planning Backups

When planning backups, think about how to do it so that you'll be able to do a full restore at any time. For instance, you shouldn't rely on just a replication slave as your backup. The slave can fall far behind its master, and thus have outdated data. The slave can also contain different data from the master, particularly with statement-based replication. We described reasons why this happens at Chapter 5. Therefore, don't rely on a slave as your only backup solution.

I prefer to do weekly full backups along with daily incremental backups and to keep all binary logs. Of course, you can change the schedule based on the actual write load. I just don't recommend leaving a really large interval between backups, because in such a case you would be at risk of losing a lot of data due to a hardware failure. Plan reasonably.

Whenever you restore data, restore from the latest full backup first, then apply the incremental backups made after the full backup in order, if they exist, and finally load any remaining changes from the binary logs.

Types of Backups

This section discusses full and incremental backups. The third element of backing up, saving binary logs, is simply this: don't delete the logs that were created after the most recent backup, and copy them to a safe place periodically if the time lag between backups is large.

Backups can be grouped along several different dimensions:

By format

    Logical

        Saves a dump of structure and data. Although this kind of backup is slow, it can be very useful because its files can be read by humans and edited manually.

    Physical

        Saves the binary files, which is usually fast. This kind of backup is very important if you cannot repeat a problem because the table is somehow corrupted. In such cases it can make sense to make binary copy of a single table and move it to the test server.

By interaction with the MySQL server

    Online

        Taken when the MySQL server is running

    Offline

        Taken when the MySQL server is stopped

By interaction with the MySQL server objects

Cold

> Taken when no operation is allowed for the MySQL server. The server should be either stopped or blocked from modifying its own files. The advantage of such backups is that they are extremely fast.

Warm

> Taken when the MySQL server is running, and prohibiting only a few operations on the objects being backed up. It is not always possible to have a consistent backup if parallel threads use database objects, so all backup methods use some kind of intelligence to keep objects being backed up secure. This method involves write locking only the objects currently being backed up, while allowing other connections to modify other objects. Read access is usually also allowed during this kind of backup.

Hot

> Taken when the MySQL server is running and all operations on backed-up objects are allowed. This is the fastest method among online backups.

By content

Full

> Backs up all objects

Incremental

> Backs up changes made after a particular time, usually the time of a previous backup

Partial

> Copies only specific objects, e.g., a few tables from a database

Tools

I won't describe all the backup tools available for MySQL, but instead describe just a few that illustrate the types of backups shown in the previous section. You are free to use your favorite, regardless of whether it's on this list.

mysqldump

> Comes with MySQL distributions and makes logical backups.

MySQL Enterprise Backup (MEB)

> A separate product available for Enterprise customers. It can create hot backups of InnoDB tables, warm backups of other storage engines, and cold backups.

Percona XtraBackup

> An open source product with functionality similar to MEB. It can create hot backups of XtraDB and InnoDB tables and warm backups of other storage engines.

cp

> The basic Unix shell command that copies files. You can use it to create cold offline backups.

Filesystem snapshot tools, such as LVM

> Creates a snapshot of file system. Should be used when the MySQL server is either stopped or prevented from writing to its own files.

Table 7-1 matches various types of backups with the tools that provide them.

Table 7-1. Backup types supported by the tools discussed in this section

Backup type/tool	*mysqldump*	MEB	XtraBackup	cp	LVM
LOGICAL	YES	NO	NO	NO	NO
PHYSICAL	NO	YES	YES	YES	YES
ONLINE	YES	YES	YES	NO	NO
OFFLINE	NO	YES	NO	YES	YES
COLD	NO	YES	NO	YES	YES
WARM	YES	YES	YES	NO	NO
HOT	NO	YES	YES	NO	NO
FULL	YES	YES	YES	YES	YES
INCREMENTAL	NO	YES	YES	NO	NO
PARTIAL	YES	YES	YES	YES	NO

Using this table, you can determine which tool is most suited to your needs. If you decide to run a solution that does not include incremental backups, do incremental backups through binary logs. For more detail and best practices related to backups, consult the books mentioned earlier in "Backups" on page 221.

Gathering the Information You Need

Information is the key to successful troubleshooting. In addition to using it for your own troubleshooting, it is critical when you open a support case. So don't ignore the sources and instruments that collect reports about problems, such as the error log.

That said, you can't log everything all the time. Logging puts a burden on your server. So you need to find a balance between the information that needs to be saved all the time and the information you can ignore until a real problem happens.

I recommend you always turn on instruments that do not need a lot of resources, such as the error logfile and operating system logs. Logging options that require light resources, such as MEM without the query analyzer, can be running constantly too. It is not thrifty to try to shave a little load off your server by turning off these instruments and giving up the help they will offer during a critical problem.

With regard to reporting tools that can decrease performance noticeably, be prepared to use them, but turn them off until a problem fires up. Use of these instruments can be implemented as an option in the application.

What Does It All Mean?

Even gigabytes of information are useless if you don't understand it. So read the error messages, suggestions from MEM, and so on. If you don't understand them, refer to the MySQL Reference Manual, books, blogs, forums, or other sources of information.

A search engine is a good companion. Just typing an error message into a search field usually turns up lots of links containing information about how other users solved a similar problem. In most cases, you are not alone.

Of course, you can always ask questions on public forums and IRC. And finally, you can buy support.

Testing

After you develop a hypothesis about what is going on and how to solve your problem, test the hypothesis and consider your results.

In my job, I meet users who are afraid of testing. There are two main reasons that people reject it: overconfidence (the user thinks that a correct guess does not require testing) and diffidence (the user is afraid of breaking something else).

But even very experienced users make mistakes, so it is risky to just rely on a guess. Always check the result of any change you make. What is quickly noticed can be quickly fixed.

Don't be shy! Just consider this: if you need to troubleshoot something, you are already experiencing a problem. If one or another test makes the problem worse, at least the test spares you from making a major change that would take even longer to fix. A mistake made during a test can be rolled back in a few seconds.

Further, discovering that a guess is wrong is valuable because you narrow the search area. Fewer options are left, so there's more chance that your next test will prove correct.

If you don't want to take any risk of harming your production setup, test in a sandbox. I recommend this especially when a test can change data, but it's also useful when you simply need to modify some configuration option. Just create a repeatable test case and run it in the sandbox.

And don't be lazy! Laziness can be a good thing when you are finding the best and shortest way to solve a problem, but it can play a bad joke on you when testing.

Being too lazy to copy the original tables to a sandbox can lead to many ineffective attempts to reproduce your problem when it cannot be reproduced with the inadequate test data. Even worse, you may end up implementing the wrong solution. So if the problem is not reproducible with a small test data set, just copy the full tables to the sandbox and experiment on them there.

Prevention

The best approach to troubleshooting is to prevent the situation in the first place. The only way to eliminate all possible problems is to completely block access to the MySQL server, which means it wouldn't do any useful work. So we can speak only about compromises.

Privileges

One important aspect of prevention is privileges. Although many test cases in this book have used the root user, this is acceptable only in test environments where you can't harm anything. When running on a production server, each person should have as few privileges as possible. Ideally, a user would have only the privileges for those objects she is going to use. For example, if a web application only selects data from a few databases, don't give write access and read access to the mysql database to the web application's user account. If you need to do a maintenance task on that database, create a separate user for it.

Such precautions will protect you from bad interventions and can even mitigate against SQL injection attacks. A successful attack will be limited in the damage it can cause.

Environment

Another important aspect is the environment for running the server: the MySQL server options and the external environment in which it runs.

When adjusting options, analyze their effects. Start with only the options whose effects you are sure of, then add others one by one and analyze how they change things. In such a scenario, if something goes wrong, you will be able to restore an acceptable work environment in a few seconds.

When planning a MySQL installation, analyze how the environment will affect it. Don't expect the MySQL server to run fast without issues when the hardware and operating system are overloaded by other processes or suffer from a corrupted disk. Plan correspondingly, and check the hardware at the first sign of problems.

When planning replication or some other complicated environment, try to diagnose in advance how the setup can affect database activities. A simple example is the differences in query behavior when row versus statement binary logging is used. Always analyze and plan correspondingly.

Think About It!

I want to finish this book by stressing the importance of reasoning. The ability to find the causes of problems comes not only from practice, but also from the skill of analyzing problems.

If you encounter a problem, I recommend you think it over thoroughly before choosing the troubleshooting techniques you believe are best suited to that particular issue.

Choosing a good action path at the first step will save you much time. And a thorough diagnosis can prevent not only the issue you noticed right away, but also other future problems stemming from the same cause.

Information Resources

Throughout this book, I have pointed to good sources of information that can help during troubleshooting. Here is short list of them, grouped by usage type. As always, I prefer those I personally use daily.

Resources Containing Information That Is Usually Useful

The official MySQL Reference Manual (http://dev.mysql.com/doc/refman/5.5/en/index .html)
> This is the first place to go for information because it documents how one or another feature is supposed to work.

Search engines
> If you can't find enough detail in the MySQL Reference Manual, try your favorite search engine. In most cases, you can copy and paste an error message and get lots of information about the problem. The planet Earth is really small, and it is hard to catch a truly unique problem.

Bug and Knowledge Databases

The Community Bug Database (http://bugs.mysql.com/)
> If you don't understand MySQL's behavior and believe it is behaving incorrectly, search the bug database. You will probably find a report with the very same problem. If you use an old version of MySQL, you can even find out whether the problem is fixed.

Oracle Customers' Bug Database (https://support.oracle.com/)
> Oracle tracks bugs reported internally or by customers using its internal bug database. If you are an Oracle customer, you can access it and find bugs that were not reported by the community. This database mostly contains real bugs, and you rarely meet reports closed as "Not a Bug" there, because they go though a careful check before they are included.

Oracle's Knowledge Management database (https://support.oracle.com/)
> Oracle makes a regularly updated knowledge database accessible to its customers. It contains product and problem descriptions in more detail than the MySQL Reference Manual. Many articles are created from customers' use cases, so you may well find the exact problem you have. Some of the articles are published there on the same day that a feature is released, so this is a really good source for actual information.

Expert Knowledge Online

If you are searching for a detailed article about one or another feature, try the following resources:

MySQL Forge (http://forge.mysql.com)
> This has information about MySQL internals, plug-in development, public worklogs, and community projects. You can find wikis describing the internals of many features, MySQL internals documentation, community add-ons, and public worklogs (plans for MySQL development in future versions).

MySQL Planet (http://planet.mysql.com/)
> This is an aggregator of English-language blogs about MySQL. All blogs belonging to active community members are combined there. You can find posts that describe one or another feature in detail and posts that go deep into internals. This is a great source for finding information about MySQL in a single place. There are also language-specific MySQL Planets; check whether one exists for your native language.
>
> I want to highlight two of the blogs you can find on this site:

MySQL Performance Blog (http://www.mysqlperformanceblog.com/)
> This blog is written by Percona engineers and contains a great amount of information about performance tuning. This is the first source you should check if you run into a performance problem.

InnoDB Team Blog (http://blogs.innodb.com/wp/)
> As can be guessed from the name, this is a blog written by members of the InnoDB team. There you can find details about InnoDB development, usage tips for new features, and internals. This is really great resource for those who use the InnoDB storage engine.

Places Where You Can Ask for Help

Forums, communities, and user groups
> I don't supply links to particular forums, because there are so many. You can start from the MySQL forum (*http://forums.mysql.com/*) or use your favorite local forum like I do. Just find out whether you have a good one in your country.

IRC, particularly #mysql at Freenode (irc://irc.freenode.net/mysql)
Many MySQL experts are here; just log in and ask your question. There are also specific channels, such as #mysql-dev (*irc://irc.freenode.net/mysql-dev*), where you can ask questions related to plug-in development or extending MySQL, or #mysql-ndb (*irc://irc.freenode.net/mysql-ndb*), where NDB experts sit. For troubleshooting issues, the most appropriate channel is #mysql (*irc://irc.freenode.net/mysql*).

Books

There are also valuable books written about MySQL. I would start with O'Reilly books (*http://shop.oreilly.com/category/browse-subjects/databases/mysql.do*) because O'Reilly always works with experts. Among the authors from this list, you can find authors of MySQL source code and top MySQL experts.

I also recommend *Expert MySQL* by Dr. Charles A. Bell (Apress), which provides information about how to debug and modify MySQL code. I touched on these topics in "When the Server Does Not Answer" on page 39 and "Core file" on page 186, but consult Dr. Bell's book if you want more details.

Index

Symbols

We'd like to hear your suggestions for improving our indexes. Send email to *index@oreilly.com*.

errors from, 185
limits for, 152–153
operating system log, 108, 224
optimizer (see MySQL optimizer)
optimizer_prune_level variable, 135
optimizer_search_depth variable, 135
optimizer_switch variable, 135
optimizing (tuning) queries, 24–30, 34, 39
options for server (see server options)
Oracle Customers' Bug Database, 229
Oracle's Knowledge Management database, 230

P

Pachev, Sasha (author)
Understanding MySQL Internals (O'Reilly), 187
page locks, 55
partial backups, 223
paths in server options, incorrect, 108–111
Percona server, xii
Percona Toolkit, 165, 219
Percona XtraBackup, 223
performance
concurrency affecting, 76–79
hardware limits affecting, 147–152
improving, general strategies for, 39
of modification queries, 35, 36–38, 63
operating system limits affecting, 152–153
other applications affecting, 153–154
server options for, 35–36, 39, 114, 132–142, 171, 174
slow query log indicating, 174–175
tuning queries, 24–30, 34, 39
tuning tables, 30–34
PERFORMANCE_SCHEMA tables, 100–101, 201–203
Performance_schema_* status variables, 204
permissions
preventing problems using, 226
problems with, 49–52
of replication user on master server, 159
server options for, 118, 131
perror utility, 19, 45, 185
PHP, coverage of, xii
physical backups, 222
ping utility, 108, 159
plug-ins (see server plug-ins)
preload_buffer_size variable, 142

privileges (see permissions)
process list (see PROCESSLIST table; SHOW PROCESSLIST statement)
PROCESSLIST table, 60, 78, 95–96
processors (see CPU)
proxy, scriptable, 175
pt-table-checksum utility, 165

Q

queries
buffers allocated for a specific query, 143–145
dynamic
viewing in query log, 3–5
viewing with output function, 2–3
failure of
causing different errors on master and slave, 170
incomplete or altered query, 170
slave failure resulting from, 166
incorrect results from
back errors in data causing, 19–24
previous updates causing, 10–16
query causing, 5–10
information about, retrieving, 16–19
modifications by (see modifications, queries for)
optimized by MySQL (see MySQL optimizer)
slow
data affecting, 34
dropping or ignoring indexes, 33
server options for, 35–36, 39
slow query log for, 174–175
tuning query for, 24–30, 34, 39
tuning tables for, 30–34
subqueries in (see subqueries)
tools analyzing
MySQL CLI, 177–181
mysql_query command, 175
mysql_real_query command, 175
scriptable proxy, 175
server plug-ins, writing, 175
slow query log, 174–175
query log (see general query log)
query_cache_size variable, 134, 142
query_prealloc_size variable, 133, 143

R

RAM
  concurrency issues with, 78
  lack of, causing server crash, 44
  limits of, 147–148
  maximum, calculating, 144
  size of, relationship to buffers, 35, 44
RBR (row-based replication), 87, 90, 93
read locks, 54
read_buffer_size variable, 133, 144
read_only variable, 126
read_rnd_buffer_size variable, 133, 144
reasoning, importance of, 227
relay log, corruption of, 161–164
REPAIR TABLE statement, 46
replicate-* options, 124
replication
  asynchronous, 155
  circular, 155, 168–170
  concurrency issues with, 86–94
  consistency between master and slave,
      checking, 164
  I/O thread for, 156
      not connecting to master, 159–160
      repeated disconnects from master, 160–
          161
      slave far behind master, 161–166
      status of, 157, 158
  inconsistency of, on master and slave, 19–
      24
  mixed, 87, 90, 93, 125
  multiple master replication, 155
  row-based, 87, 90, 93
  semi-synchronous, 156
  server options for, 124–126
  slave status for, 157–158
  SQL thread for, 156
      data inconsistent between master and
          slave, 167–168
      different configuration on master and
          slave, 171
      different errors on master and slave,
          170
      nonreplicated writes to slave, 168–170
      query causing slave to fail, 166
      query incomplete or altered, 170
      relay lay corruption indicated by, 161–
          164
      slave lagging behind master, 171–172
  status of, 157, 158
  starting between two servers, 185
  statement-based, 87–91, 90, 125
  transactional and nontransactional tables,
      mixing, 91–93
reserved words, as names, 2
resources (see books and publications;
          hardware resources; website
          resources)
restarts, errors caused by, 20, 22
restoring from backups, 222
ROLLBACK statement, 63
row locks, 55, 57–63
  showing for multistatement transactions,
      63–69
  timeout for, 127
row-based replication (RBR), 87, 90, 93, 125
rows affected, number of, 16
rows changed, number of, 17
rows matched, number of, 17
rows, in EXPLAIN EXTENDED output, 24
RWLOCK_INSTANCES table, 100

S

safe-user-create option, 131
sandbox environment, 181–185
SBR (statement-based replication), 87–91, 90
Schwartz, Baron (author)
  High Performance MySQL (O'Reilly), 221
scriptable proxy, 175
secure_auth variable, 132
secure_file_priv variable, 132
security, server options for, 131
SELECT queries (see queries)
Select_* status variables, 204
semaphores, 86
semi-synchronous replication, 156
server
  checking if reachable, 159
  connection issues, 39
  crashed, 39–44
      by waiting InnoDB semaphores, 86
  creating new instance of, 185
  failing to start, 108–111
  other applications affecting, 44
server options
  for buffers, 132–135, 142–145
  for caches, 134
  for case of database objects, 121

(see also InnoDB storage engine; MyISAM storage engine)
  server options for, 126–130, 137–142
  substitution of, if one fails to start, 110
stored functions, binary logging affecting, 111
stored procedures, queries called from, 181
subqueries
  dependent, 7, 10
  replaced by index lookup in optimizer, 27
  troubleshooting, 7, 43
swapping
  checking for, 148
  large buffers leading to, 35
  preventing, 147–148
syntax errors, 1–5, 113
sysbench utility, 212–214

T

table locks, 55–57, 127
Table Monitor, 192, 200
tables
  checking and recovering from errors, 129
  nontransactional (see nontransactional tables)
  opening, number of file descriptors affecting, 79
  size of, 128
  transactional (see transactional tables)
  tuning, 30–34
Tablespace Monitor, 192, 201
table_definition_cache variable, 135, 142
table_open_cache variable, 135, 142
tcpdump utility, 160, 161
telnet utility, 159
testing
  methods for, 209–211
  role in troubleshooting, 225–226
  tools for, 211–218
Thread Pool Plugin, 138
THREAD table, 82
threads
  caches shared between
    large buffers affecting, 36
    performance affected by, 79
  killing, 84
  for replication
    I/O thread (see I/O thread for replication)

SQL thread (see SQL thread for replication)
  server options for, 134, 142, 143
THREADS table, 100, 101
thread_cache_size variable, 134, 142
thread_stack variable, 134, 143
timeouts, 59, 76, 127, 130–131
tmp_table_size variable, 134, 144
transactional tables
  handling of invalid data inserts, 112
  mixing with nontransactional tables, 91–93
transactions, 54, 63–73
  (see also concurrency)
  deadlocks, 69–72, 79–86
  implicit commits, 72–73
  isolation level for, 54
  multiple statements in
    showing row locks, 63–69
  rolling back, 127
  transactional and nontransactional tables, mixing, 91–93
  uncommitted, locks held by, 69
triggers, queries called from, 181
tuning queries, 24–30, 34, 36–38, 39
tuning tables, 30–34
type, in EXPLAIN EXTENDED output, 24

U

ulimit option, 152
Understanding MySQL Internals (O'Reilly), 187
unique values, duplicate values occurring in, 19–24
UPDATE queries (see modifications, queries for)
uptime status variable, 40
USER() function, 50, 51

V

variables for server options (see server options)
vm.overcommit_ratio option, 152
vmstat utility, 148

W

wait_timeout variable, 130
warm backups, 223
warnings

About the Author

Sveta Smirnova is a Principal Technical Support Engineer in the Bugs Verification Group of the MySQL Support Group at Oracle.

Colophon

The animal on the cover of *MySQL Troubleshooting* is is a Malayan badger (*Mydaus javanensis*), also known as a Javan stink badger, a Sunda stink badger, a teledu, or an Indonesian stink badger. The genus *Mydaus* includes one other species, the Palawan stink badger (*M. marchei*). The stink badgers were long considered part of the badger family, but recent DNA studies have shown that they are more closely related to the skunks.

Stink badgers have brownish-black fur, with a white or yellow cap and a long skunk-like stripe down the back. Their long muzzles are capped by pig-like snouts, and they have long curved claws on their front feet. They measure 12–20 inches long (including a very short tail) and may weigh up to 8 pounds.

Stink badgers are found in Indonesia, Malaysia, and the Phillipines. They live in forests and nearby open areas, and reside at many elevations on the mountainous islands. The nocturnal animals live in underground burrows, which they may dig themselves or appropriate from (or share with) porcupines. They eat eggs, insects, plants, and carrion; their claws and snouts are used to dig and root for earthworms. They usually have a litter of two or three, but little else is known about their social lives and breeding.

Lydekker commented on the species' "evil odour" in his *Royal Natural History*, calling the spray from its rear glands "foetid in the extreme." The secretions are used for defense against predators, which include the Javan hawk-eagle, feral cats, and tigers.

The cover image is from Lydekker's *Royal Natural History*. The cover font is Adobe ITC Garamond. The text font is Linotype Birka; the heading font is Adobe Myriad Condensed; and the code font is LucasFont's TheSansMonoCondensed.

Get even more for your money.

Join the O'Reilly Community, and register the O'Reilly books you own. It's free, and you'll get:

- $4.99 ebook upgrade offer
- 40% upgrade offer on O'Reilly print books
- Membership discounts on books and events
- Free lifetime updates to ebooks and videos
- Multiple ebook formats, DRM FREE
- Participation in the O'Reilly community
- Newsletters
- Account management
- 100% Satisfaction Guarantee

Signing up is easy:

1. **Go to: oreilly.com/go/register**
2. **Create an O'Reilly login.**
3. **Provide your address.**
4. **Register your books.**

Note: English-language books only

To order books online:
oreilly.com/store

For questions about products or an order:
orders@oreilly.com

To sign up to get topic-specific email announcements and/or news about upcoming books, conferences, special offers, and new technologies:
elists@oreilly.com

For technical questions about book content:
booktech@oreilly.com

To submit new book proposals to our editors:
proposals@oreilly.com

O'Reilly books are available in multiple DRM-free ebook formats. For more information:
oreilly.com/ebooks

O'REILLY®

Spreading the knowledge of innovators   oreilly.com

Have it your way.

Milton Keynes UK
Ingram Content Group UK Ltd.
UKHW050838290224
438644UK00008B/577